PAPER IN HARMONY
A Collection of Origami Instrumentalists
Second Edition

Marc Kirschenbaum

Fit to Print Publishing, Inc.
New York, New York

For Todd

Paper in Harmony, Second Edition
Copyright © 2019, 2000
Fit To Print Publishing, Inc.

All rights reserved. No part of this publication may be reproduced, stored in a retrieval system or transmitted in any form or by any means, electronic, mechanical, photocopying, recording or otherwise, without the permission of the copyright holder.

ISBN 978-1-951146-04-7

The diagrams in this book were produced with Macromedia's Freehand, and image processing was done with Adobe Photoshop. The Backtalk family of typefaces was used for the body text and the cover uses Florida Serial with PT Sans. Ellen Cohen assisted with the cover design and provided valuable artistic assistance. The late Bernhardt Crystal wrote the foreward, reprinted in this new edition.

Contents

Foreword	5
Introduction	7
Symbols and Terminology	8
Dollar Bill Guitarist	12
Leaping Guitarist	15
Violinist	20
Bassist	33
Guitarist	44
Pianist	53
Drummer	70
Harpist	85
Clarinetist	96
Conductor	105
Dancing Couple	114
Saxophonist	125
Original Beatle	133
Seated Guitarist	140
Materials and Methods	158
Ratio Information	166

Foreword

For forty-three years I have been the fortunate Director of an art gallery in New York. I acquire objects of art from all over the world - and for each one, the criterion is "Is it beautiful?" Does it speak to me, to my sense of beauty, in its form, its use of materials? Now, I have found such beauty in the art of Origami.

One day, my friend Marc Kirschenbaum handed me a small object made of paper. On first inspection I recognized its form as that of a tiny bird. A closer look revealed it to be a U.S. dollar bill, which had been folded over and over until it had grown a head, a tail and wings. It almost seemed to fly out of my hand!

This experience - a small but intense emotion of surprise, admiration and pleasure, was my introduction to the world of Origami.

Marc has created works in this book that capture the metamorphosis from an unassuming square sheet of paper to intricate forms of musicians. His models dispel the notion of what is possible through the act of merely folding paper.

Originating in Japan centuries ago, origami originally referred to "paper folded into objects." It is an art form in the truest sense, as belonging to that rare pantheon of things made by human talent and creativity. Paintings, sculpture, literature, music, poetry, dance - of a quality that embodies the finest workmanship and performance - and any expression of human effort that shows excellence. My first glimpse upward to take in the majesty of Michelangelo's Sistine Chapel, and my intake of breath in wonder at the perfection of the tiny bird in my hand, are alike in their recognition of art.

It is with a sense of deep appreciation for the hands that first took a flat surface and began to fold, and refold it, until it became a three-dimensional object, representing something else other than the one-dimensional surface it began with. "Subject comes before form," is the working maxim for any artistic endeavor. It is as if I were to decide to write a sonnet, which must have fourteen lines, the last two summing up the idea set forth in the first twelve – without having an idea of what I wanted to say. First must come the idea, the subject, and then the form - as in the example of the exquisite object I'm holding in the palm of my hand - a bird. Thus, the effort of creating this object is in the unspoken command "subject before form" and in the true spirit of art!

Bernhard Crystal
WASHINGTON IRVING GALLERY

Introduction

Twenty years has passed since the first edition of *Paper in Harmony* was created. This series of musicians still stands as a unique entry in the world of origami art. Two new pieces are added in this revision and more tips and techniques are included. The presentation is also given a more modern look.

The earlier origami of master folders has inspired this work. Most notable are the musician folds of Neal Elias. In the 1970's, Elias developed a technique known as box-pleating (the *Dollar Bill Guitarist* and *Leaping Guitarist* are examples of the application of this technique). By employing long rectangles (and on occasion, odd shapes), appendages could be formed along the length of the rectangle to create forms of unprecedented complexity. Elias exploited his abilities in a series of instrumentalists that were representative of famous musicians. These included a model of *Andrés Segovia* (a guitarist seated on a bench) and *Yehudi Menuhin* (a violinist dressed in formal garb). Asides from his sheer technical mastery, these works were excellent examples of composition, in the way different elements were integrated into a single model.

About a decade later, Robert Lang, another American origami master, took the subject matter into a different direction. Lang's approach was to create a common look for each of his musicians (in contrast to the tailored approach Elias took with each of his subjects). By creating a motif, the sum became greater than its parts, making for a very effective presence when these works are viewed together. The other exciting element to Lang's instrumentalists was that they each employed an action mechanism.

In Japan, origami master Takashi Hojo has also taken on instrumentalists as subject matter. By using multiple sheets of paper, an unprecedented range of color and texture is achieved. As with Elias's work, Hojo's instrumentalists take on a unique approach with each musician and are even more focused though the level of ornateness he achieves. The musicians contained here have an unusually streamlined look with distinctive cowl-shaped heads. Most are formed from a single square and have a similar look and feel. Surely, there are more unexplored directions to be taken; use these models to inspire you as the masters have influenced this collection.

Symbols and Terminology

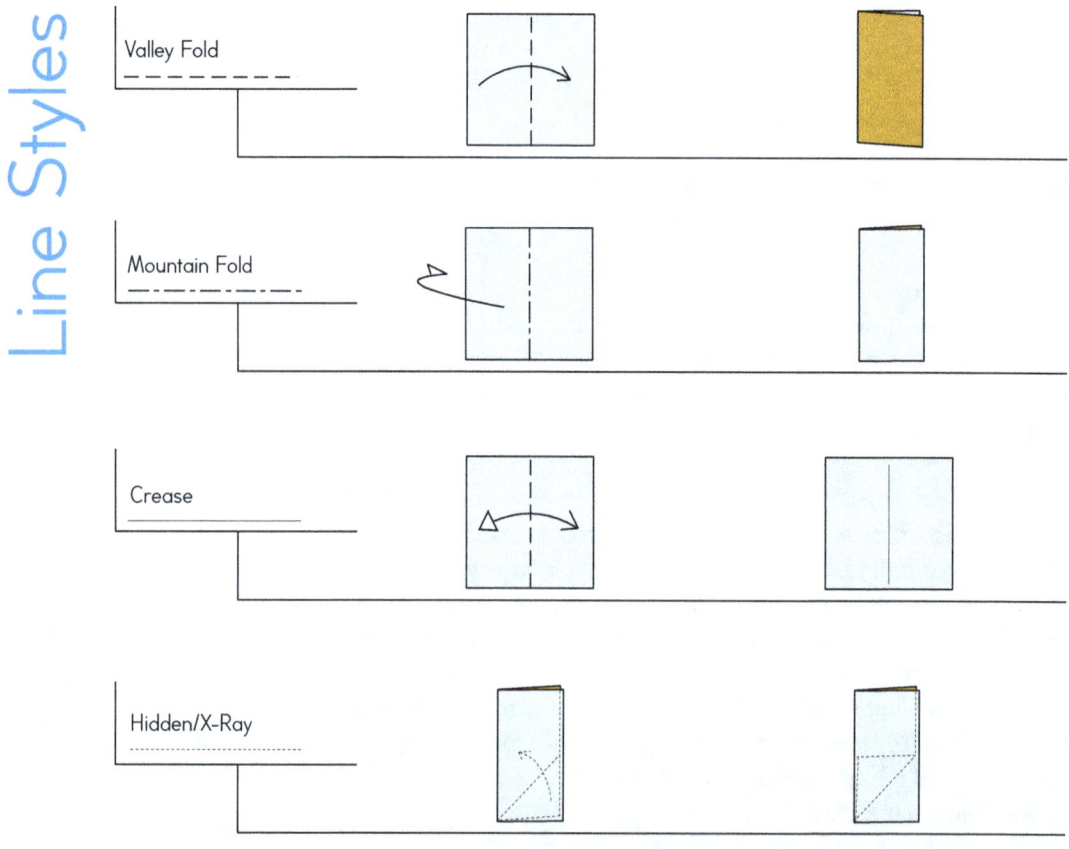

Line Styles

Valley Fold

Mountain Fold

Crease

Hidden/X-Ray

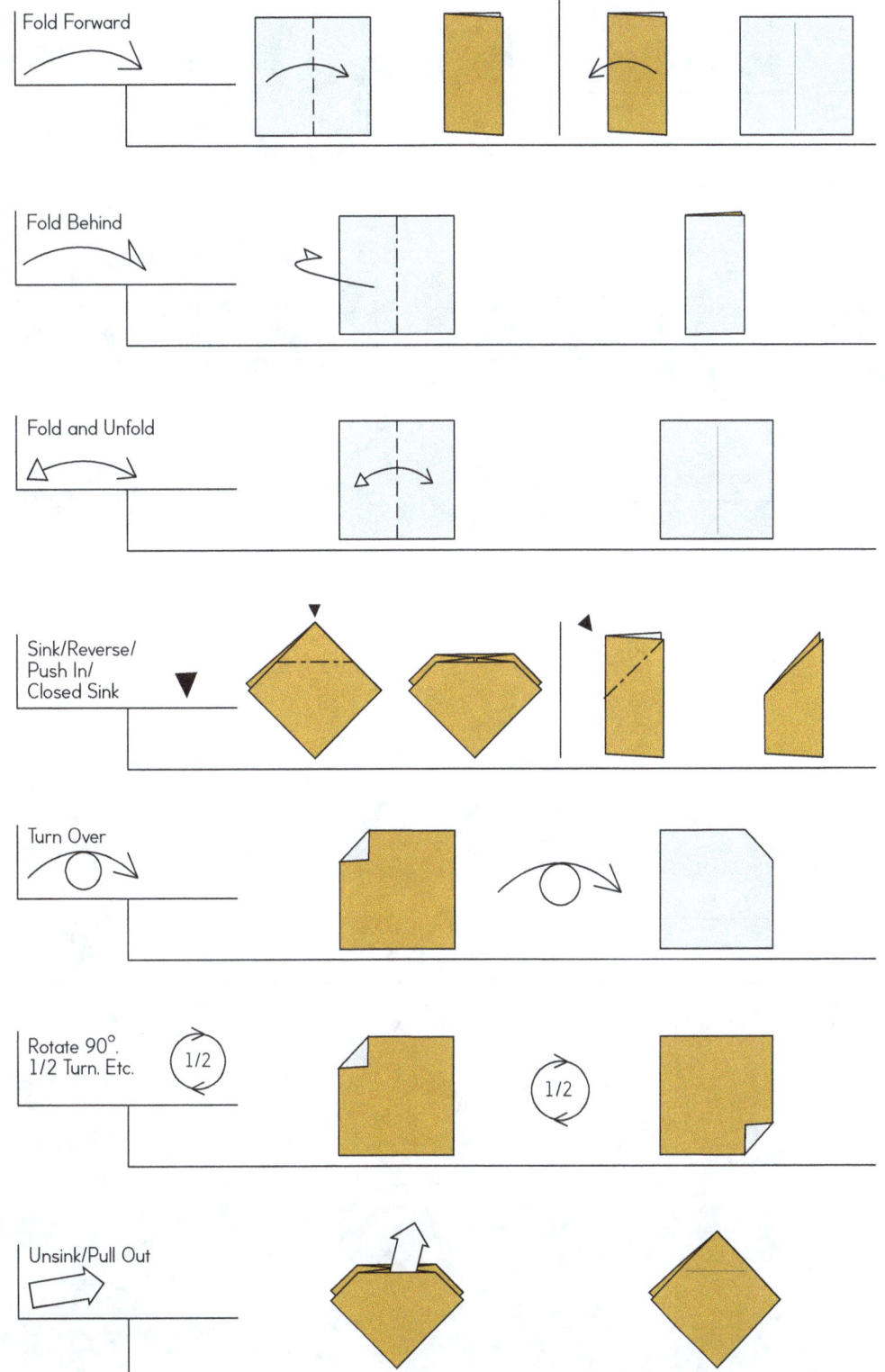

Maneuvers

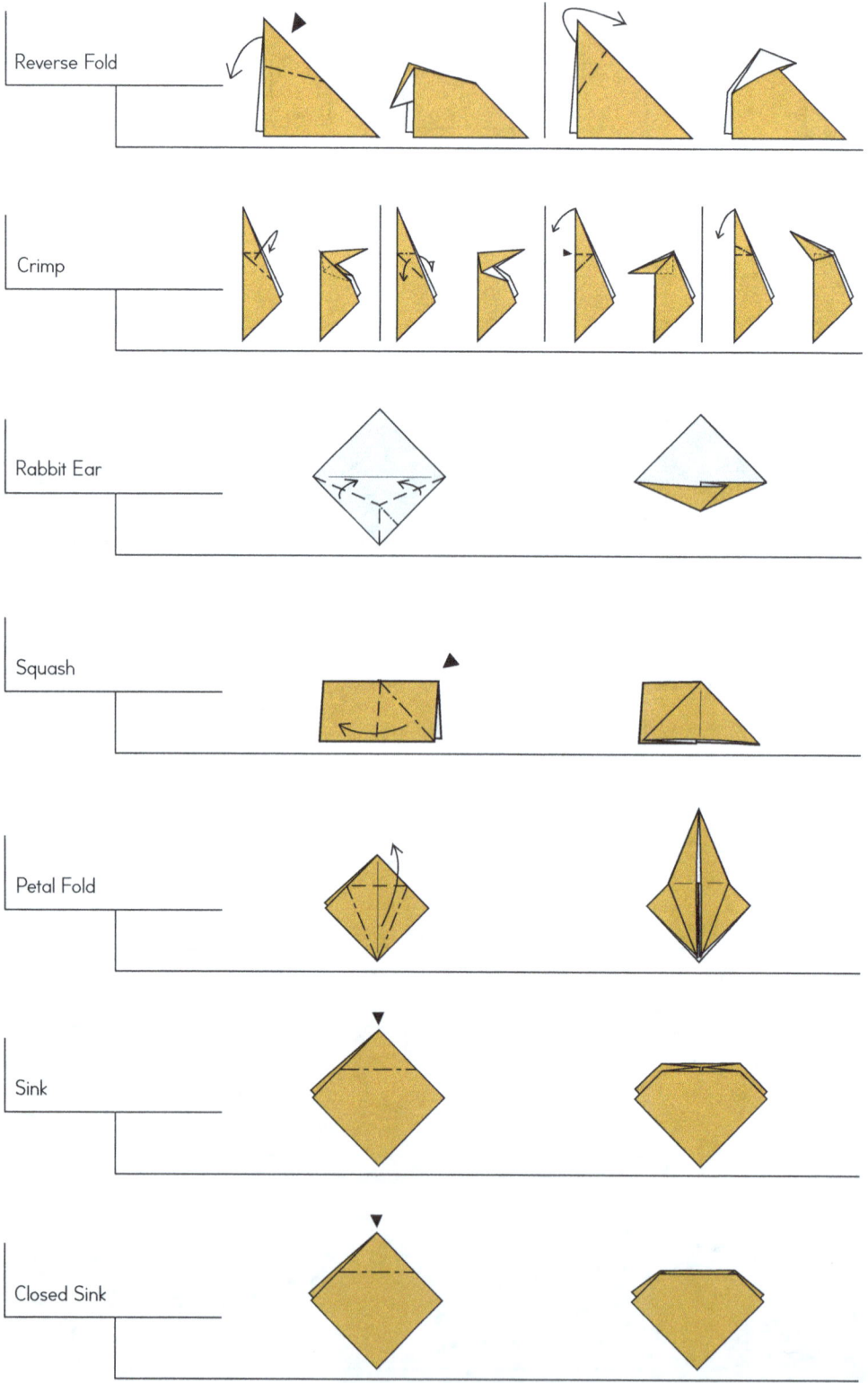

Reverse Fold

Crimp

Rabbit Ear

Squash

Petal Fold

Sink

Closed Sink

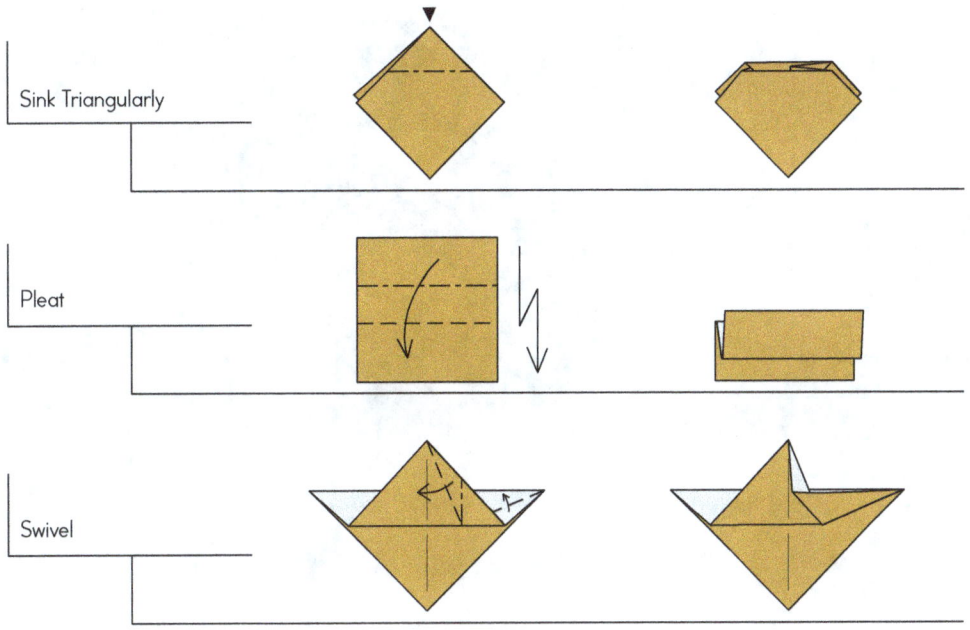

Dollar Bill Guitarist

About

This *Dollar Bill Guitarist* was developed in 1983 as a novel payment for guitar lessons. It is loosely based on Neal Elias' *Andrés Segovia* (his famous origami model of a guitarist seated on a bench). The Elias version was folded from a 3x1 rectangle, but with the bench eliminated, it could be folded from standard currency. This dollar bill version won a spot in the national Origami by Children competition.

Tips

Although this model was designed to be folded from a dollar bill, it is recommended to practice with larger paper. The proportions needed are approximately 3x7, and most types of paper are suitable for this model. When folding from real currency, dampen the model and secure the sections with twist ties to avoid the layers from spreading apart. At the end, you can leave it to dry with a heavy weight for permanent results.

If you are new to the box-pleated works of Neal Elias, step 1 might seem strange. The first thing to do is perform all the precreasing. The horizontal precreases do not go all the way up to the center because of the odd proportions of the bill. Collapsing your paper might seem intimidating at first, but keep in mind that most of the folds shown form naturally; that is, you can ignore most of the short folds. Collapse the bottom first (since it is easier), unfold and collapse the top section next. After that, the model should fall into place quite easily.

Step 10 features another standard Elias move. The result is much like a flap that has been sunk multiple times in and out. In terms of execution, form the indicated mountain fold pinch. A similar mountain fold is formed at the rearmost layer. Pull the pleats apart, forming a horizontal mountain fold between the two pinches. If you now pull down the corner, a flap should emerge, and should flatten nicely.

dollar bill guitarist

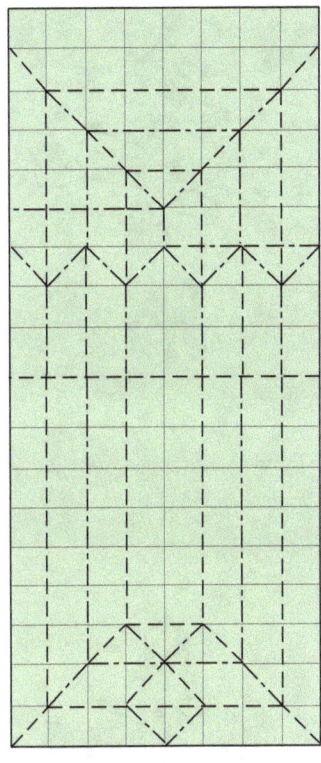

1. Precrease a dollar into 8ths vertically and 8ths at the top and bottom. Collapse as indicated.

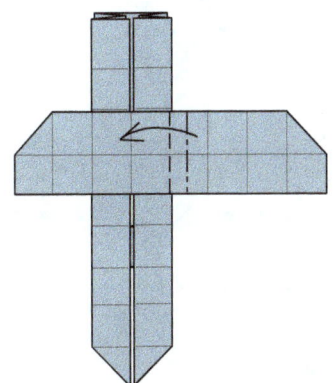

2. Pleat the guitar.

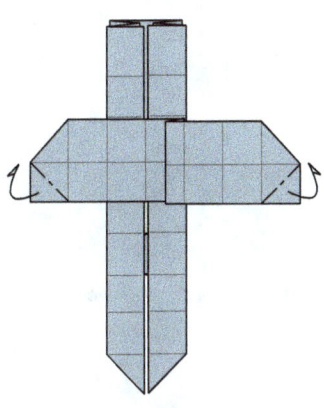

3. Shape the ends with mountain folds.

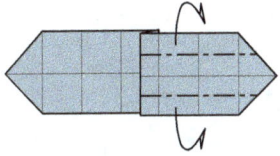

4. Swivel the sides of the neck in.

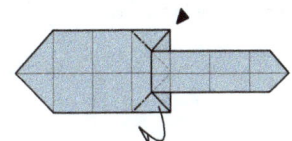

5. Reverse fold at the top and mountain fold at the bottom.

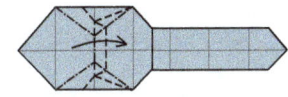

6. Form the mountain folds first, and collapse the body towards the neck.

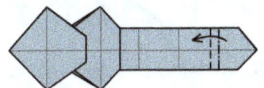

7. Pleat the headstock over.

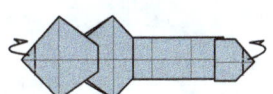

8. Shape the ends with mountain folds.

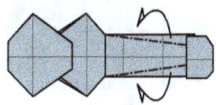

9. Swivel in the sides.

dollar bill guitarist

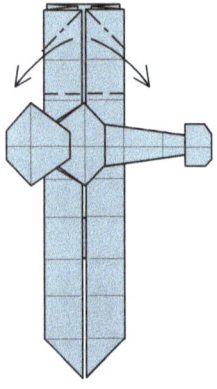

10. Stretch the pleats downwards.

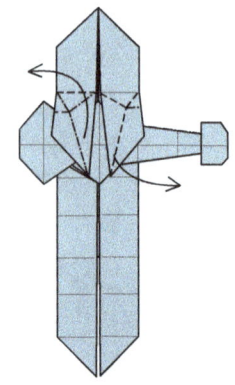

11. Rabbit ear the arms.

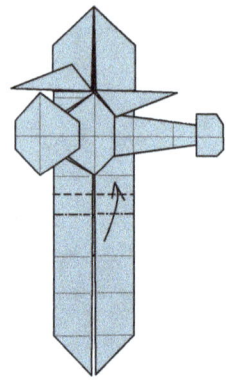

12. Form a pleat at the waist.

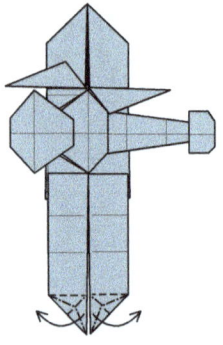

13. Valley fold up and rabbit ear the feet.

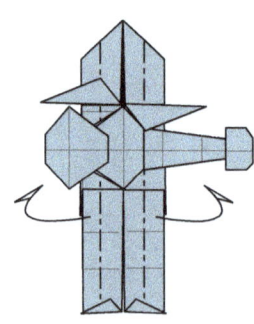

14. Mountain fold the sides inwards.

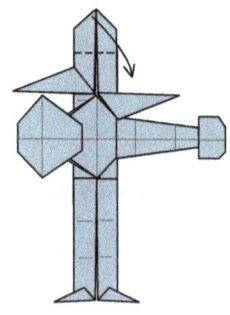

15. Valley fold the head down.

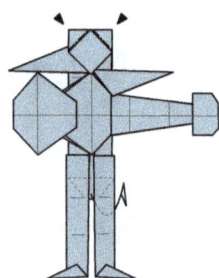

16. Reverse fold the corners of the head. Petal fold the flap up through the legs.

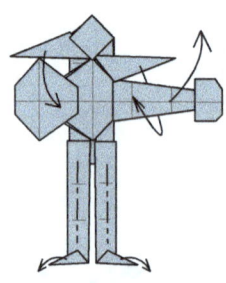

16. Position the arms and guitar into playing position. Open out the feet and add additional shaping as desired.

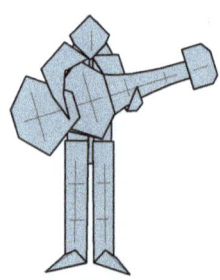

17. Completed *Dollar Bill Guitarist*.

Leaping Guitarist

About

This is a reworking of the *Dollar Bill Guitarist*, developed between debates at a Model United Nations gathering. This time a 2x1 rectangle was used, but the basic structure is the same. It was tough figuring out which portions of the player's leg should be towards the forefront to create the leaping effect. The guitar was fun to design and was a model of the times (during heavy metal's heyday).

Tips

If you were able to get through the *Dollar Bill Guitarist*, the first step should feel straightforward.

In step 11, the term *swivel* is introduced, which is basically a fold that terminates with a squash fold. The important part of this step is to get the sides to fall along the center. These folds will naturally fan out at the waist, and the preexisting pleat will fan out over there as well.

Have fun shaping the guitar and player to taste.

leaping guitarist

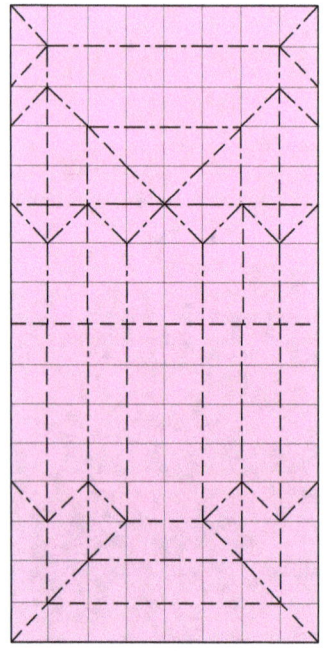

1. Precrease a 2x1 rectangle into 8ths and 16ths, and then collapse as shown.

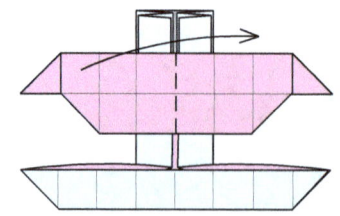

2. Valley fold over.

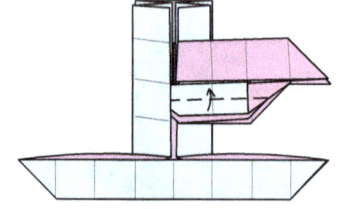

3. Valley fold the single layer up.

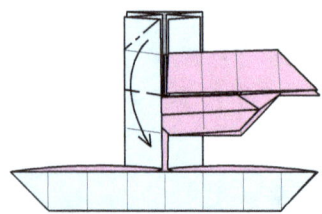

4. Stretch the flap down.

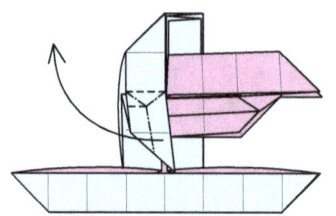

5. Swing the flap up and rabbit ear over.

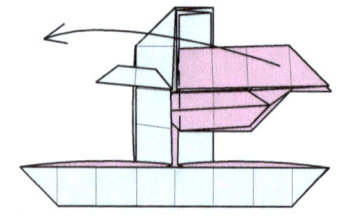

6. Swing over.

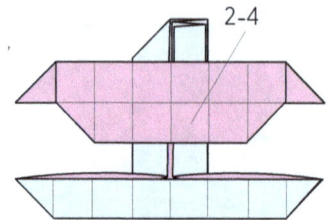

7. Repeat steps 2-4 in mirror image.

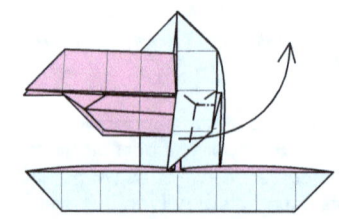

8. Rabbit ear over.

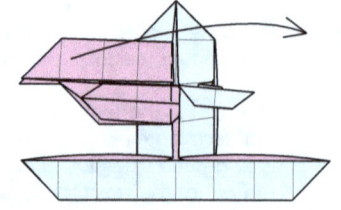

9. Swing over.

leaping guitarist

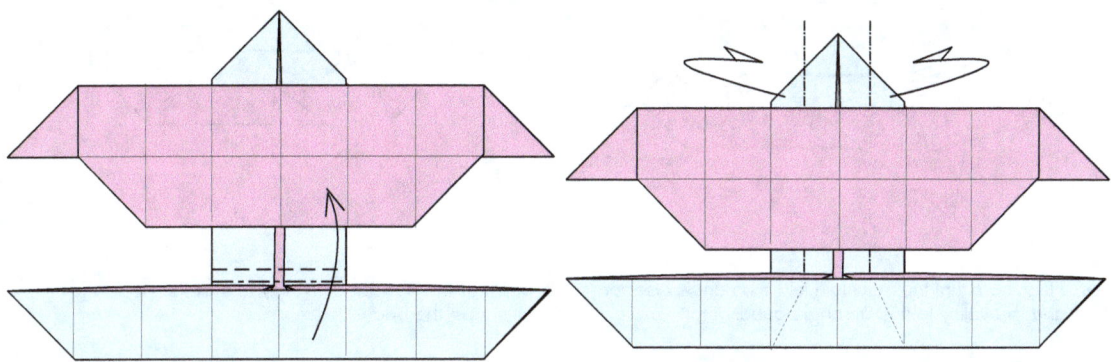

10. Form a tiny pleat at the waist.

11. Mountain fold the sides in, allowing a swivel to form at the waist.

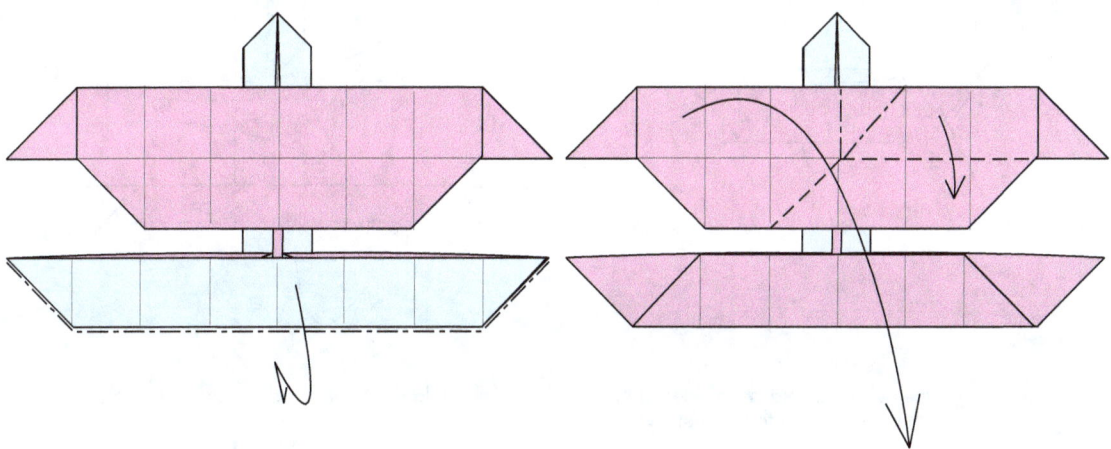

12. Wrap around a single layer.

13. Squash fold the guitar.

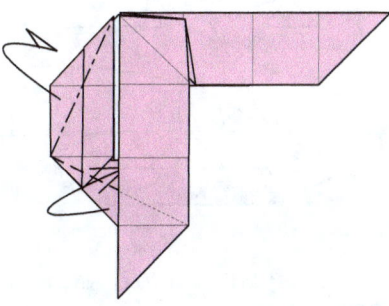 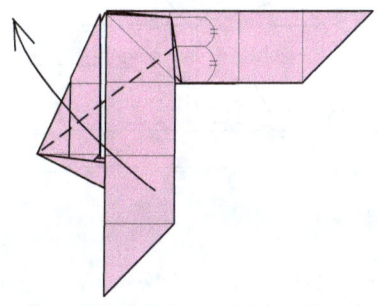

14. Valley fold and mountain the indicated edges.

15. Valley fold over.

17

leaping guitarist

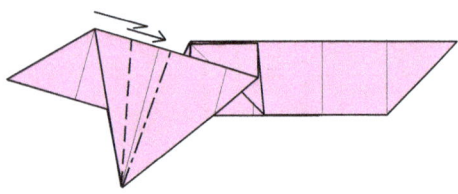

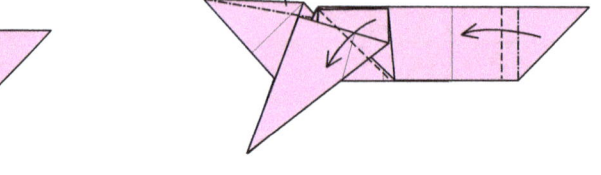

16. Pleat, such that the mountain fold is an angle bisector and the valley fold is an angle quadsector.

17. Pleat the headstock. Valley fold at the neck and shape the body.

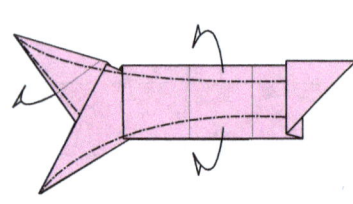

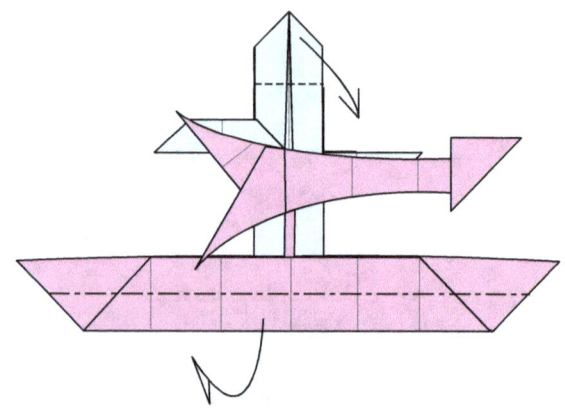

18. Further shape the body and fold in the sides of the neck (tiny squashes will form at the headstock).

19. Valley fold down the head. Mountain fold along the legs.

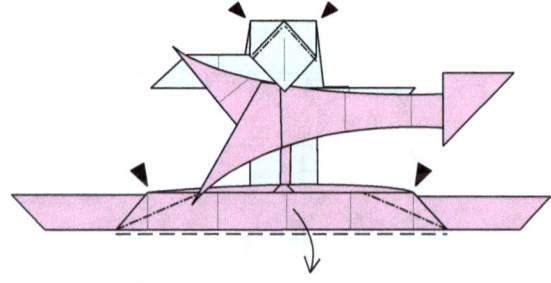

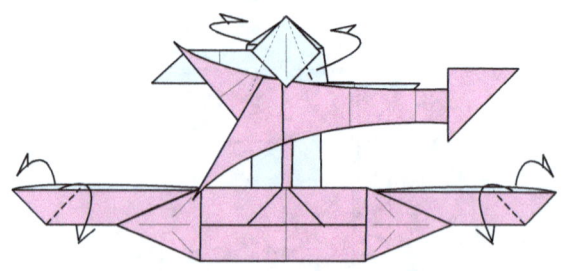

20. Reverse fold the corners of the head. Swing down the top layer of the legs forming spread squashes.

21. Outside reverse fold the feet. Mountain fold the sides of the neck.

leaping guitarist

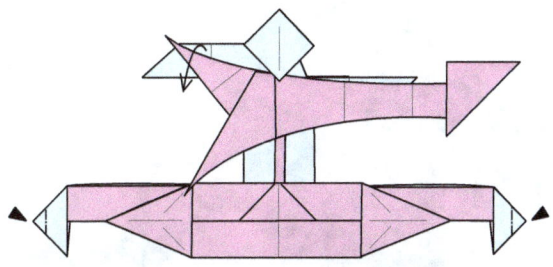

22. Bring the arm around the guitar. Sink the corners of the feet.

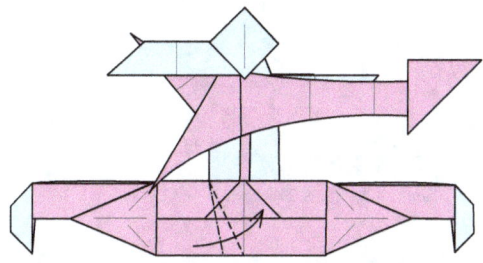

23. Pleat one leg.

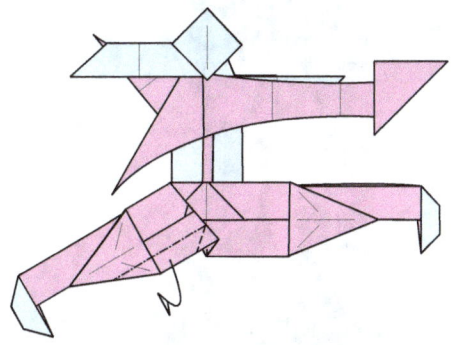

24. Swivel under.

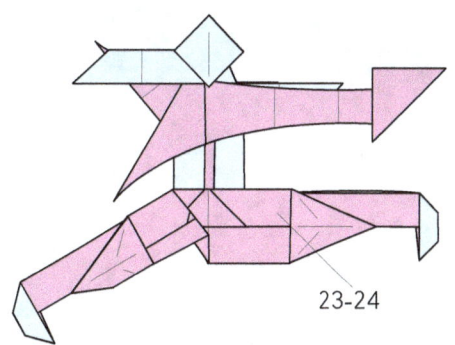

25. Repeat steps 23-24 on the other side.

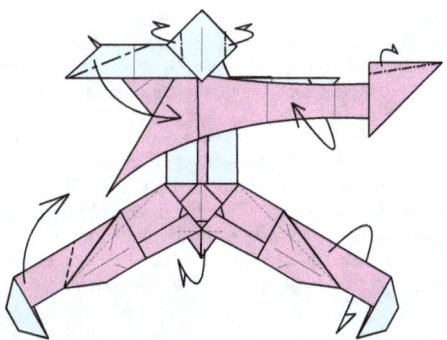

26. Pleat the legs into position. Wrap the arms into position. Shape the guitar and head to taste.

27. Completed *Leaping Guitarist*.

Violinist

About

This is the first model that defined the look that the rest of the instrumentalists were to take on. A big part of creating this look was an accident. While designing the model, forming the player's head was forgotten. Fortunately, there was enough paper between the player's arms to form this essential appendage, and the paper seamed to coalesce into a hooded form. This original look allows the viewer's own feelings to be projected onto the work.

The creative process for this model was still drawn from the works of Neal Elias, specifically his *Yehudi Menuhin* (which was formed from a "T" shaped rectangle) and transferred that symmetry onto a square. If you could imagine the squashes at the corners in the beginning of the sequence opened out, you will have a "T" shaped form. The extra paper needed for the violin formation was accounted for with the hem that was placed in step 5. It is only at step 76 where those Elias roots are evident.

Tips

The hem from step 5 is exactly $1/5^{th}$ of the square. The first steps can be eliminated if you find it easier to use a ruler or other means.

Step 68 is easier than it looks. You can grasp at the colored paper in the pockets below the triangle. Pulling them out will reveal a shallow triangular flap that can be flattened onto the surface of the triangle.

violinist

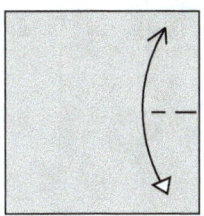 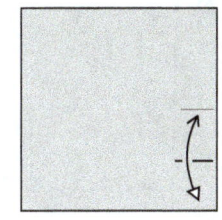 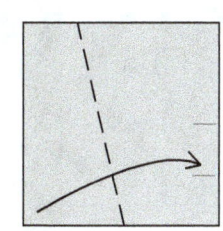 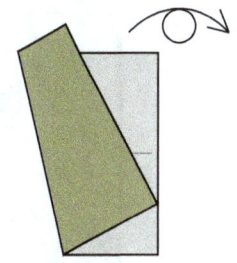

1. Pinch in half.
2. Pinch again.
3. Valley fold the corner to the crease.
4. Turn over.

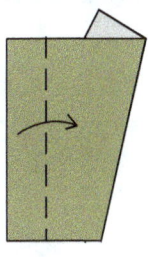 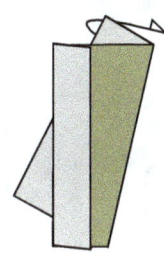 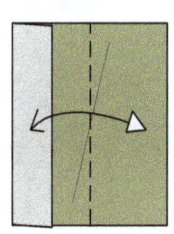 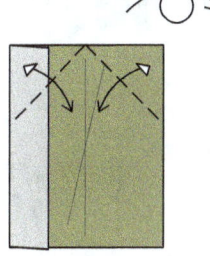

5. Valley fold to the intersection of raw edges.
6. Unfold.
7. Precrease in half.
8. Precrease again. Turn over.

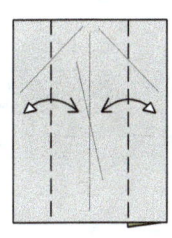 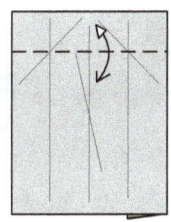 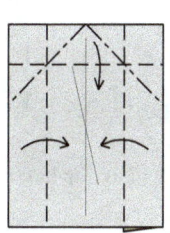 

9. Precrease to the center.
10. Precrease through the intersection of creases.
11. Collapse using the existing creases.
12. Turn over.

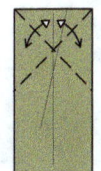 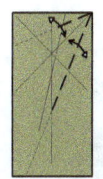 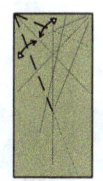 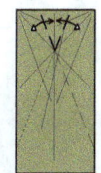

13. Precrease the top layer.
14. Precrease along the angle bisectors as far as indicated.
15. Repeat in the opposite direction.
16. More precreasing along angle bisectors.

violinist

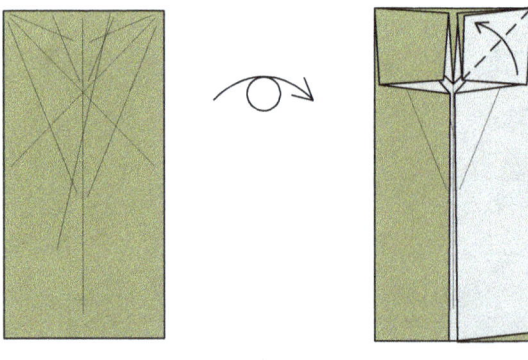

17. Turn over.

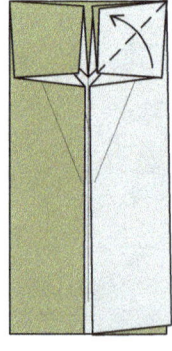

18. Lightly valley fold the flap upwards.

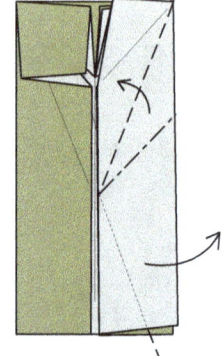

19. Swivel the single layer using the exiting creases as a guide.

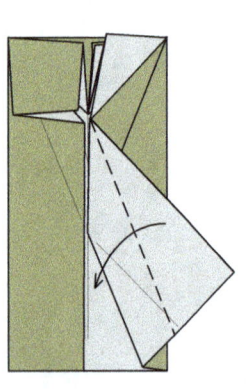

20. Valley fold to the center.

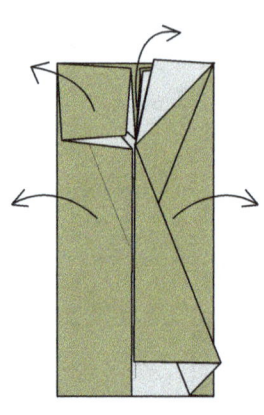

21. Open out the sides and top.

22. Turn over.

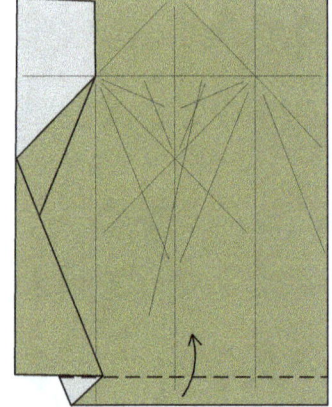

23. Valley fold the bottom edge up to match with the left corner.

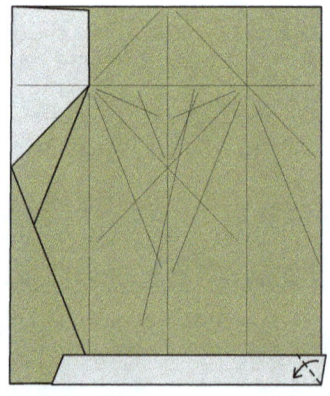

24. Valley fold the corner.

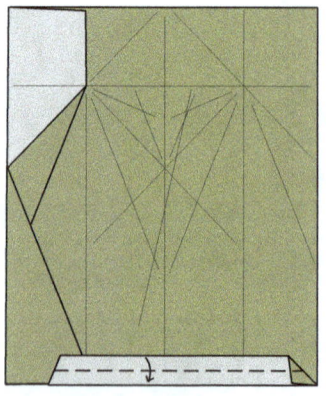

25. Valley fold down.

v i o l i n i s t

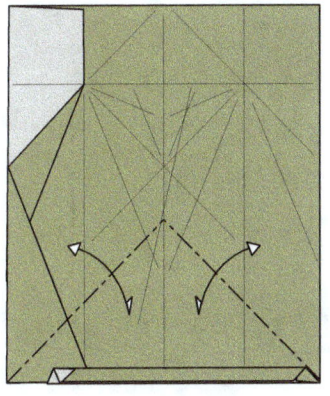

26. Precrease with mountain folds.

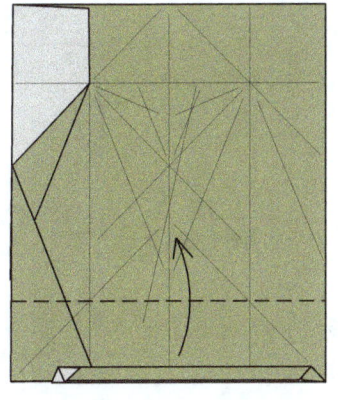

27. Valley fold through the intersection of creases.

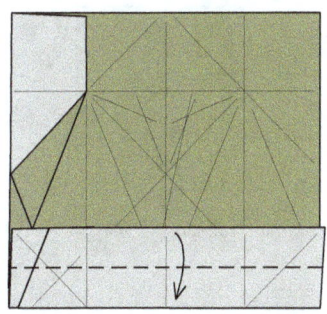

28. Valley fold down.

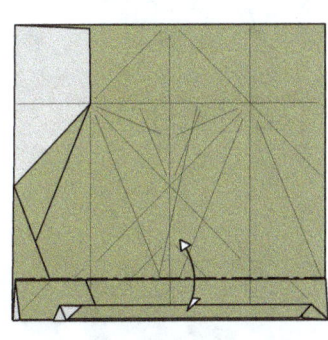

29. Precrease with a mountain fold along the folded edge.

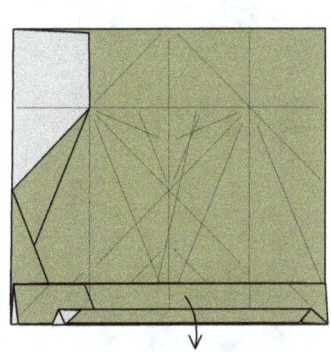

30. Unfold the pleat.

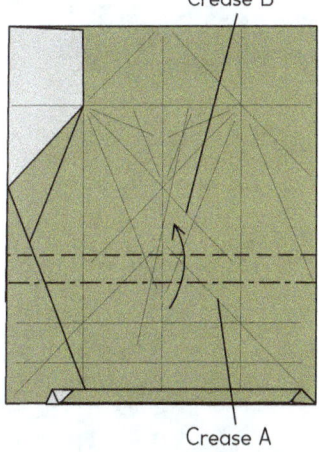

31. Using the mountain fold from step 29, pleat such that crease A lies on crease B.

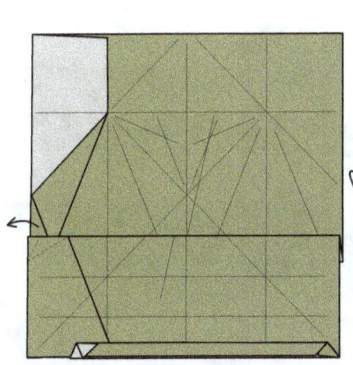

32. Swivel out the side layer.

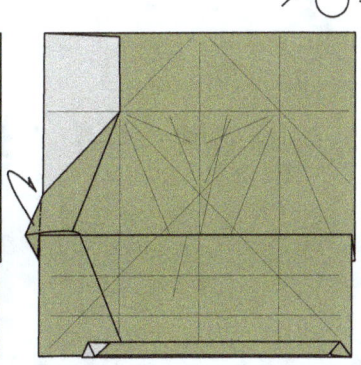

33. Tuck the resulting flap into the side. Turn over.

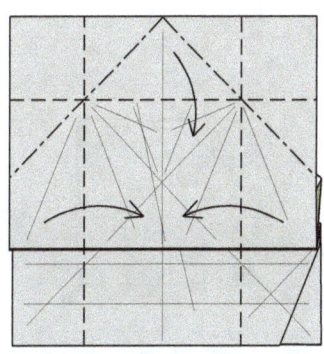

34. Collapse (like step 11).

23

violinist

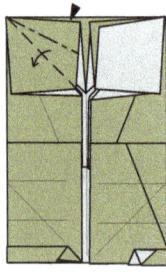

35. Squash fold.

36. Petal fold.

37. Valley fold down the small flap.

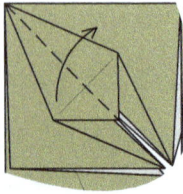

38. Valley fold over.

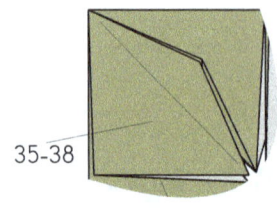

39. Repeat steps 35-38 on the indicated flap.

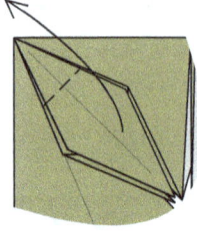

40. Stretch upwards. The tiny hidden flaps will disappear in the process.

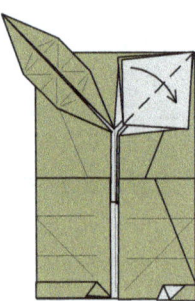

41. Valley fold down lightly.

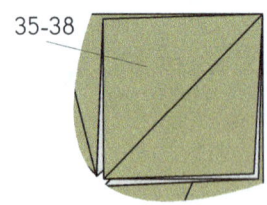

42. Repeat steps 35-38 on the indicated flap.

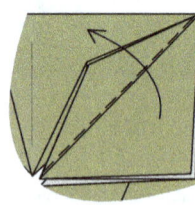

43. Swing back up.

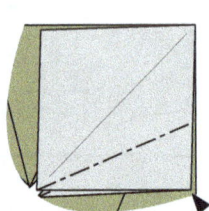

44. Reverse fold.

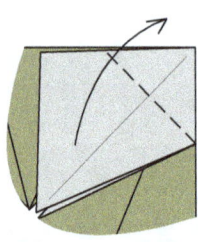

45. Valley fold upwards. The top half will stretch flat as in step 40.

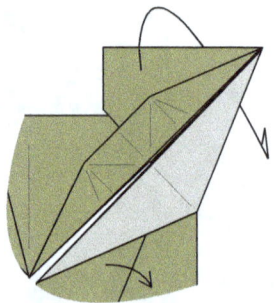

46. Unwrap the single layer. The model will not lie flat.

violinist

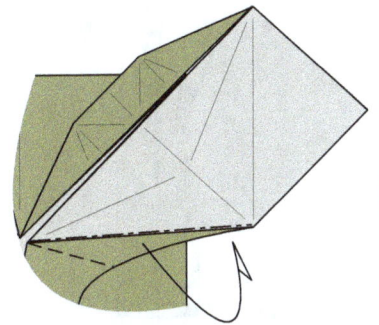
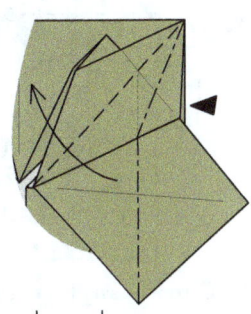

47. Pleat the paper under to flatten.

48. Valley fold down.

49. Spread squash.

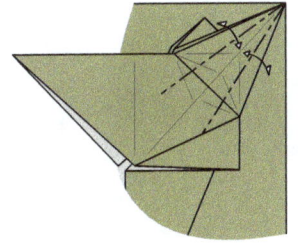
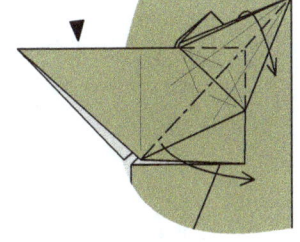
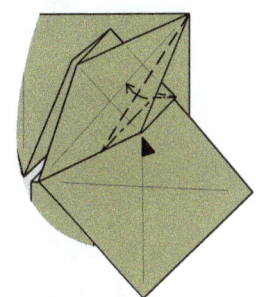

50. Precrease the top layer with mountain folds.

51. Open out the bottom while swinging over the top.

52. Valley fold to the crease while spread squashing.

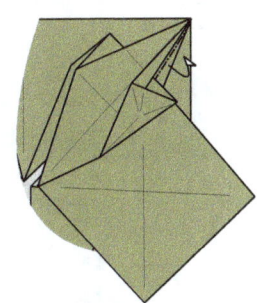
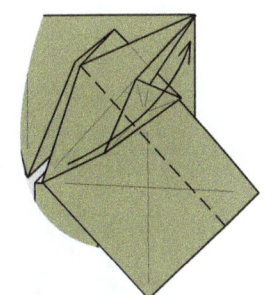
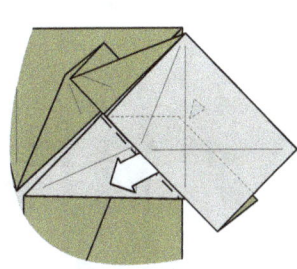

53. Repeat step 52 behind.

54. Valley fold up to the corner.

55. Unsink the indicated region.

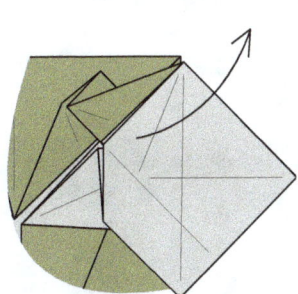
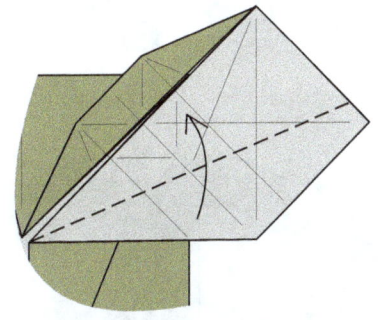
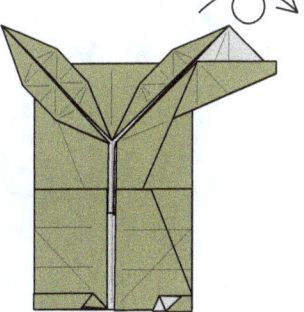

56. Stretch outwards, undoing the center ridge.

57. Valley fold to the center.

58. Turn over.

25

violinist

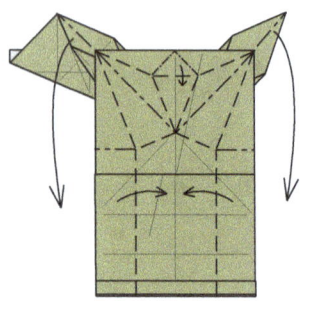

59. Collapse using the existing creases as a guide.

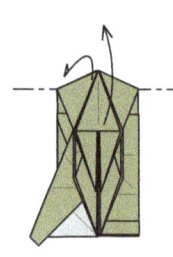

60. Swing the two points upwards.

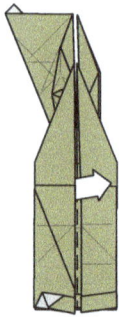

61. Unsink a single layer.

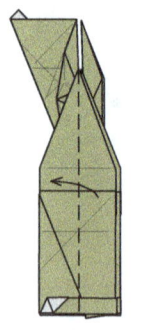

62. Valley fold over.

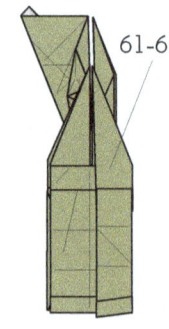

63. Repeat steps 61-62 on the other side.

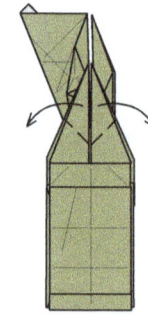

64. Valley fold the two points outwards.

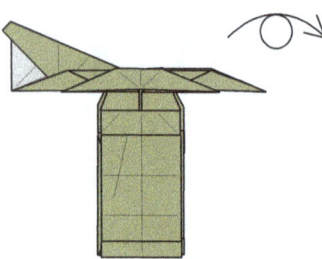

65. Turn over.

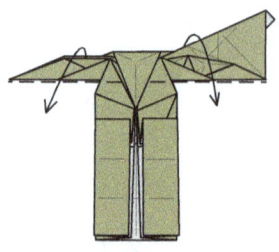

66. Open out the two points.

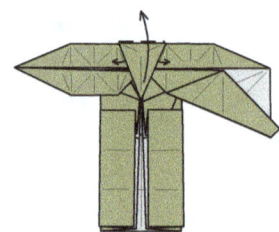

67. Release the top point upwards. The model will not lie flat.

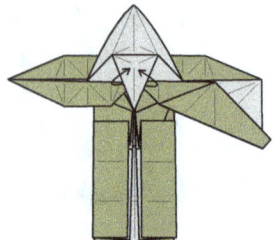

68. Pull out the hidden corners to the surface.

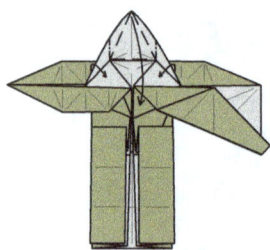

69. Collapse the top point flat.

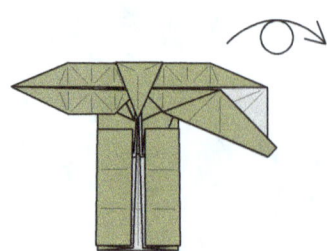

70. Turn over.

26

violinist

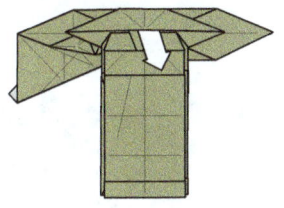

71. Unsink.

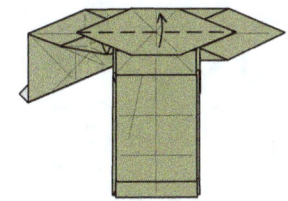

72. Valley fold upwards.

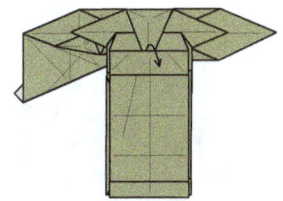

73. Unsink the remaining portion of the triangle to the surface.

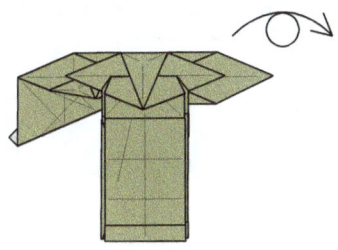

74. Turn over.

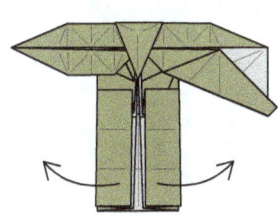

75. Spread apart the bottom pleats. The model will not lie flat.

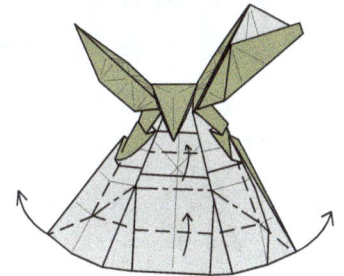

76. Pleat the bottom edge upwards while stretching the corners outwards.

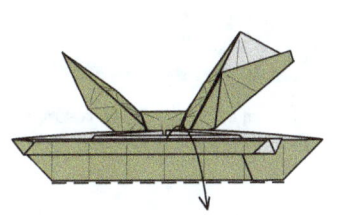

77. Swing down the top layer.

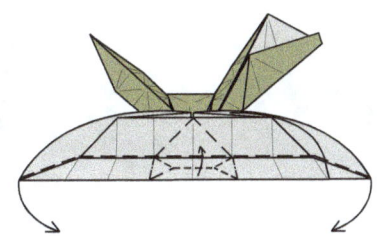

78. Collapse downwards, adding the indicated folds. Do not flatten.

79. Pull the indicated layer up.

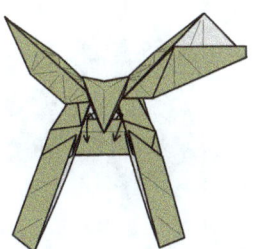

80. Wrap a single layer around from behind.

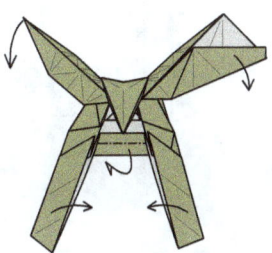

81. Mountain fold the bottom edge under as far as possible and flatten.

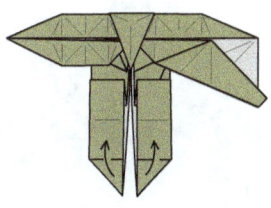

82. Valley fold the bottom corners up.

27

violinist

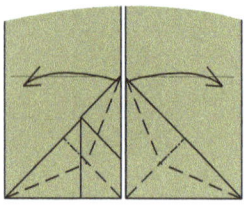

83. Rabbit ear outwards.

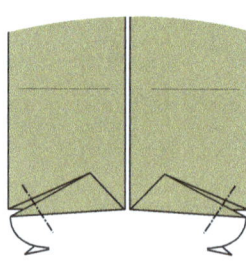

84. Reverse fold the tips.

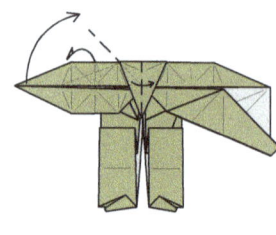

85. Swing the arm upwards, allowing the indicated flaps to swing along with it.

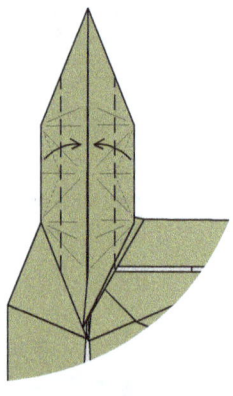

86. Valley fold the sides inward, such that the folds line up with the hidden edges behind.

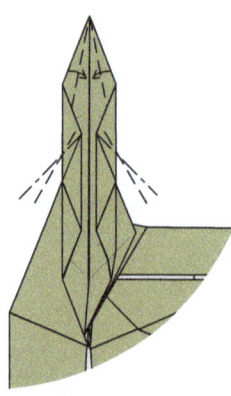

87. Valley fold the sides to the center, allowing the paper to pleat where indicated.

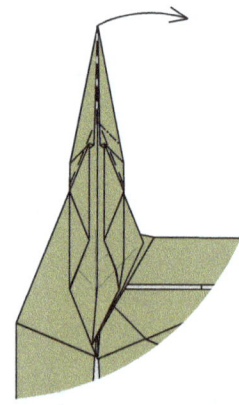

88. Rabbit ear the flap. The resulting edges should match with the flap behind.

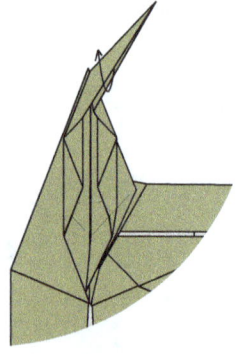

89. Pull out the inner layers, and wrap them around to the surface.

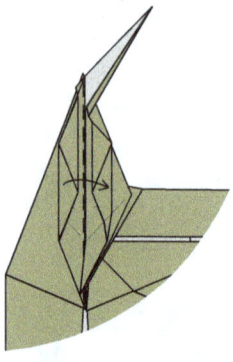

90. Valley fold over.

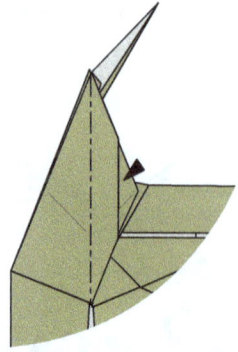

91. Closed sink.

violinist

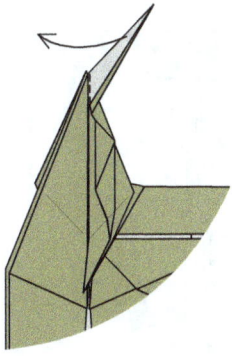
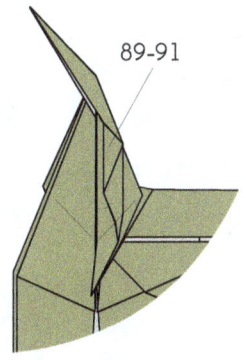
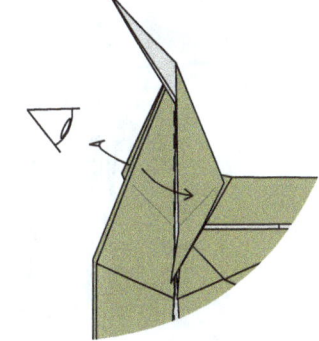

92. Swing over.

93. Repeat steps 89-91 on the other side.

94. Spread apart the two larger layers.

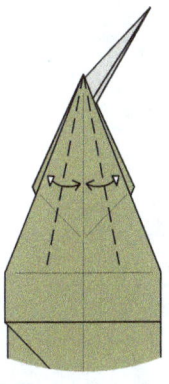
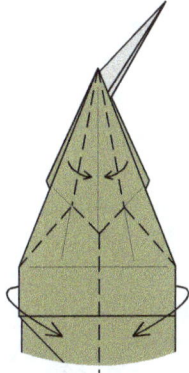
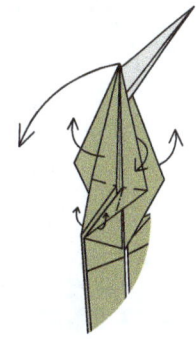

95. View from step 94. Precrease along the angle bisectors.

96. Start to collapse the sides inwards by adding the indicated folds.

97. Twist the arm down back into the position from step 85, noting which layers swing upwards, and which layer swings down.

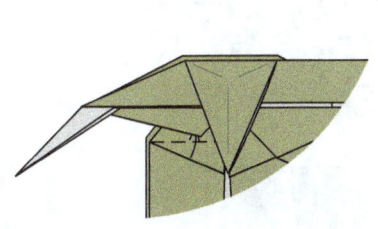
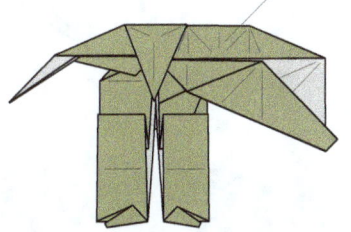
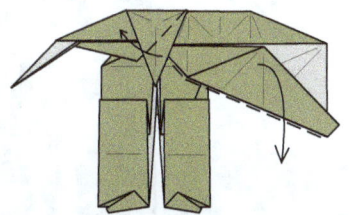

98. Valley fold up the small flap.

99. Repeat step 85, and then steps 94-98 on the other side.

100. Lightly swing over the center flap. Open out the large flap at the right. The model will not lie flat.

violinist

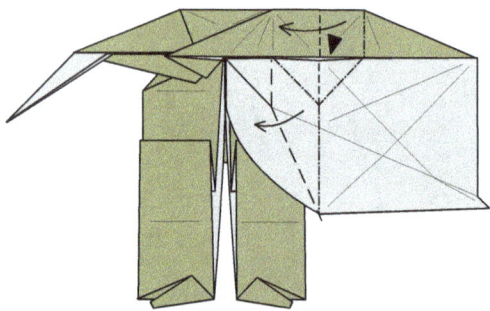

101. Collapse inwards, replacing the folds formed in step 55.

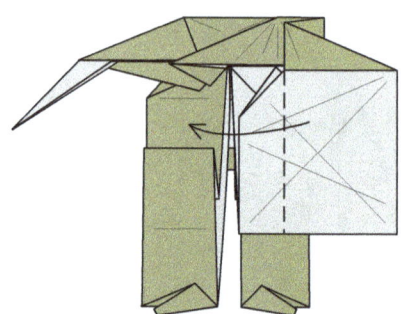

102. Swing over.

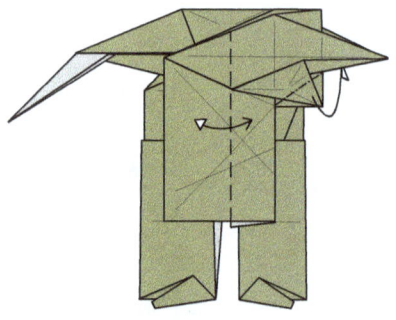

103. Precrease the large flap to match up with the folded edge behind. Tuck the protruding corner at the armpit into the arm as far as possible.

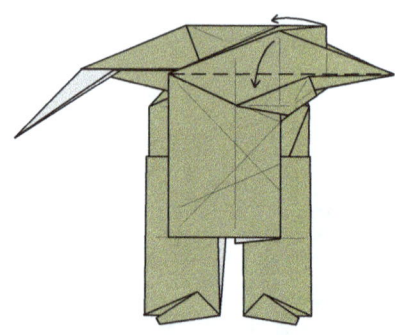

104. Swing down the top layer, allowing the top corner to squash flat.

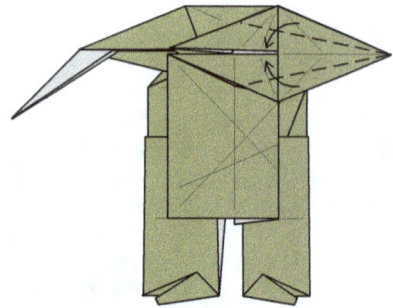

105. Valley fold to the center.

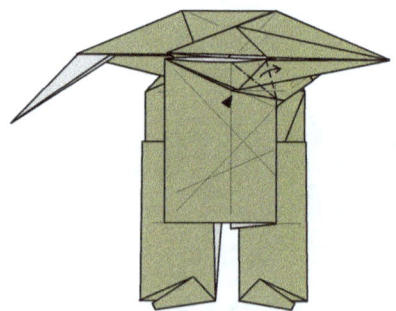

106. Spread squash the indicated area. Do not flatten yet, as the next step will show where the remainder of the folds go.

violinist

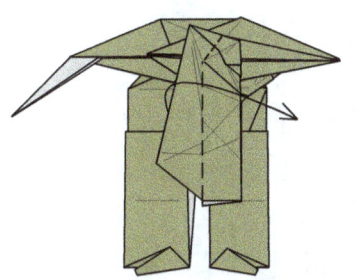

107. Flatten.

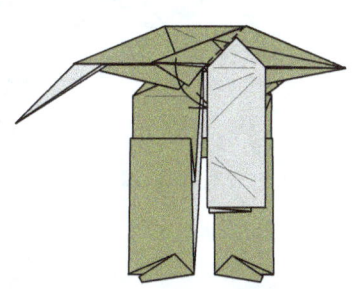

108. Swing down the center point under the violin.

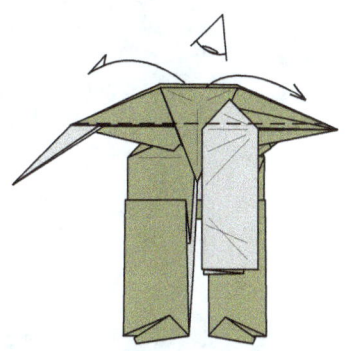

109. Spread apart the top layers.

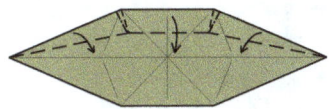

110. Valley fold to the center, inserting tiny rabbit ears.

111. Unsink.

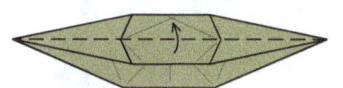

112. Valley fold up.

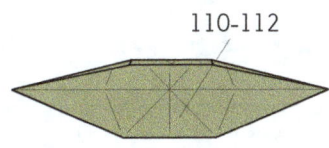

113. Repeat steps 110-112 on the thicker bottom section.

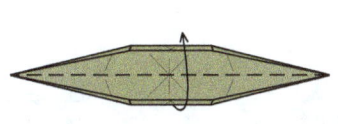

114. Close back up.

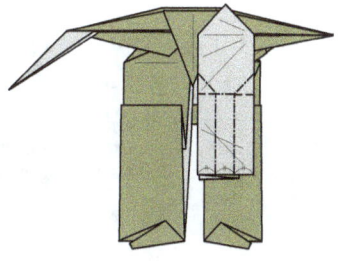

115. Collapse the violin into a 3-D form as indicated.

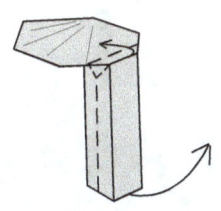

116. Rabbit ear the sides of the neck while raising it upwards.

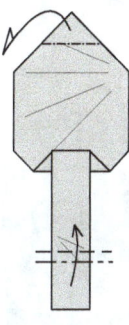

117. Round off the top. Pleat the bottom.

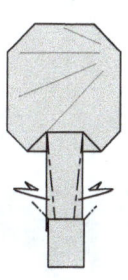

118. Round the neck with swivel folds (do not crease sharply).

violinist

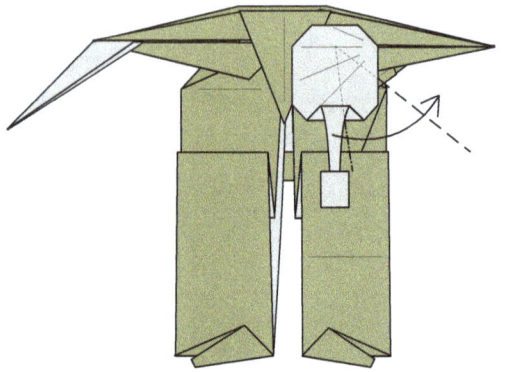

119. Pleat the violin upwards.

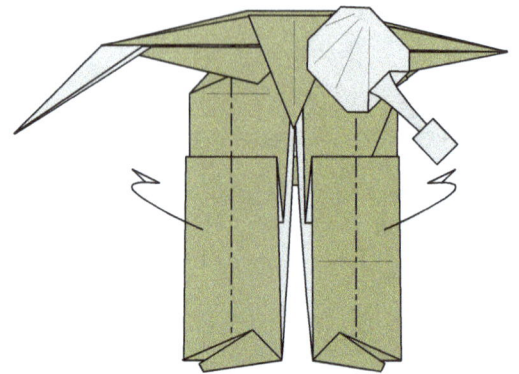

120. Mountain fold the sides in half.

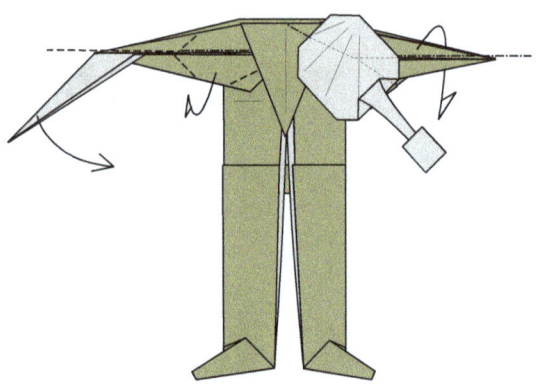

121. Rabbit ear one arm to lie below the violin. Rabbit ear and thin the other arm into position.

122. Raise and open out the layers of the head. Open out the feet. Shape the bow and violin. Add additional rounding to the body.

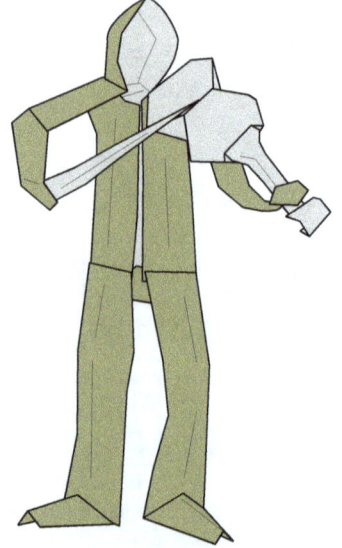

123. Completed *Violinist*.

Bassist

About

This bassist uses the boxy style of Neal Elias, albeit with a different approach. Generally, box pleated models have appendages that are pulled from a rectangle that has been pleated like a fan. However, by step 9, the sort of pleat used is nonstandard. Nonstandard folds are used to deal with this, but by step 49, the top of the model is restructured in the conventional pleated style.

The player's appendages come from out of the bass (many similar models would connect the bass via an umbilical cord of paper). Since both the bass and the player are oriented the same way, this is convenient. The color changes between the bass and player is important to maintain the illusion of separation.

The feet were designed first, and the model is developed upward from there. The folding sequence reflects this unusual approach.

Tips

The triangular sink in step 14 is basically a standard "open" sink. You are sinking through a three-sided polygon, hence "sinking triangularly."

The wrap procedure in step 102 might be the most difficult part of this model. The concept is simple, but preventing the model from tearing can be a challenge. The trick is to grasp the head at its weakest point, which is along the center.

When you shape the player and bass in step 118, keep in mind that the pleats that connect the bass to the player are loose. It is important to stretch the bass away from the player to create the illusion they are separate.

bassist

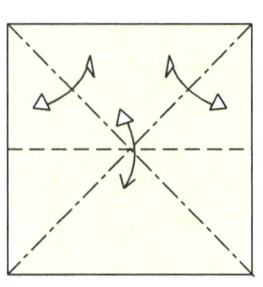
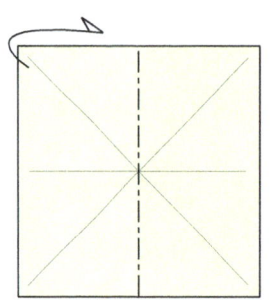
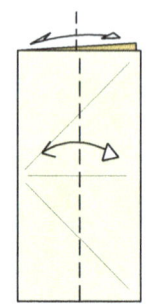
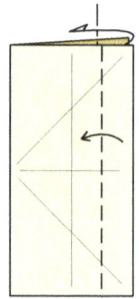

1. Precrease with mountain and valley folds.

2. Mountain fold as lightly as possible.

3. Precrease, front and back.

4. Valley fold to the previously formed crease. Repeat behind.

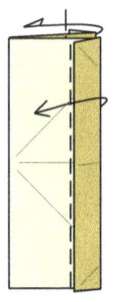
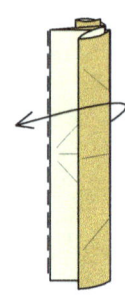
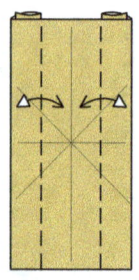
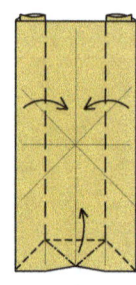

5. Valley fold along the existing creases.

6. Open out the center fold.

7. Precrease.

8. Collapse as shown.

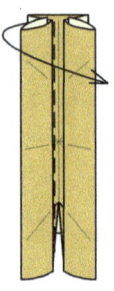
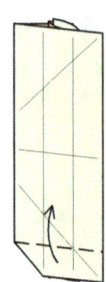
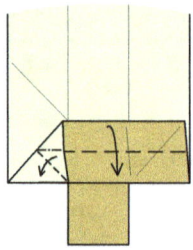
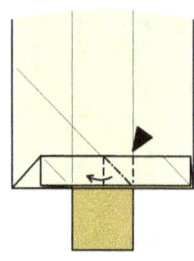

9. Unravel one side.

10. Valley fold up.

11. Valley fold down while swiveling over.

12. Squash, allowing the pleat to flatten out.

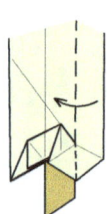
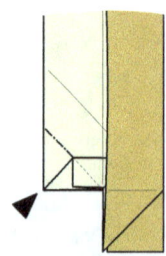
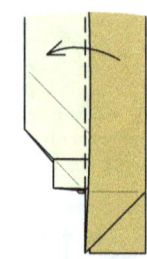
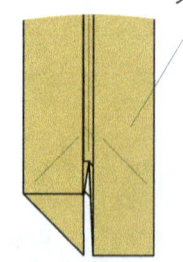

9-15

13. Flatten.

14. Sink triangularly.

15. Swing over.

16. Repeat steps 9-15 in mirror image.

bassist

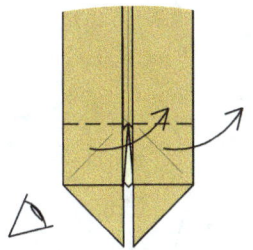
17. Swing the flaps upwards at a 90º angle.

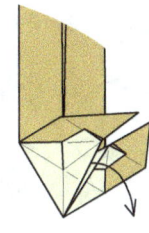
18. Pull out paper from the center.

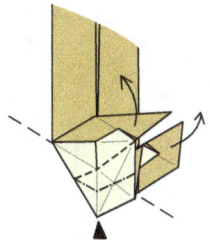
19. Swing the flaps upwards while spread squashing the center.

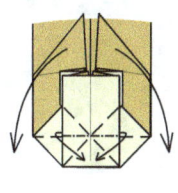
20. Swing down the flaps while reverse folding at the bottom.

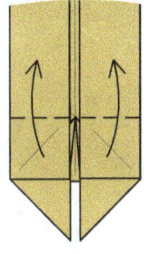
21. Swing the flaps back up while stretching the internal pleats flat.

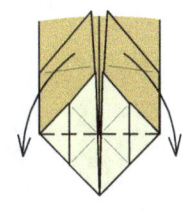
22. Swing back down.

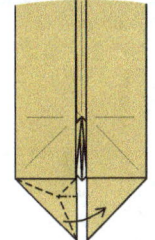
23. Rabbit ear.

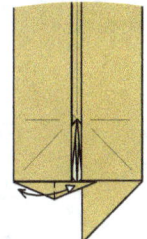
24. Precrease.

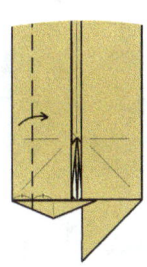
25. Valley fold to the precrease.

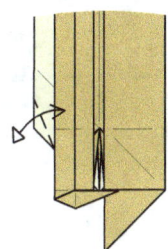
26. Precrease.

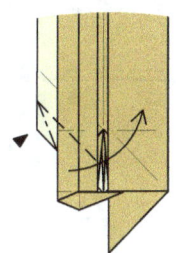
27. Valley fold over, allowing the corner to squash flat.

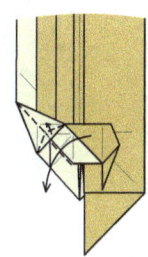
28. Swing back down, while closing up part of the squash.

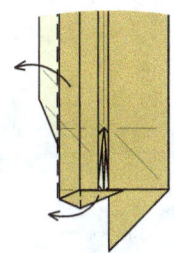
29. Swing back over.

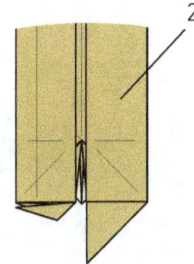
30. Repeat steps 23-29 in mirror image.

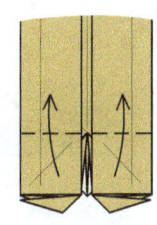
31. Swing up.

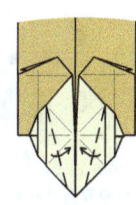
32. Valley fold the corners to the center.

bassist

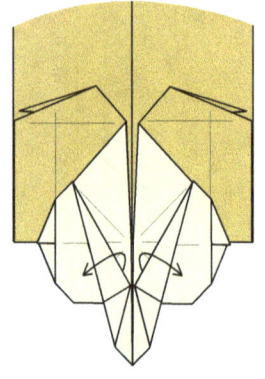

33. Bring the single layers to the surface (closed sink).

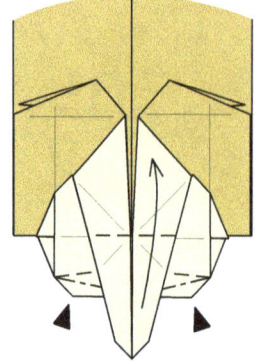

34. Raise the center flap while spread squashing the side corners.

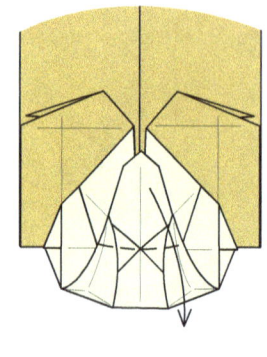

35. Swing back down to flatten.

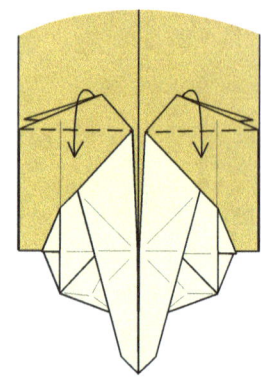

36. Valley fold down.

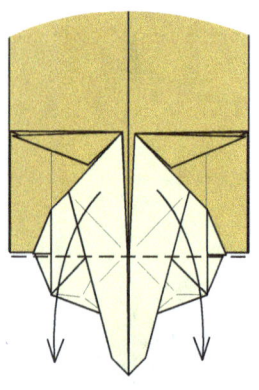

37. Swing back down.

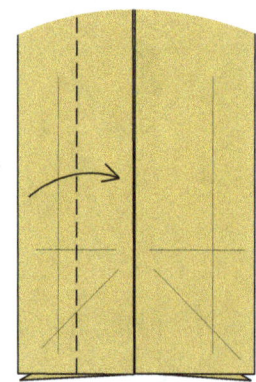

38. Valley fold in half.

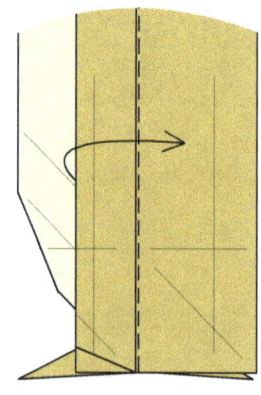

39. Swing over.

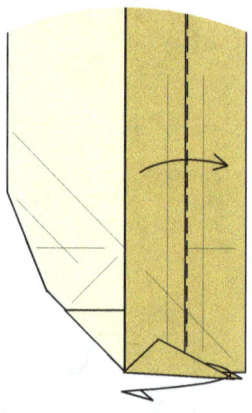

40. Swing over the top layer.

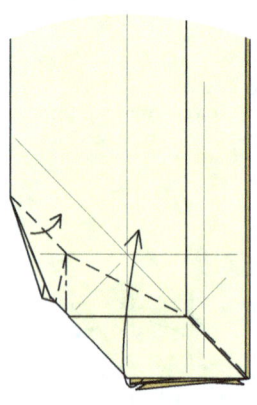

41. Valley fold up while opening out the side squash. The model will not lie flat.

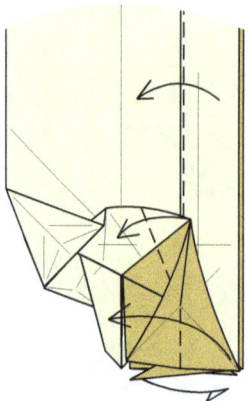

42. Swing the single layer back over, allowing the layers at the bottom to collapse flat.

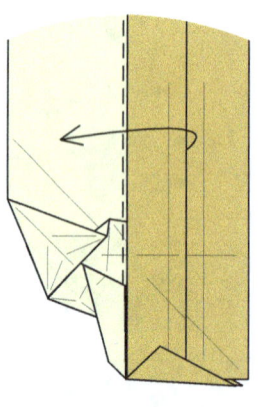

43. Swing back over.

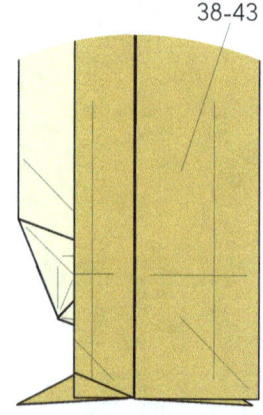

44. Repeat steps 38-43 in mirror image.

bassist

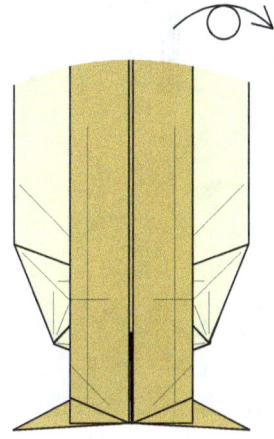
45. Turn over.

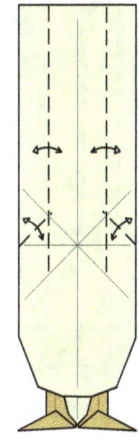
46. Precrease.

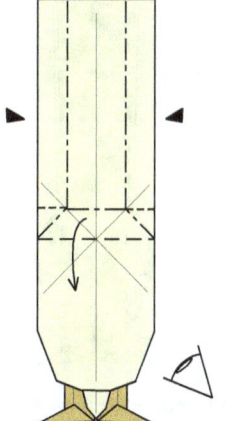
47. Collapse the sides upwards into a box shape.

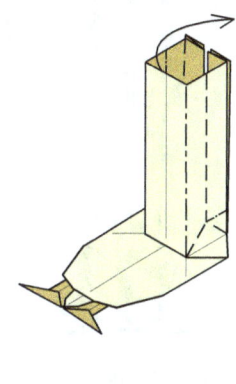
48. Rabbit ear the flap on both sides to flatten it.

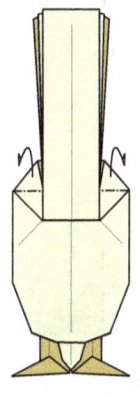
49. Mountain fold behind.

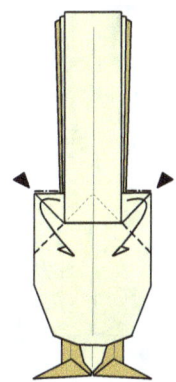
50. Reverse fold the corners.

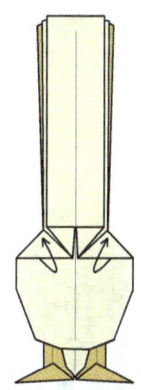
51. Bring the single layer to the surface (closed sink).

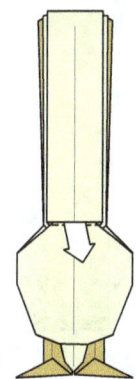
52. Unsink the hidden triangle.

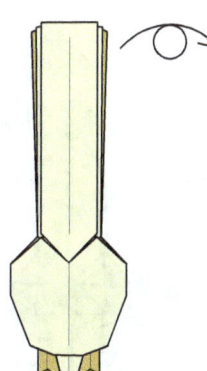
53. Turn over.

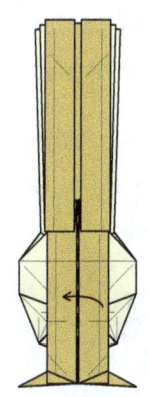
54. Swing over, releasing the trapped colored layers.

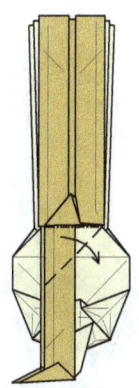
55. Swivel the corner down.

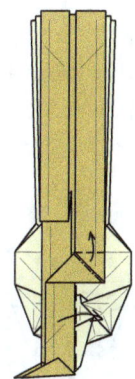
56. Swivel up.

37

bassist

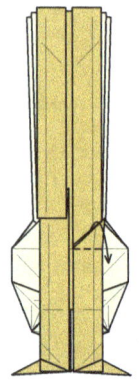
57. Swing down.

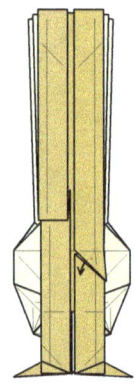
58. Pull out a layer.

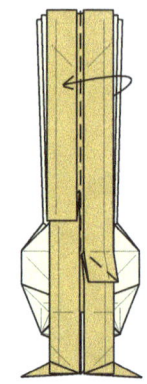
59. Open out the top layer.

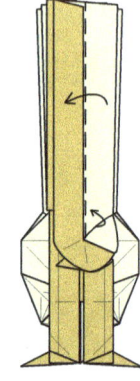
60. Swing over the next layer, pulling out paper from the crimp.

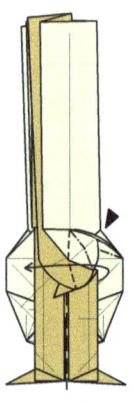
61. Swing over the bottom, allowing the indicated area to spread squash.

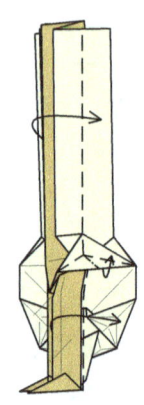
62. Close up the squashed area and swing everything back over to flatten.

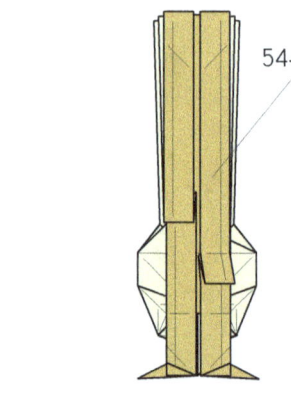
63. Repeat steps 54-62 in mirror image.

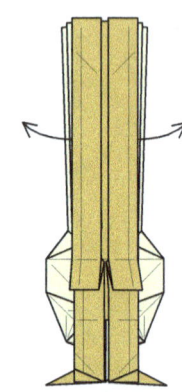
64. Pull out a single layer from each side.

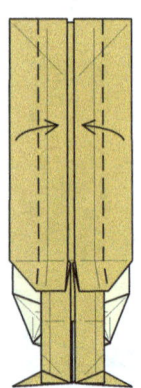
65. Valley fold the sides to the center.

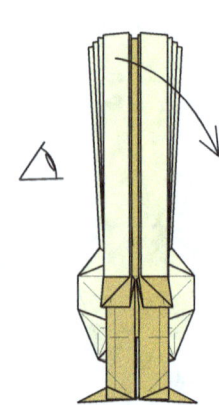
66. Spread apart one side.

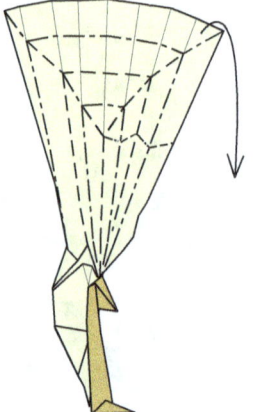
67. Stretch the corner down while pleating the top edge down.

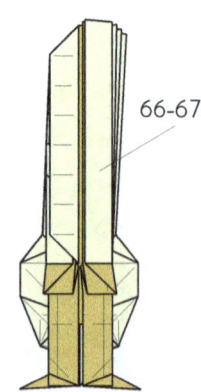
68. Repeat steps 66-67 on the other side.

bassist

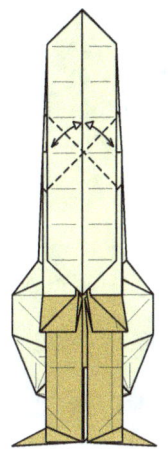
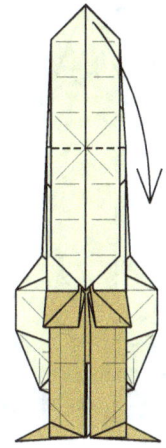
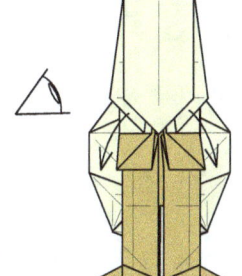
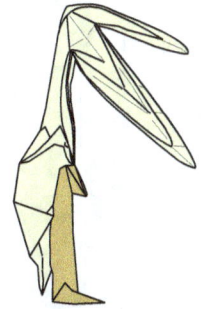

69. Precrease through all layers.

70. Valley fold down.

71. Pull the two points down, allowing the inner pleats to stretch.

72. Completed stretching.

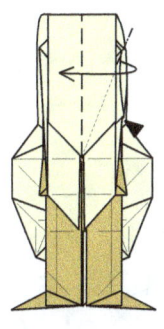
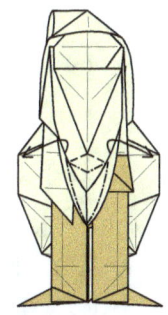
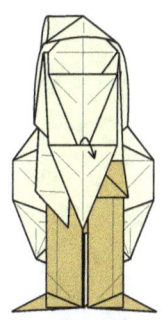
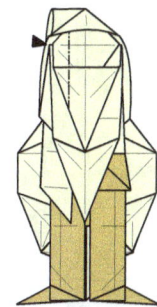

73. Swing over, allowing the center section to spread squash.

74. Pull apart the sides, allowing the bottom to spread squash.

75. Pull the hidden corner to the surface.

76. Sink triangularly.

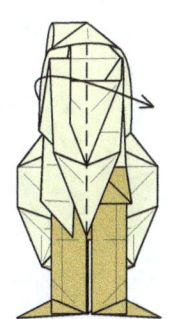
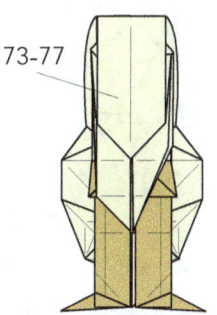
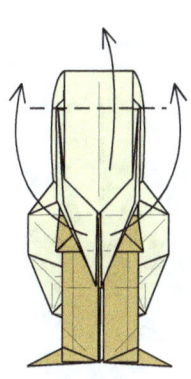
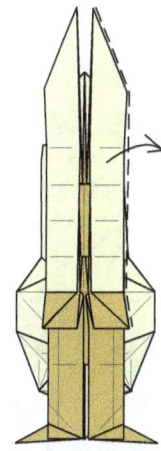

77. Close back up.

78. Repeat steps 73-77 in mirror image.

79. Swing the three flaps upwards.

80. Swing the top layer over. The model will not lie flat.

bassist

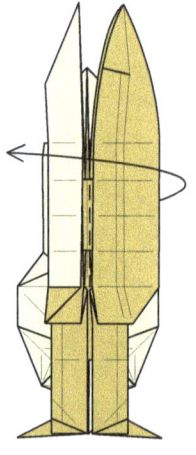
81. Swing over two layers.

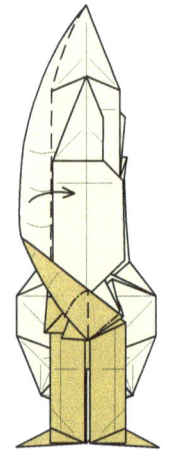
82. Valley fold over, reversing at the bottom.

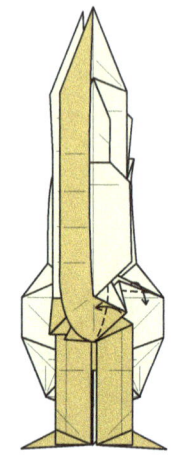
83. Swivel over as much as possible.

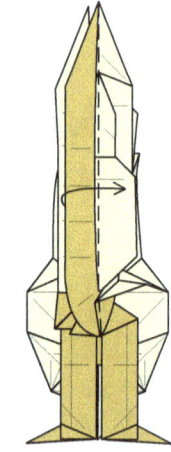
84. Close back up.

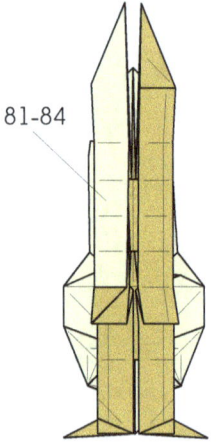
85. Repeat steps 81-84 in mirror image.

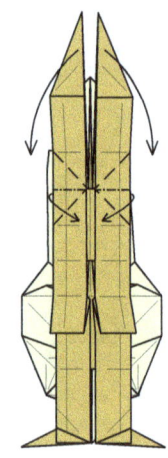
86. Swing down while reverse folding.

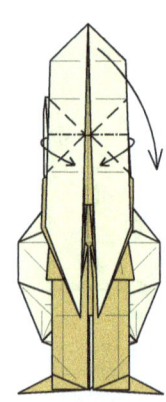
87. Swing down while reverse folding.

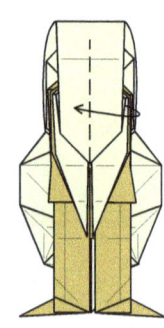
88. Swing over the top layer.

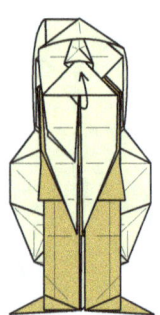
89. Wrap the single layer from behind.

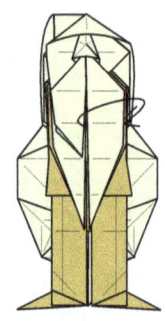
90. Wrap the single layer around.

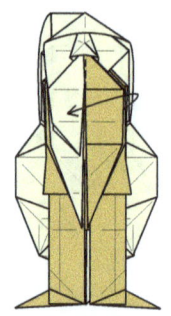
91. Swing over one flap.

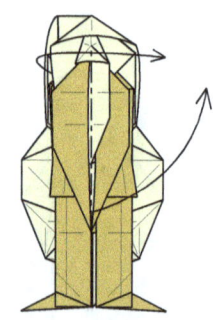
92. Reverse the flap upwards while closing the model back up.

bassist

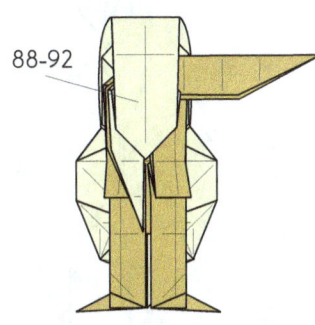

93. Repeat steps 88-92 in mirror image.

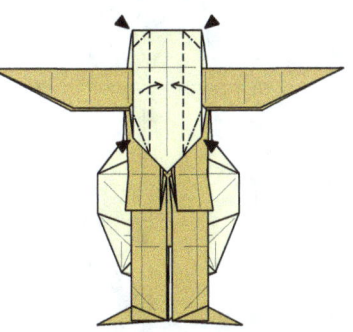

94. Valley fold the sides to the center, squashing at the top and spread squashing at the bottom.

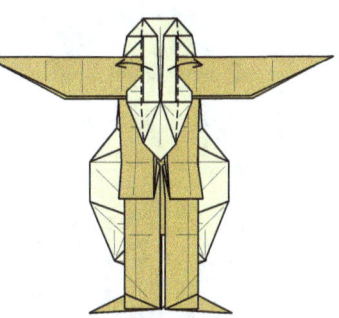

95. Valley fold the sides outwards.

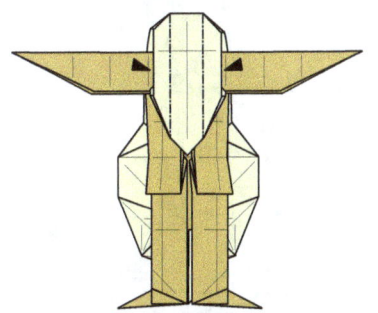

96. Closed sink the sides.

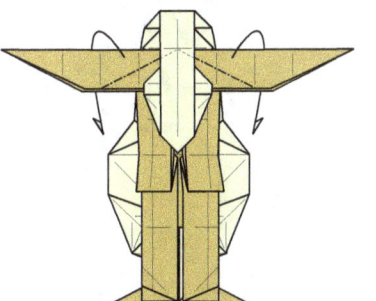

97. Mountain fold the arms.

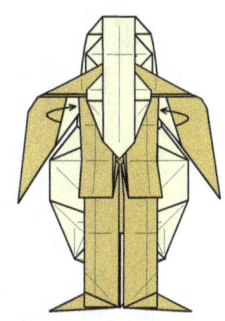

98. Wrap a single layer over the white area.

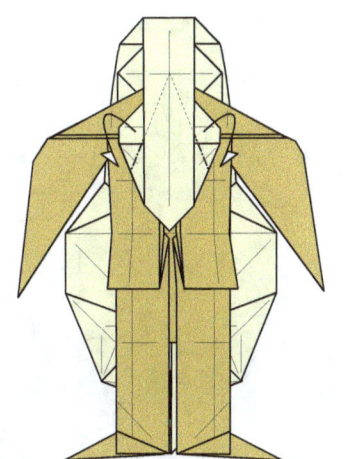

99. Mountain fold the sides.

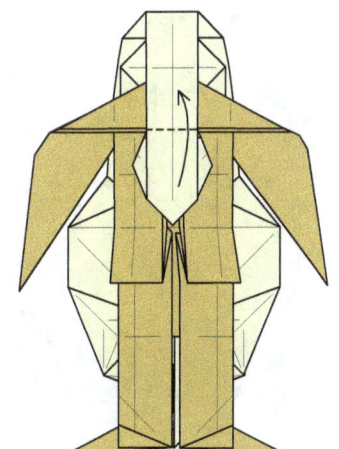

100. Valley fold up.

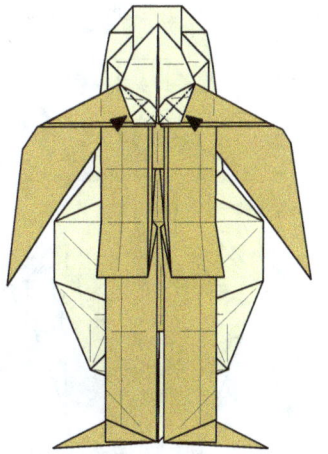

101. Reverse fold the sides.

41

bassist

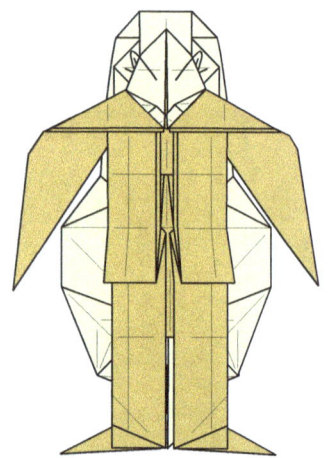

102. Carefully wrap a single layer around.

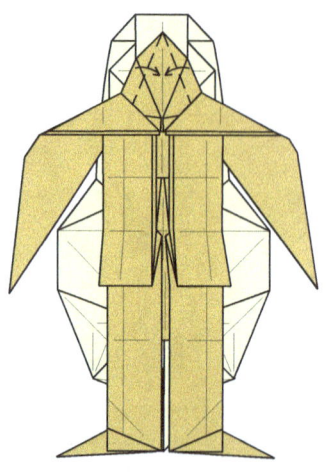

103. Valley fold to the center.

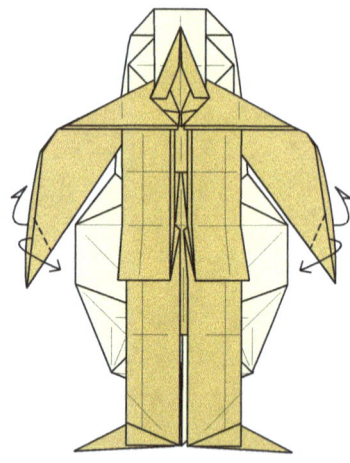

104. Outside reverse fold.

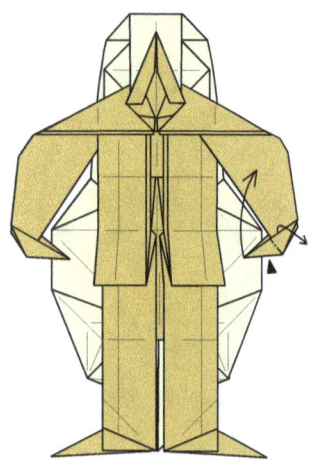

105. Squash one of the hands.

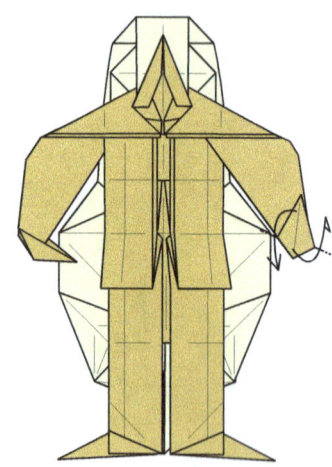

106. Flip the hand down.

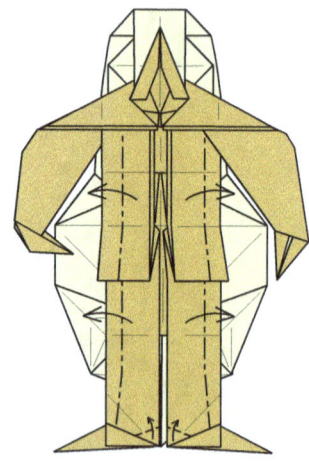

107. Slide the top layers outwards.

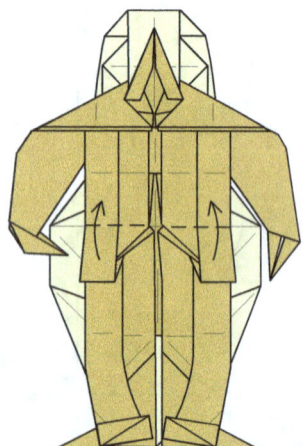

108. Valley fold the flaps upwards.

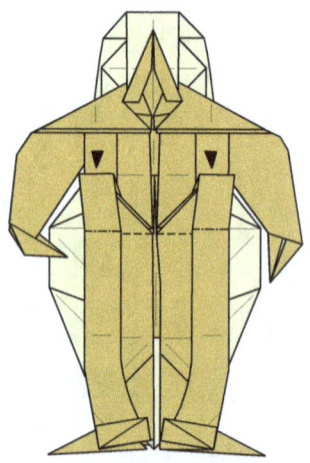

109. Closed reverse fold the flaps.

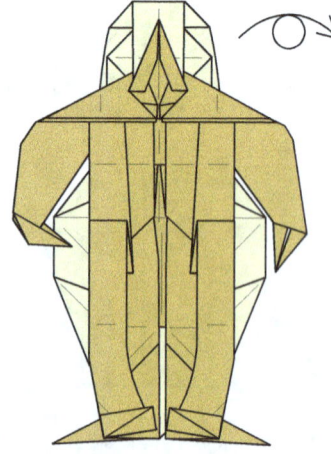

110. Turn over.

bassist

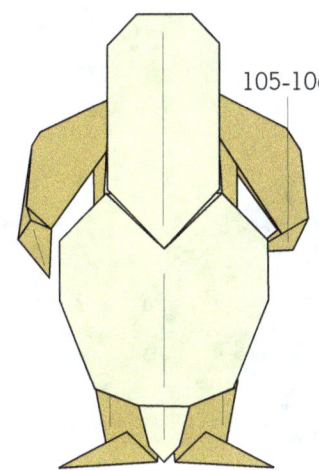

111. Repeat steps 105-106.

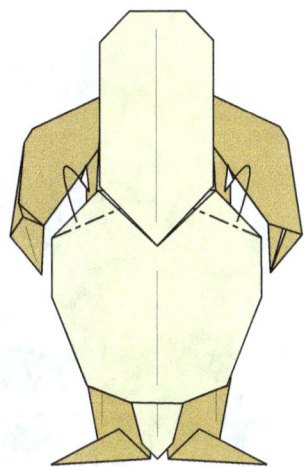

112. Mountain fold.

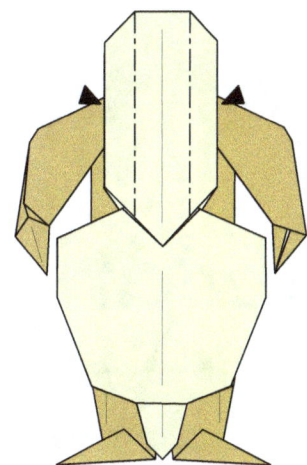

113. Sink triangularly.

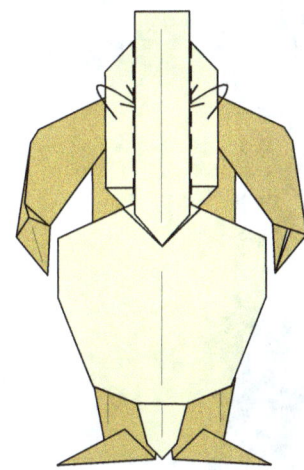

114. Valley fold into the pockets.

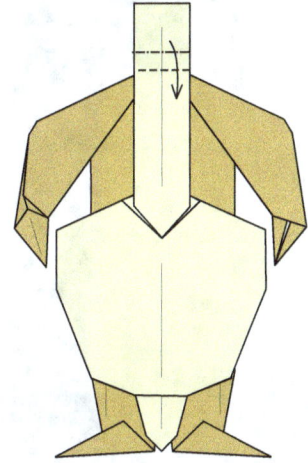

115. Pleat the headstock.

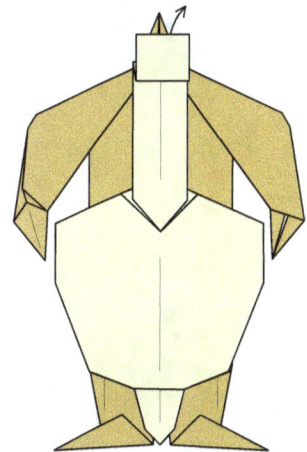

116. Stretch a single layer upwards from behind.

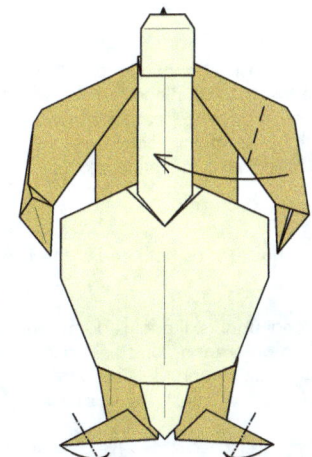

117. Valley fold over the arm. Reverse fold the feet.

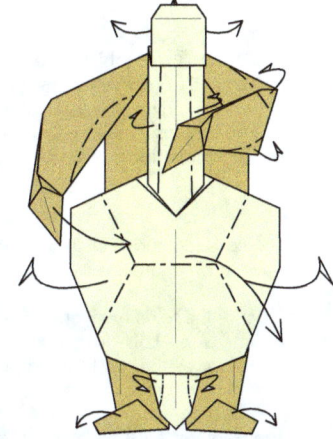

118. Shape the man and bass. Open out the head and feet.

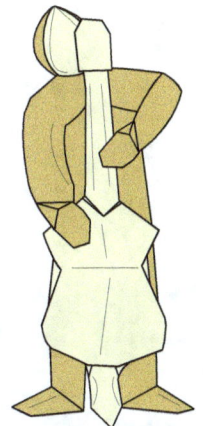

119. Completed *Bassist*.

Guitarist

About

Unlike the *Bassist*, this *Guitarist* features a distinct appendage to form the instrument. Compared to layouts where the guitar is integrated, this version is efficient, and has the advantage of having a bit more freedom of movement. The guitar was initially too large, and the proportion problem was solved by truncating the grossly large appendage with a mountain fold.

Tips

The spread squash in step 18 is slightly unusual, as both end of the flap have to be opened out.

Most of the folds here are non-orthogonal (that is, the folds do not lie at either 90° or 180° from each other). The precreasing and sinking in steps 27-31 gives the model that box pleated look though. Just keep in mind that the most critical of all these folds is the innermost pair of sinks.

The pleat in step 42 is meant to give the player a waistline. This pleat should be as shallow as possible, so as not to pull too much paper away from the arms.

guitarist

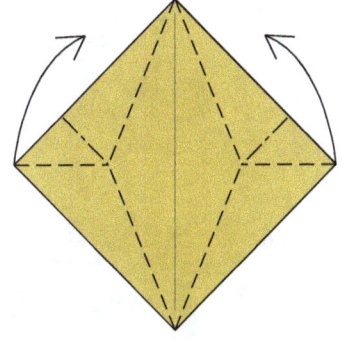

1. Rabbit ear both sides upwards.

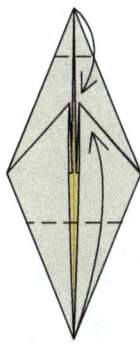

2. Valley fold towards the center flaps.

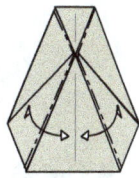

3. Precrease using mountain folds.

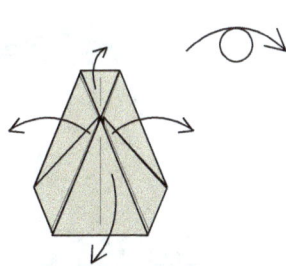

4. Unfold completely. Turn over

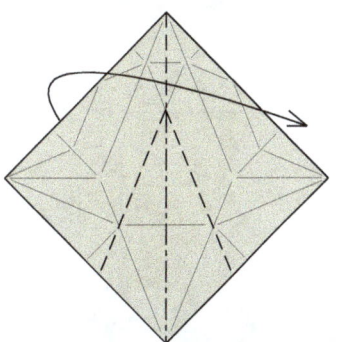

5. Collapse, using the existing creases as a guide.

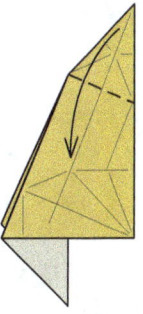

6. Valley fold to the intersection of creases.

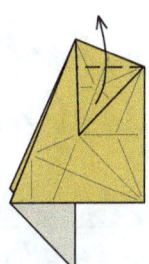

7. Valley fold up.

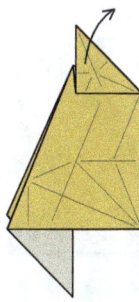

8. Open out the pleat.

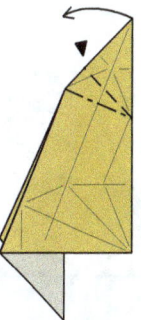

9. Reverse fold in and then out along the existing creases.

45

guitarist

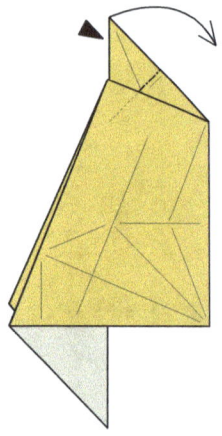

10. Reverse fold.

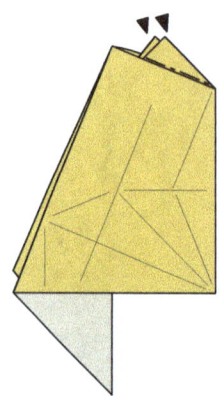

11. Reverse fold twice.

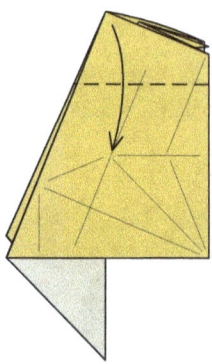

12. Valley fold to the intersection of creases.

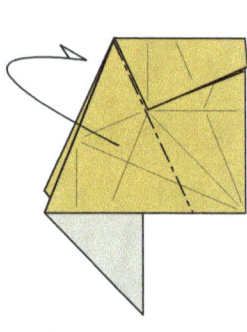

13. Mountain fold, so as to run along the interior folded edge.

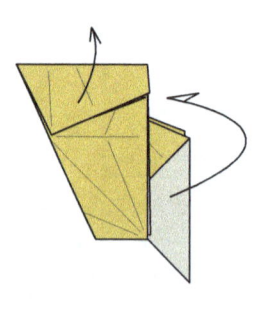

14. Open out the last two folds.

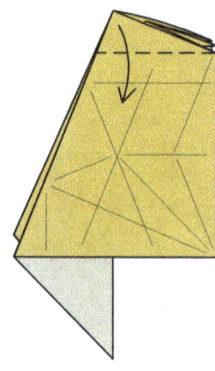

15. Valley fold down, using the interior thickness as a guide.

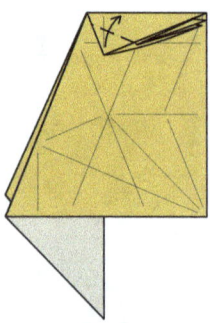

16. Valley fold to the top edge (this fold meets with the interior cluster of flaps).

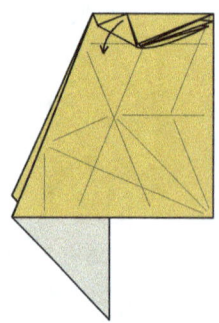

17. Unfold.

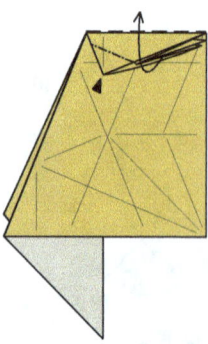

18. Spread squash, using the existing crease as a guide.

g u i t a r i s t

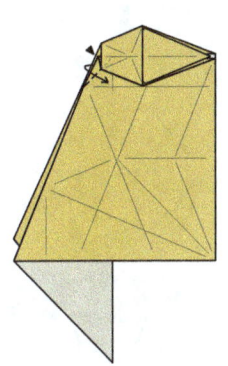

19. Reverse fold.

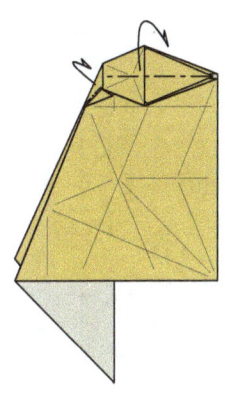

20. Mountain fold in half, reversing the left edge to match the front.

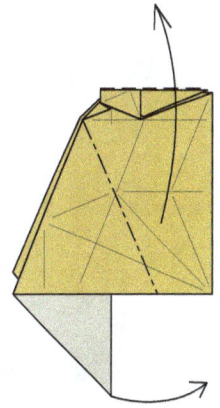

21. Open out, squashing the bottom flap over.

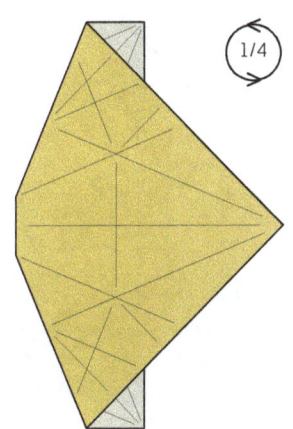

22. Rotate the model.

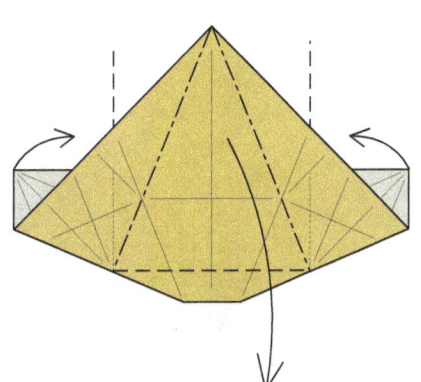

23. Petal fold down.

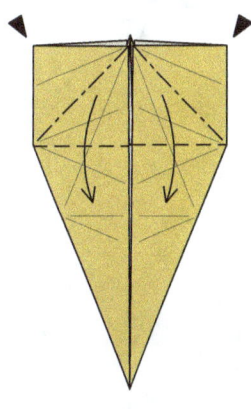

24. Squash the corners down.

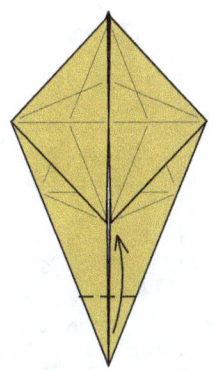

25. Valley fold up to the two points.

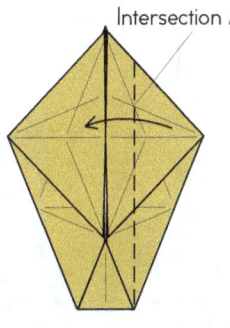

26. Valley fold though intersection A.

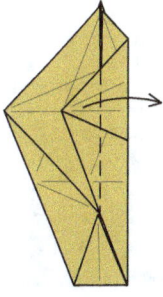

27. Valley fold over, so the fold lies over the center of the model.

47

guitarist

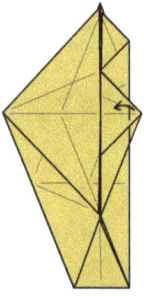

28. Valley fold over, to be flush with the folded edge below.

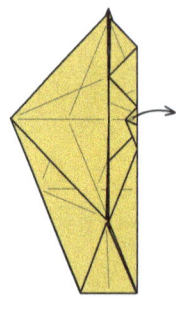

29. Unfold the pleat.

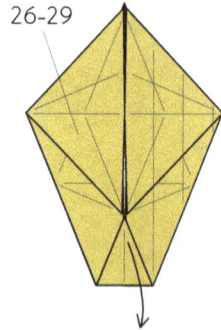

30. Repeat steps 26-28 on the other side. Swing down the bottom point.

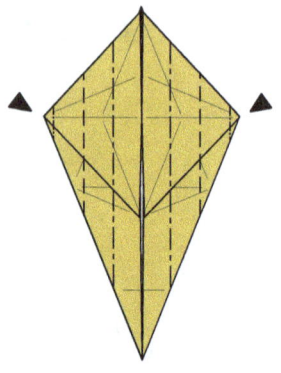

31. Sink triangularly along the existing creases.

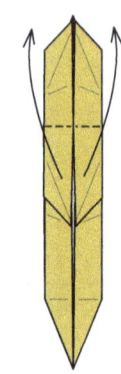

32. Swing the two points up.

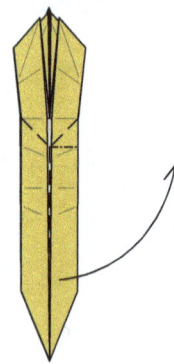

33. Rabbit ear the long flap.

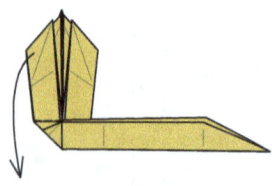

34. Swing down one flap.

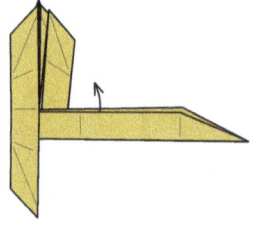

35. Pull out all of the layers from the foremost side of the flap (which will become convex at its end).

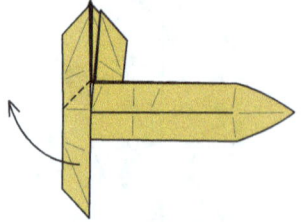

36. Lightly valley fold the bottom point outwards.

guitarist

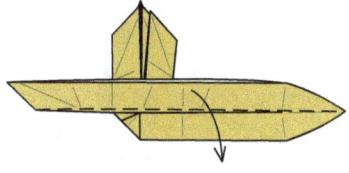
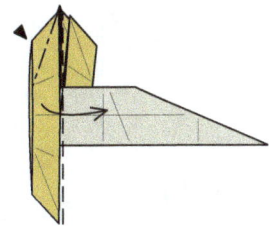

37. Bring down one layer, which will allow the right side to flatten and cause the left side to open out.

38. Rabbit ear the left appendage down.

39. Open out the left side, spread squashing the top. The bottom will not lie flat.

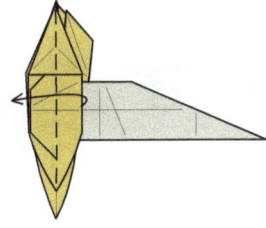
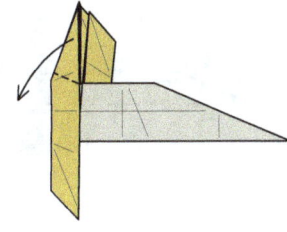
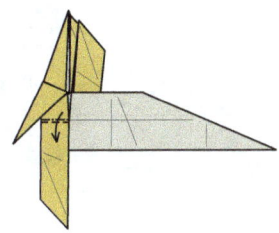

40. Close back up.

41. Valley fold the arm outwards.

42. Pulling paper from under the arm, pleat the top layer down. The mountain fold lies along an existing crease.

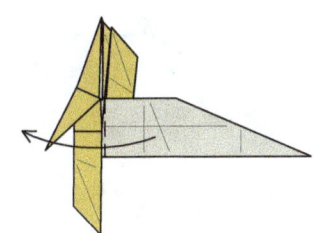
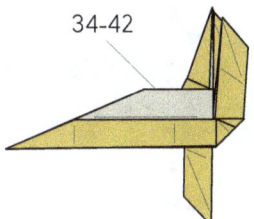
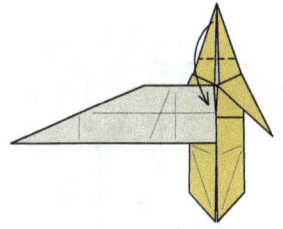

43. Swing the guitar over.

44. Repeat steps 34-42 in mirror image.

45. Valley fold the tip of the head to the center crease.

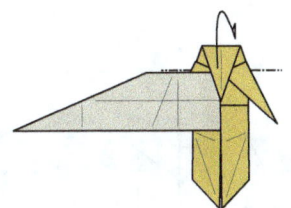
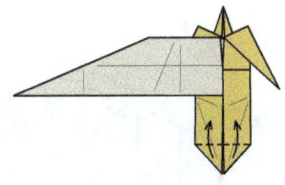
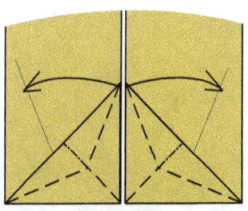

46. Mountain fold the head assembly back as far as possible.

47. Valley fold the feet upwards.

48. Detail of the feet. Rabbit ear the feet outwards.

guitarist

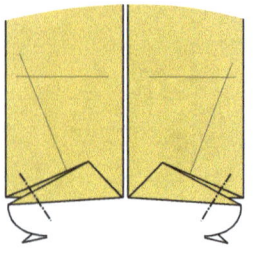 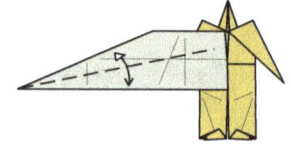 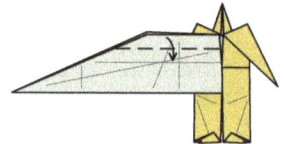

49. Reverse fold the tips of the feet.

50. Precrease the guitar along the angle bisector.

51. Valley fold the top layer to the center crease.

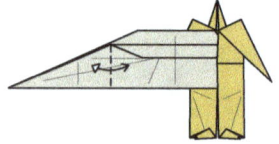 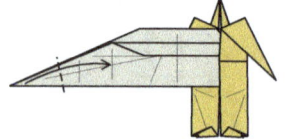 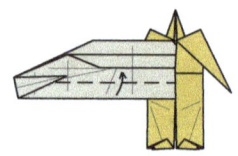

52. Precrease lightly.

53. Valley fold the tip to the intersection of creases.

54. Valley fold up a single layer to the center, allowing a swivel fold to form at the left.

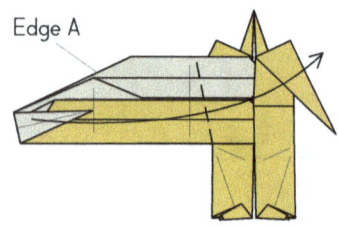 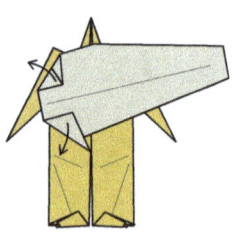

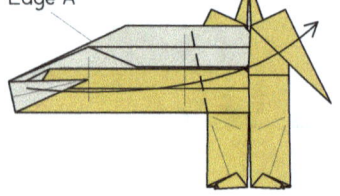

Edge A

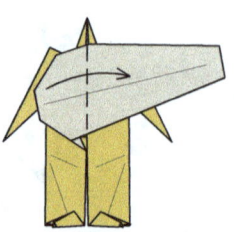

55. Valley fold over, such that edge A lies straight.

56. Valley fold the corners towards the center.

57. Note how the interior edges are parallel with the center crease. Unfold the two corners.

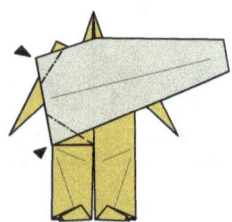 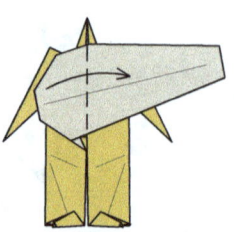 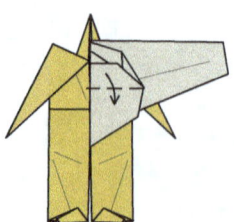

58. Reverse fold.

59. Swing over lightly.

60. Valley fold down one layer.

guitarist

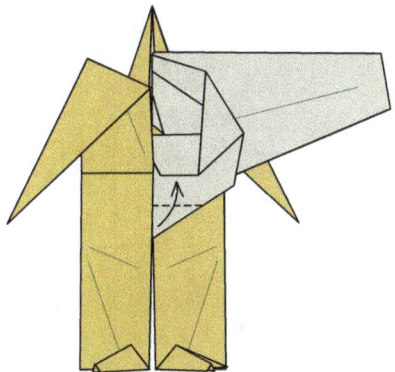

61. Pull up a single layer to the center, releasing the trapped paper at the right.

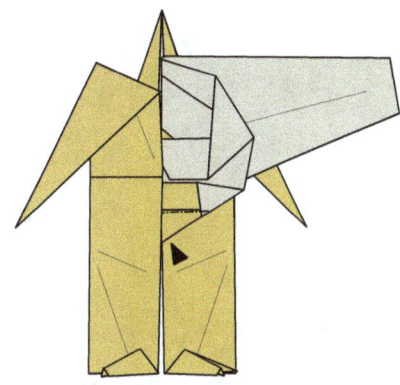

62. Sink at the center.

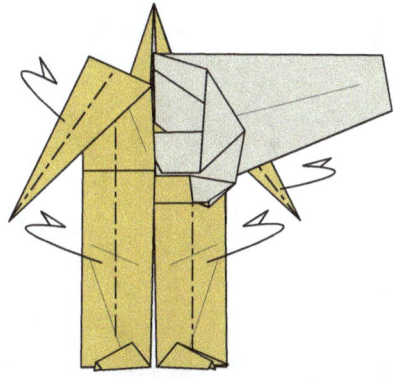

63. Mountain fold the sides of the body while thinning the arms.

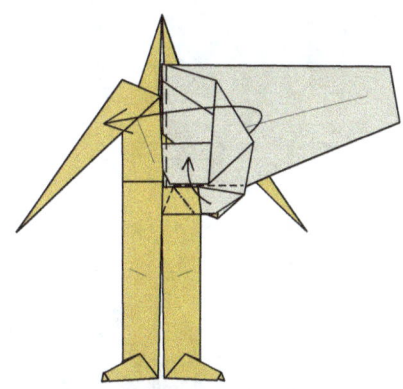

64. Swing the guitar body back over while swiveling up a layer.

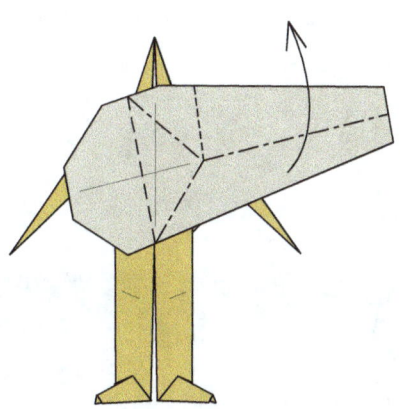

65. Rabbit ear the guitar neck. Note how the fold intersects with the center of the player.

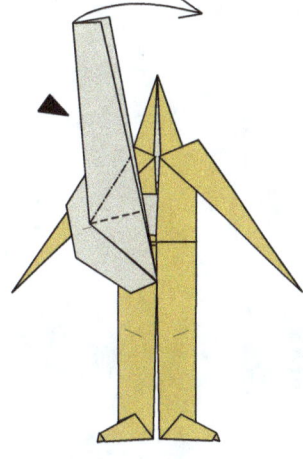

66. Squash fold the neck flat.

51

guitarist

67. Petal fold the neck.

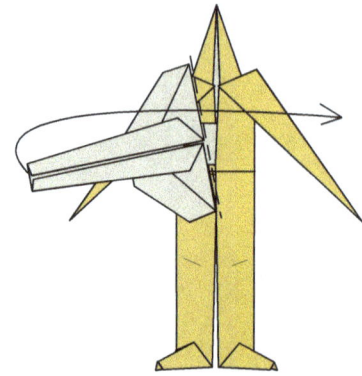

68. Swing the neck section over.

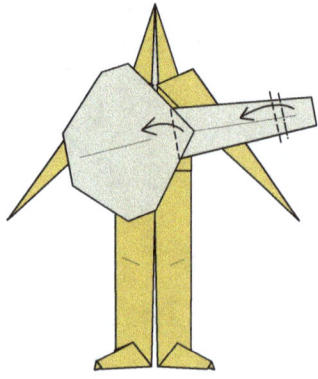

69. Valley fold over the base of the neck. Make a tiny pleat at the headstock.

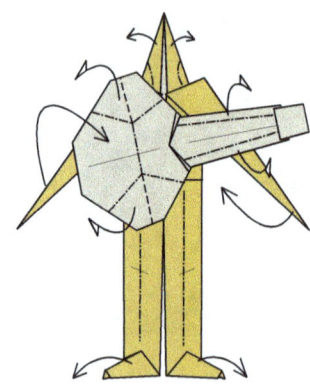

70. Open out the head and feet. Shape the guitar and player's body. Position the arms to taste.

71. Completed *Guitarist*.

Pianist

About

This *Pianist* took the longest to design, having gone through various unsuccessful drafts. Eventually an early draft of a base for the *Drummer* was used. This in turn was like an earlier model of a *Rat*. The lower jaw was converted to the to the stool, the upper jaw to the arms and head, the ears to the legs, the front legs to the prop and lid, and the tail to the legs.

Tips

The stretch procedure depicted in steps 20-22 is the most difficult part of this model. To understand it better, you might try skipping steps 21-22 to see how they affect the model. You will notice how that inner ridge of paper gets in the way of flattening. You actually have to spread it apart for the initial stretch to work.

Steps 89-93 used to be a single step. Basically you are spread squashing the flap from step 89 to create a new set of folded edges that lie on the piano's body more neatly. To make the sequence more digestible, step 89 was added so you can work on one edge of the lid at a time. It is best not to commit yourself to the mountain fold in step 90, until you know you have it positioned well. Nevertheless, you can always add additional shaping to the lid with mountain folds if you feel it is aesthetically necessary.

pianist

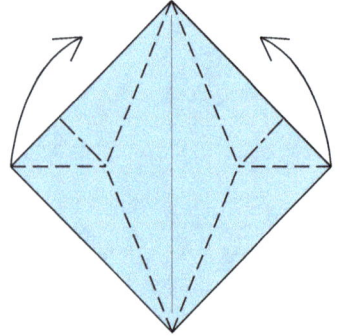
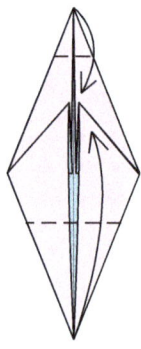
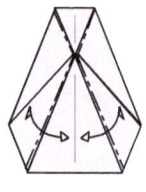

1. Rabbit ear both sides upwards.
2. Valley fold towards the center flaps.
3. Precrease using mountain folds.

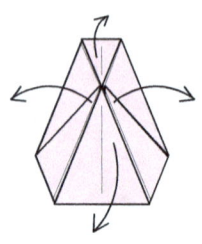
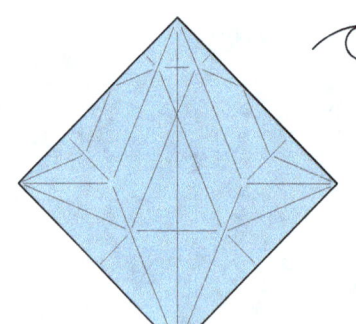
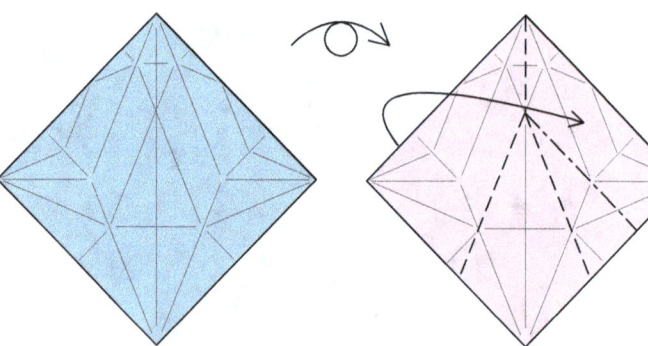

4. Unfold completely.
5. Turn over.
6. Rabbit ear.

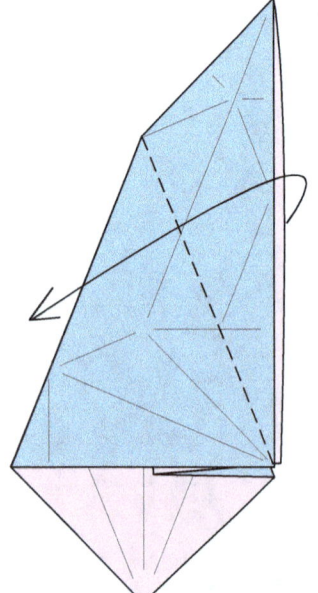
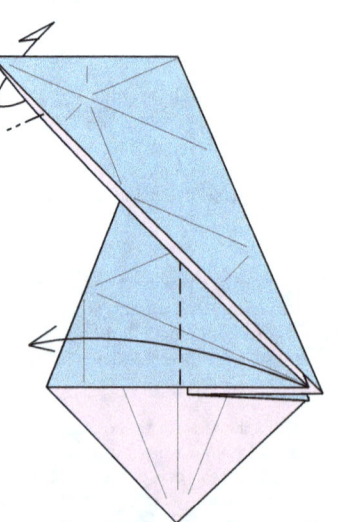
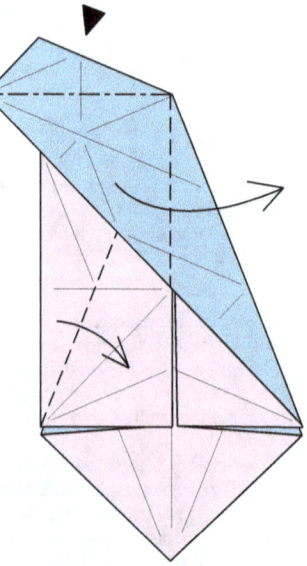

7. Valley fold.
8. Fold out the single layer, pulling up at the top.
9. Asymmetrical squash.

pianist

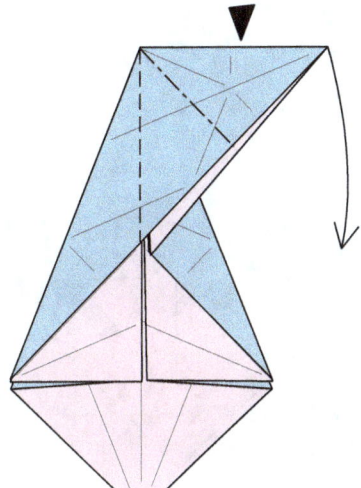

10. Squash fold.

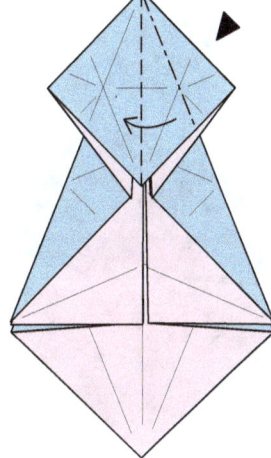

11. Squash fold one side.

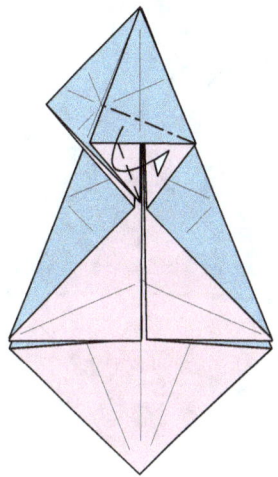

12. Swivel fold under.

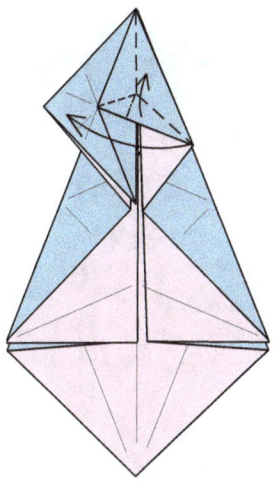

13. Swing over, while incorporating a reverse fold.

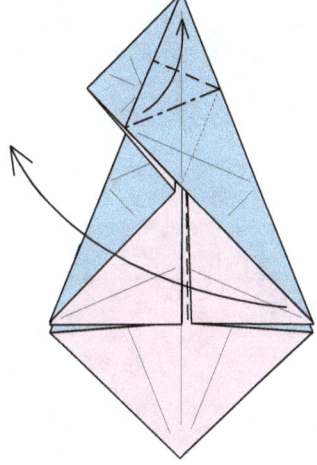

14. Valley fold the corner up to the top point, allowing the side flap to open out. The flap will not lie flat.

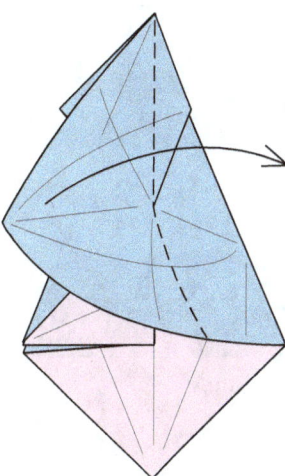

15. Valley fold over the flap to flatten.

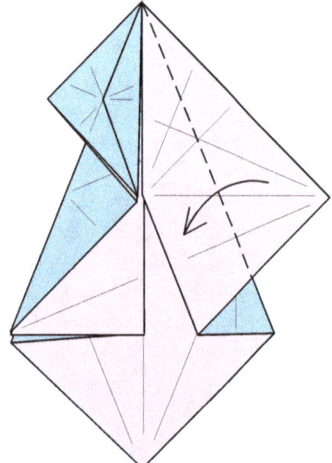

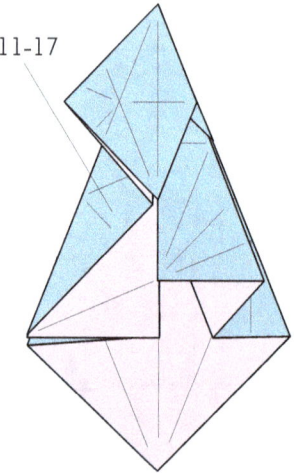

16. Valley fold the raw edge to the center.

17. Swing over the flap while reverse folding the top point down.

18. Repeat steps 11-17 in mirror image.

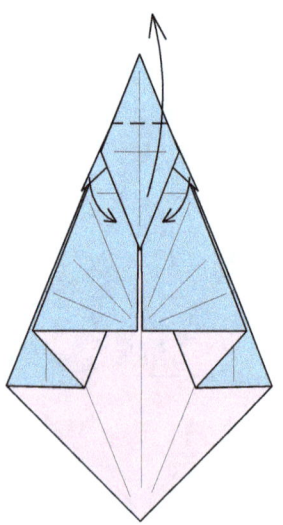

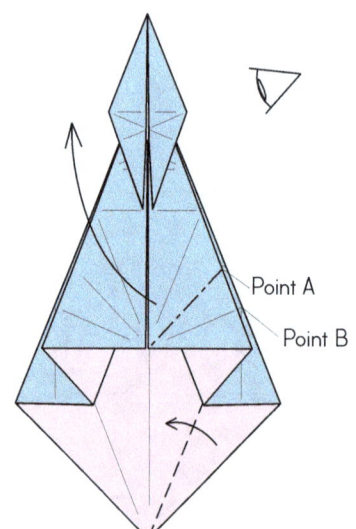

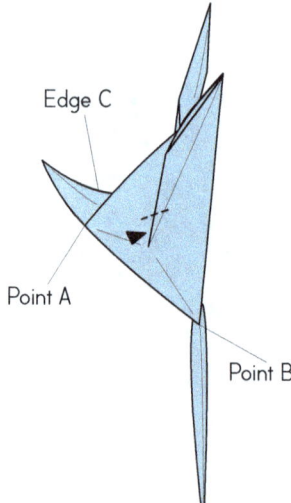

19. Stretch the center flap while allowing the small side flaps to come together.

20. Stretch the side apart, forming a fold between point A and point B. Do not flatten.

21. View from previous step. Squash a portion of the ridge flat, such that the resulting fold meets with a portion of raw edge C.

— p i a n i s t —

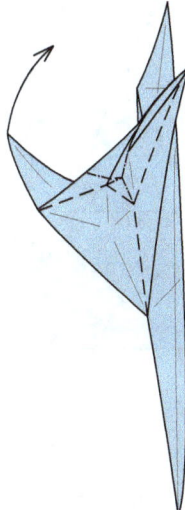

22. Collapse the flap flat.

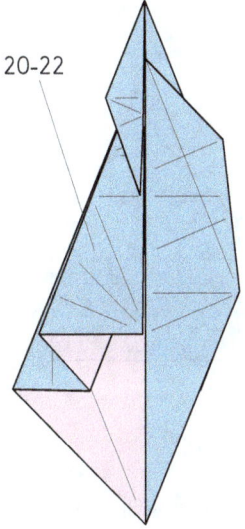

23. Repeat steps 20-22 on the other side.

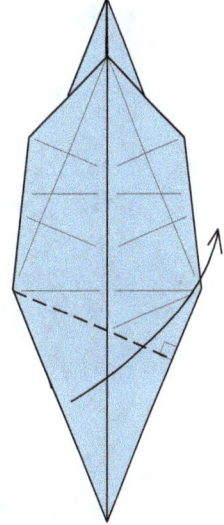

24. Valley fold the bottom flap up.

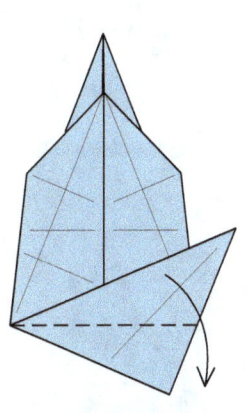

25. Valley fold down.

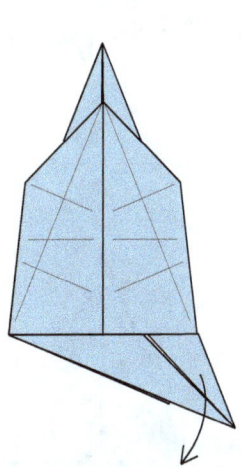

26. Unfold the pleat.

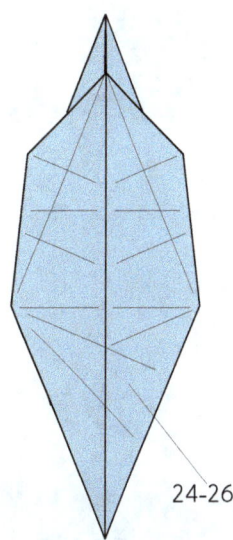

27. Repeat steps 24-26 in mirror image.

57

pianist

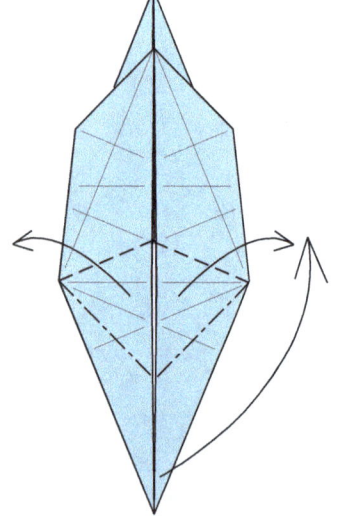

28. Spread apart the flap while pulling it upwards.

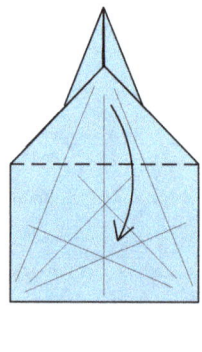

29. Valley fold down the corner.

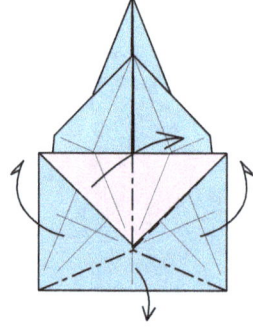

30. Collapse downwards into a rabbit-ear formation.

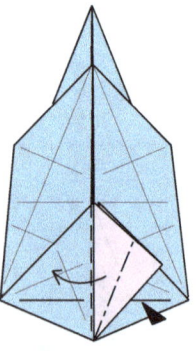

31. Squash the center flap.

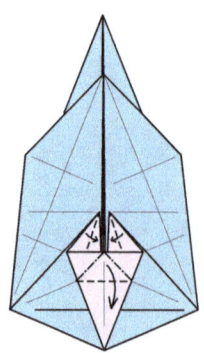

32. Petal fold.

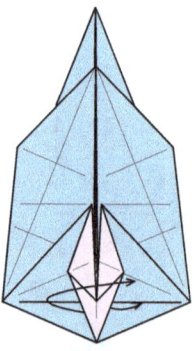

33. Unwrap the single layer.

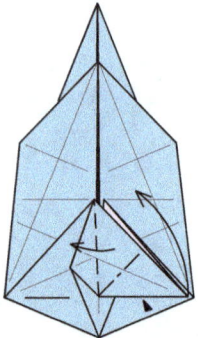

34. Squash the center flap.

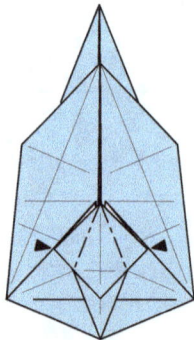

35. Reverse fold the sides.

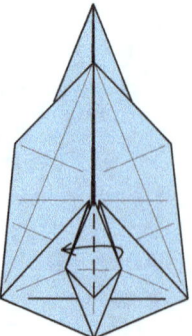

36. Swing over one flap.

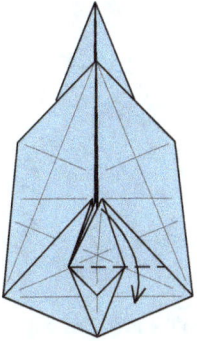
37. Valley fold down.

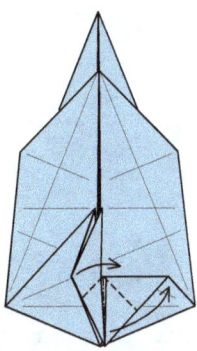
38. Swing over while incorporating a reverse fold.

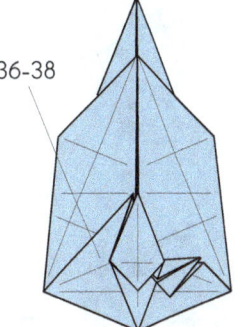
39. Repeat steps 36-38 in mirror image.

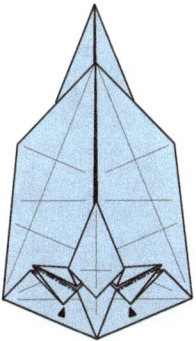
40. Reverse fold the corners.

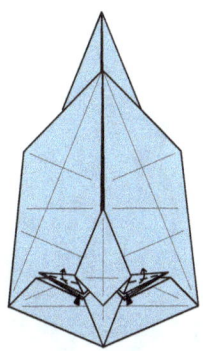
41. Reverse fold the top layer.

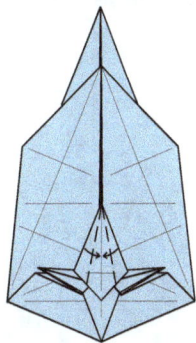
42. Valley fold to the center.

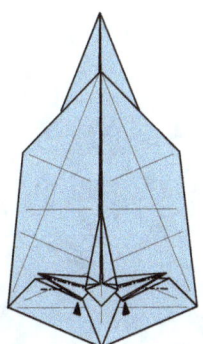
43. Reverse fold.

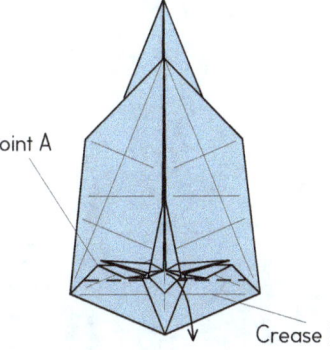
44. Pull down, so point A lies on crease B.

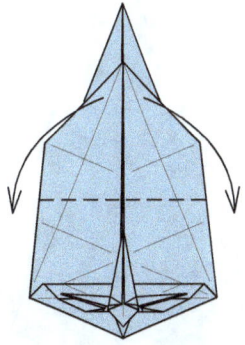
45. Swing down the large flaps.

pianist

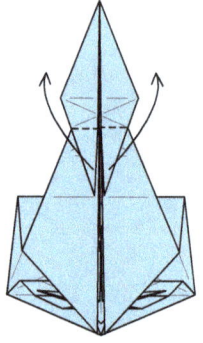

46. Lightly valley fold the two flaps up.

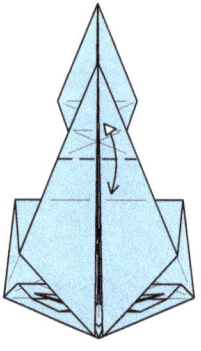

47. Precrease, using the existing creases as a guide.

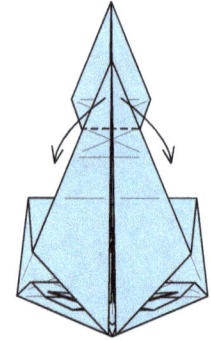

48. Swing the two flaps back down.

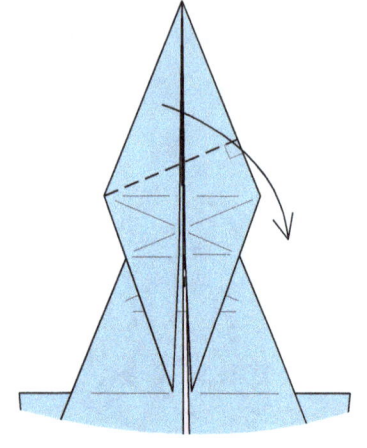

49. Valley fold over.

50. Valley fold back up.

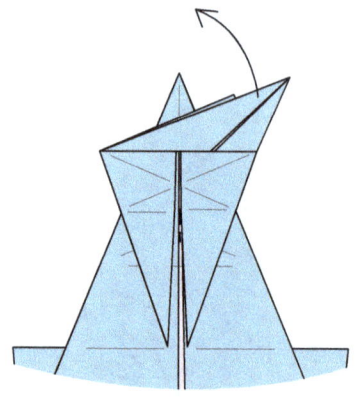

51. Unfold the pleat.

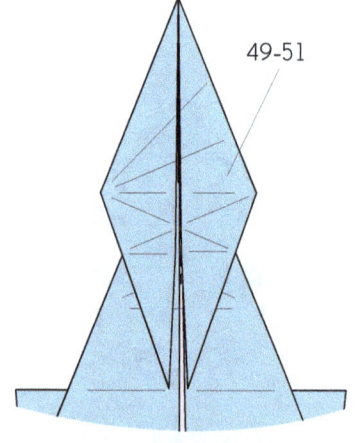

52. Repeat steps 49-51 in mirror image.

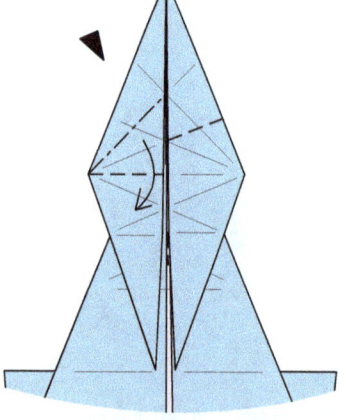

53. Form an asymmetrical squash.

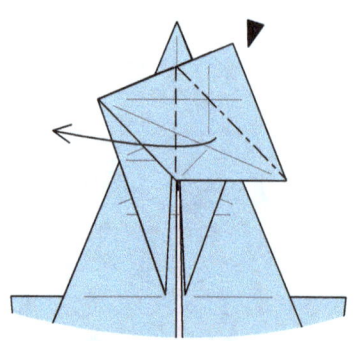

54. Squash fold again.

pianist

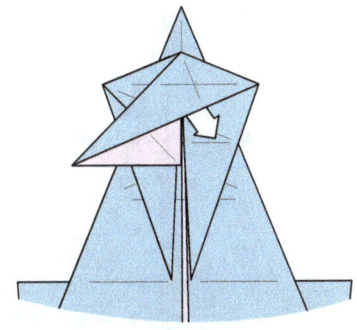

55. Pull out the single layer to match with the other side.

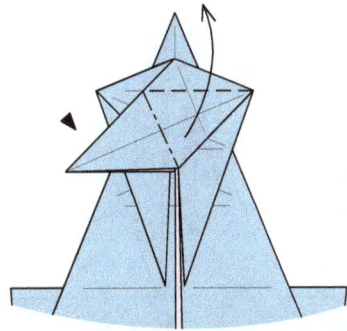

56. Squash fold.

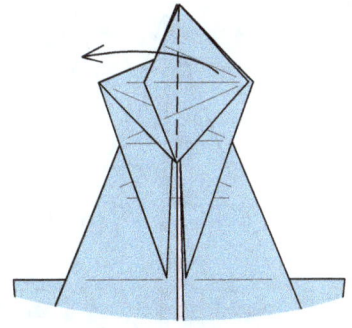

57. Valley fold over.

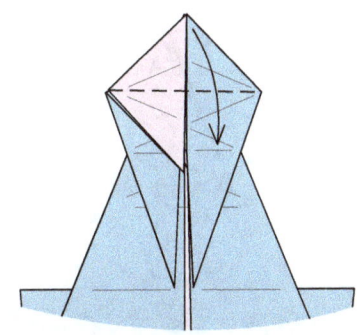

58. Valley fold down.

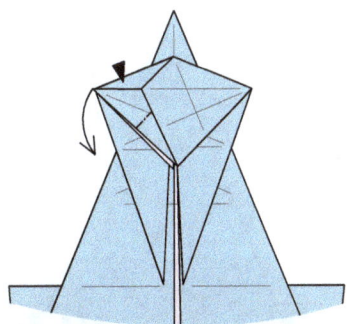

59. Reverse fold.

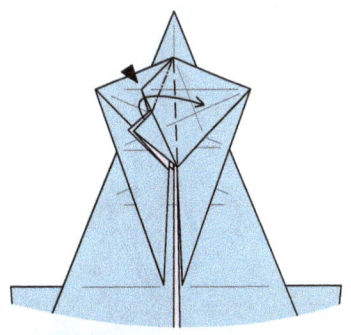

60. Spread apart the bottom layers evenly, allowing the center to spread squash flat.

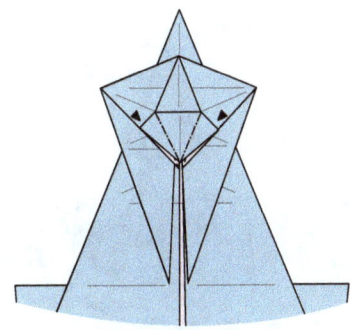

61. Reverse fold at the bottom.

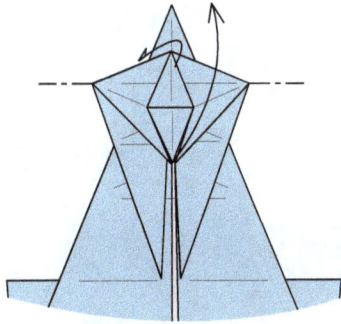

62. Swing the three points up, allowing the top point to swing down.

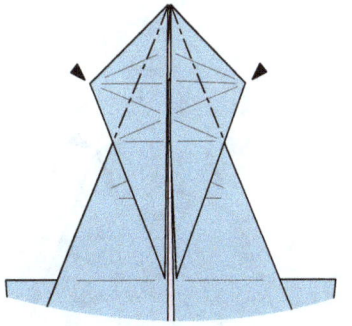

63. Sink the sides triangularly.

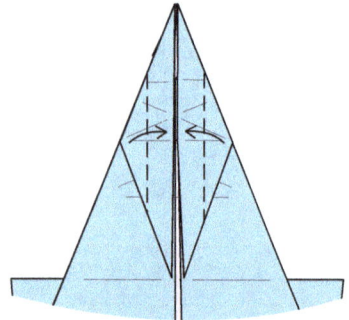 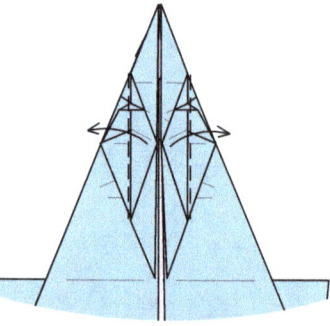 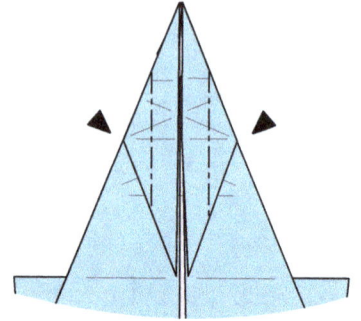

64. Valley fold the corners to the center, allowing tiny squashes to form.

65. Fold the corners back.

66. Closed sink the corners.

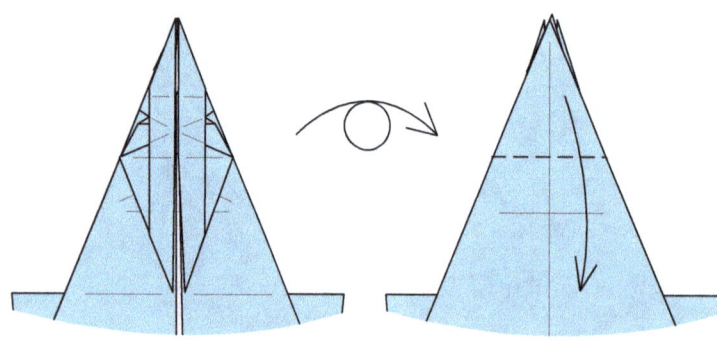 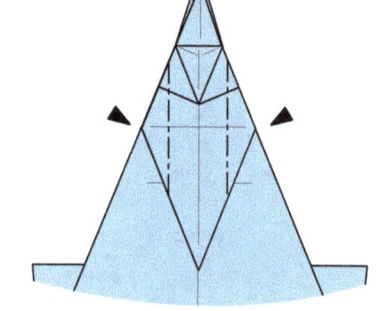

67. Turn over.

68. Valley fold down the top flap.

69. Closed sink the sides to match the back.

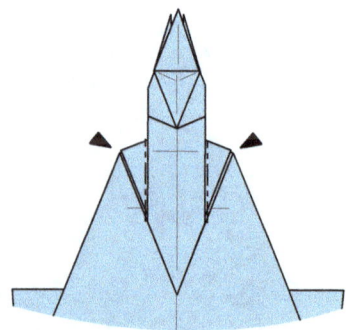 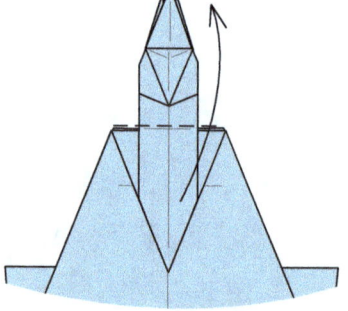 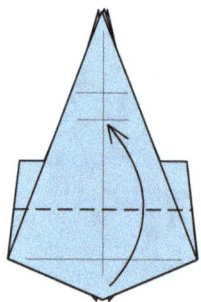

70. Open sink the trapped corners.

71. Swing the flap back up.

72. Valley fold the bottom corner to the crease.

pianist

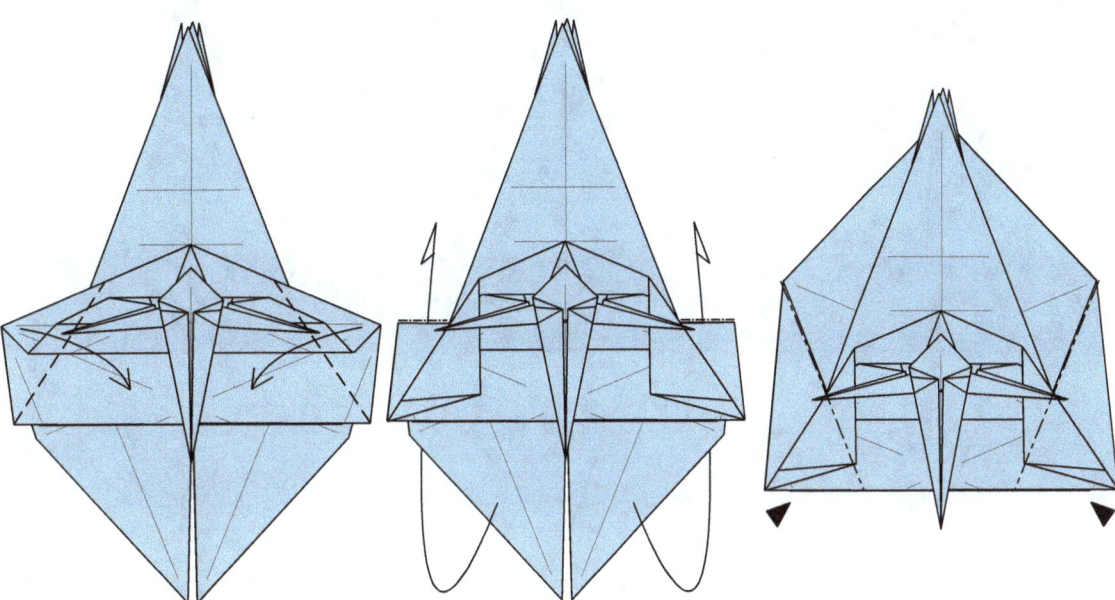

73. Valley fold the corners inward. Note that in step 74, the resulting edges meet the interior corners.

74. Swing the large flaps upwards.

75. Closed sink the corners, using the interior folded edges as a guide.

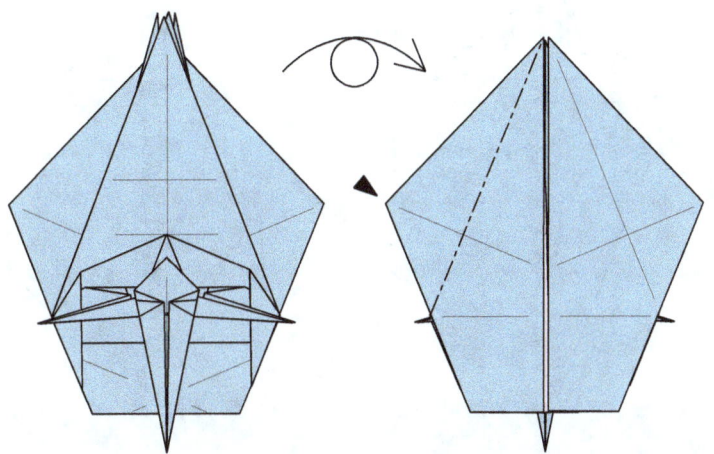

76. Turn over.

77. Sink the left side triangularly.

78. Flip the top flaps back down.

pianist

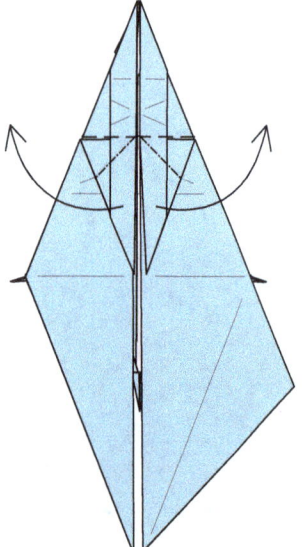

79. Pleat the flaps upwards.

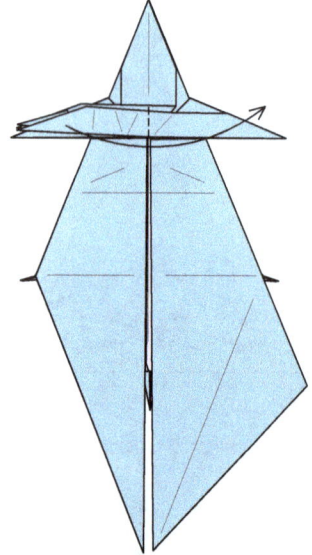

80. Stretch the center flap over to the left, releasing the trapped layers.

81. Swing over, releasing the trapped layers on the other side.

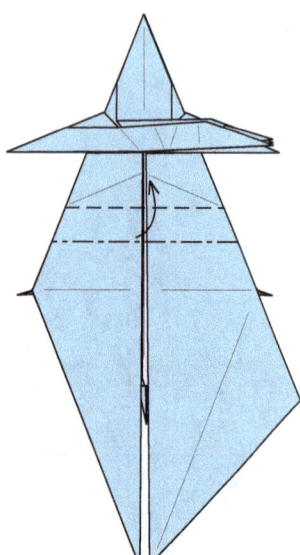

82. Pleat through all layers. The valley fold is preexisting, and the mountain fold meets the intersection of creases.

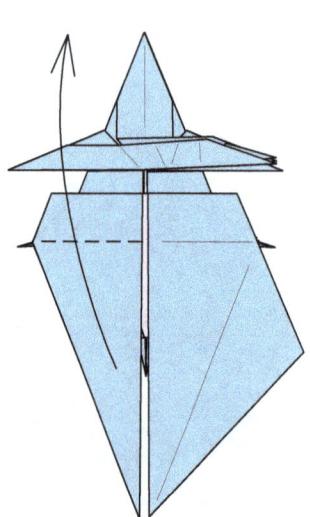

83. Swing the left flap up.

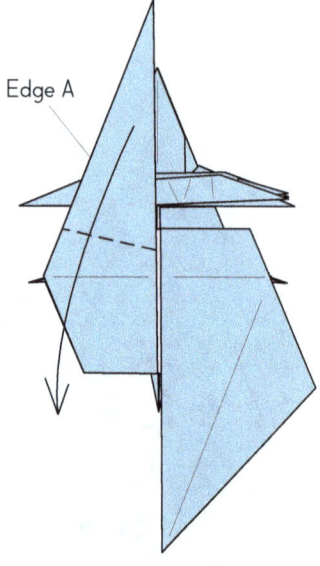

Edge A

84. Valley fold down, such that edge A lies parallel to the center.

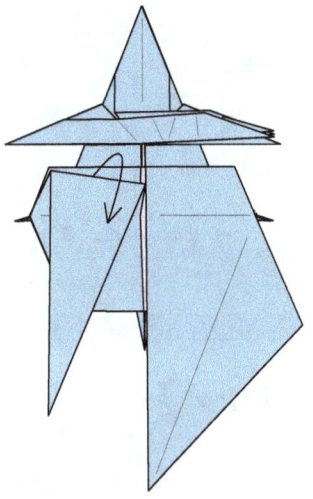 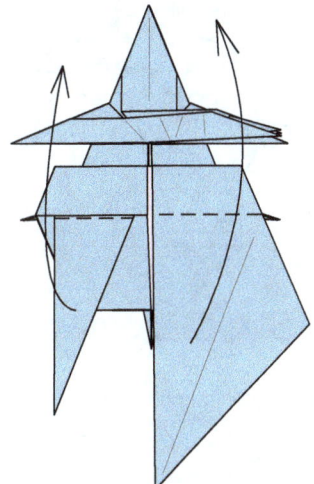 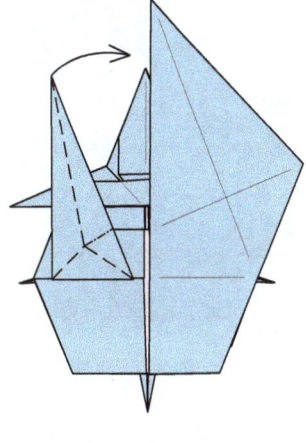

85. Bring the single layer to the surface. This is in effect, the same as reversing the flap in and then out.

86. Swing the two flaps up.

87. Rabbit ear the smaller flap over to the right.

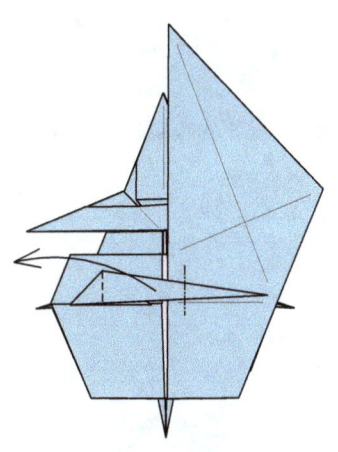 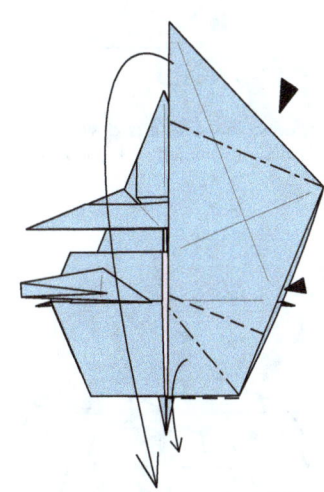 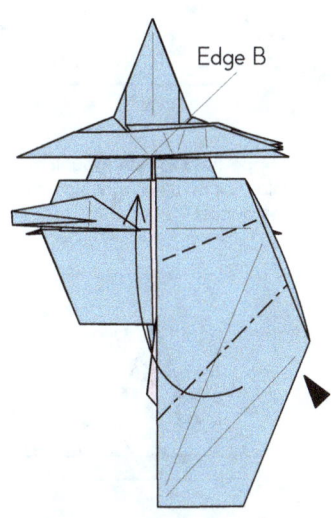

88. Swing the flap over to the left, adding a mountain fold (which can be adjusted later).

89. Swing down the large flap while squashing. Do not be too concerned with how the layers behind collapse.

90. Spread squash the flap upwards, such that the mountain fold aligns with edge B.

pianist

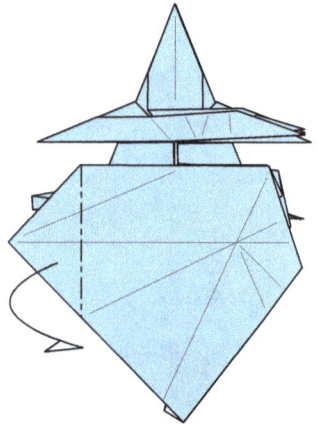

91. Mountain fold.

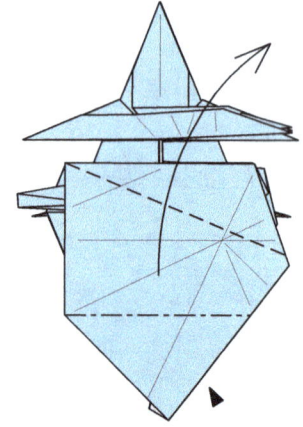

92. Lightly squash upwards.

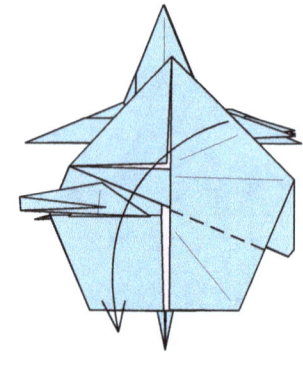

93. Swing back down.

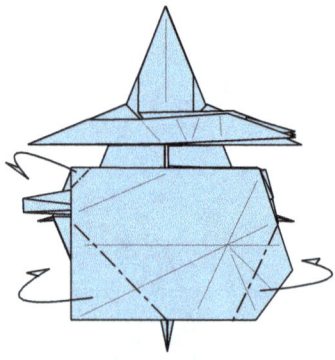

94. Shape the top with mountain folds, tucking the right side into the pocket.

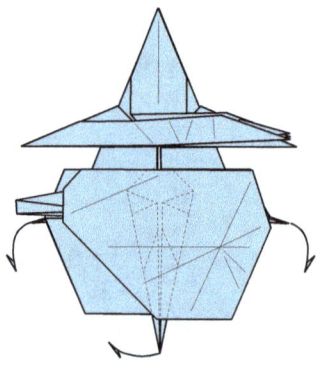

95. Swing the side legs down. Reverse the center leg down.

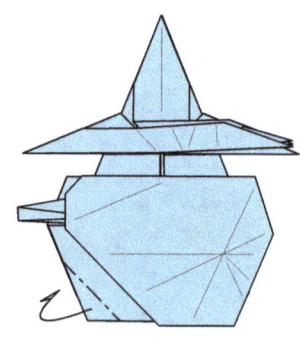

96. Shape the side with a mountain fold.

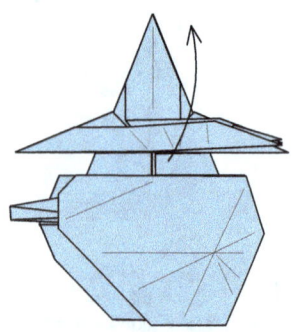

97. Make the model 3-D by letting the pleat from step 82 lie at 90°.

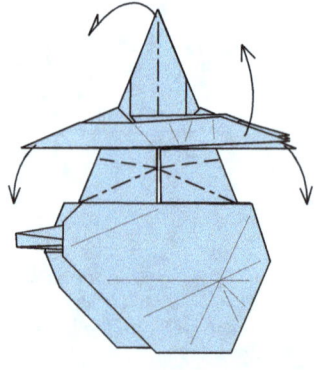

98. Rabbit ear. The sides will not flatten completely.

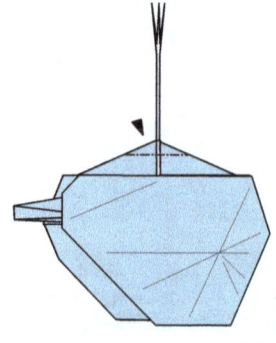

99. Sink the front of the keyboard.

pianist

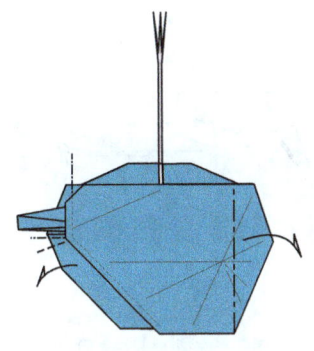 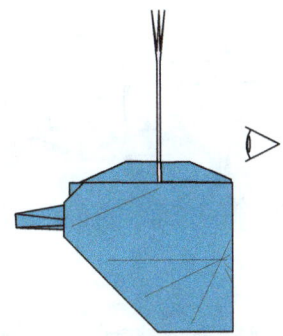 

100. Make the sides 3-D with mountain folds (and a crimp).

101. Completed piano body.

102. View from previous step. Lightly open out the back leg.

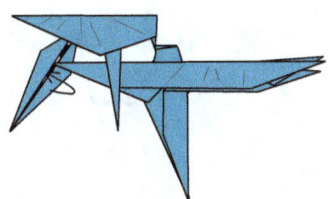 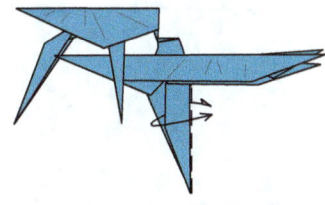

103. Close back up, tucking the flap into the pocket.

104. Pull through two layers at each side. The layers should now be evenly distributed.

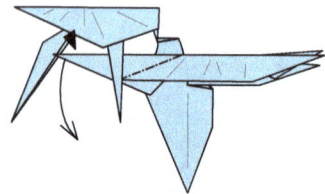

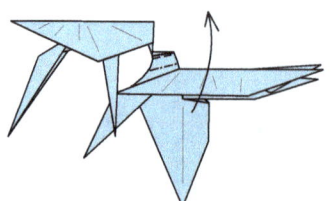

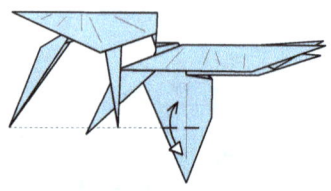

105. Reverse fold both legs down (divide the layers evenly when reversing).

106. Pull the body closer to the keyboard, allowing the connecting joint to buckle.

107. Precrease the base of the seat so it is even with the piano legs.

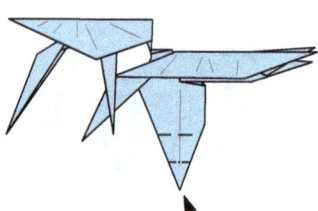

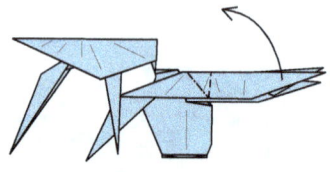

108. Spread squash the base flat into an octagonal shape.

109. Crimp the body upwards.

pianist

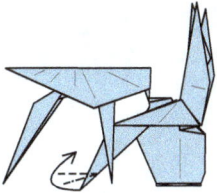

110. Crimp the feet up.

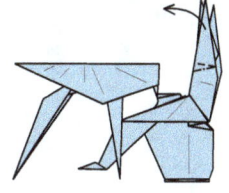

111. Crimp the arms an neck foward.

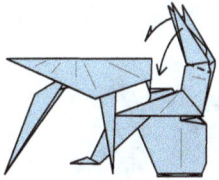

112. Stretch the arms down.

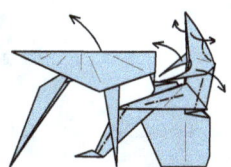

113. Open out the head and shape the player's body. raise the piano top and insert the prop into its pocket.

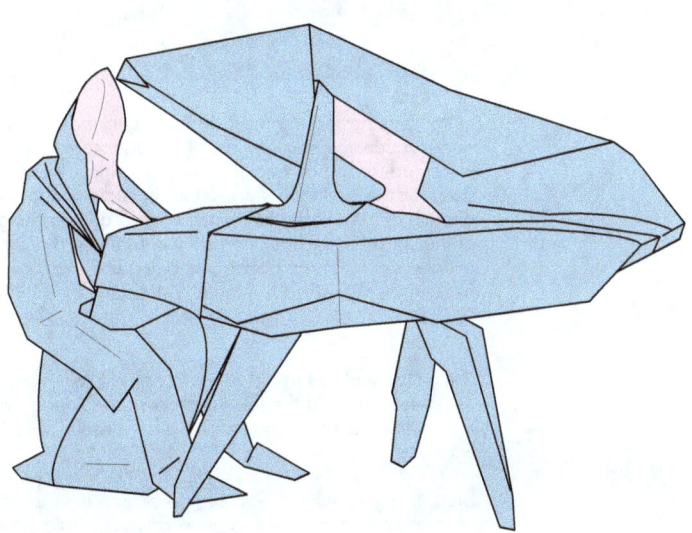

114. Completed *Pianist*.

69

Drummer

About

In sprite of having the most appendages, the *Drummer* was one of the easier models to develop, and it is easier to fold than it looks. The player is formed from a corner of a square, using a similar pattern to the one used for the *Guitarist*. More paper is dedicated to the drum section, being a much larger instrument. Since each drumhead originates from the edge of the square (which is necessary to facilitate a color change), none of the middle portion of the paper was being used for anything useful. So, this excess paper is used to create a stand for the model.

Tips

The difficulty of this model is not from the folding sequence, but rather from the sheer length of the folding process. A folder's stamina does contribute to a model's difficulty, and taking a few breaks while folding can often work wonders.

Step 46 suggests the indicated procedure is similar to a closed sink. If you were to swing the thick flap outwards, you could closed sink it to achieve the same result.

Steps 71-72 and steps 85-88 provide landmarks to create drumheads of various sizes. It would be okay to skip the precreasing and use your judgement to form the squashes in steps 73 and 89.

drummer

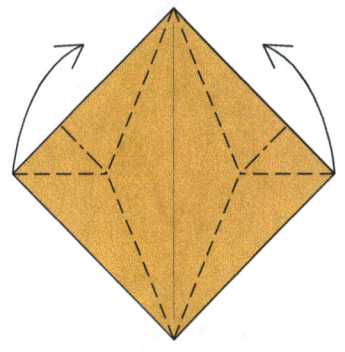

1. Rabbit ear both sides upwards.

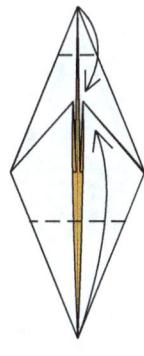

2. Valley fold towards the center flaps.

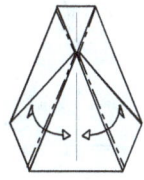

3. Precrease using mountain folds.

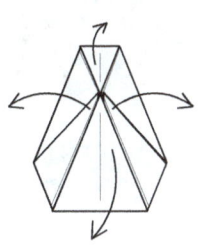

4. Unfold completely.

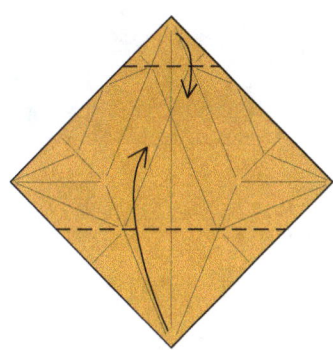

5. Valley fold towards the intersection of creases.

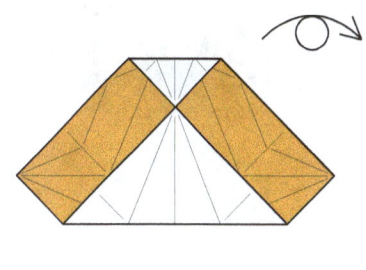

6. Turn over.

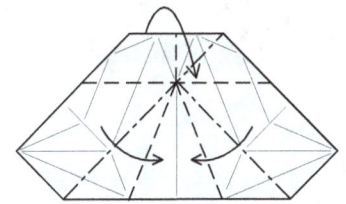

7. Collapse.

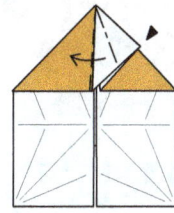

8. Squash fold.

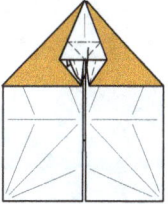

9. Petal fold under.

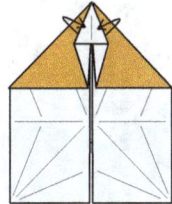

10. Wrap around a single layer at each side.

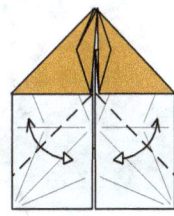

11. Precrease.

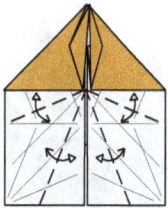

12. Precrease again. The upper creases only go through a single layer.

drummer

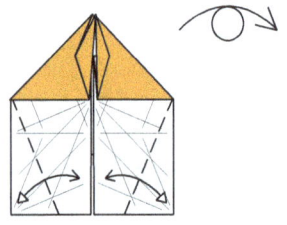

13. Precrease. Turn over.

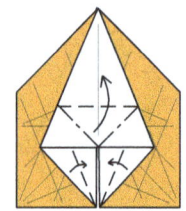

14. Petal fold.

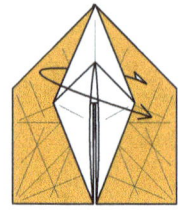

15. Unwrap the trapped layer.

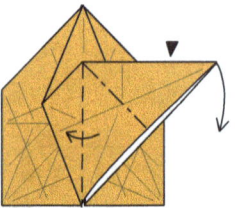

16. Squash fold.

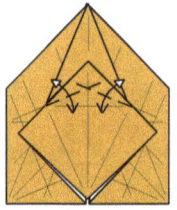

17. Precrease along the angle bisectors.

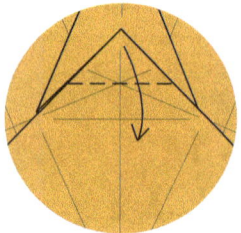

18. Valley fold through the intersection of creases.

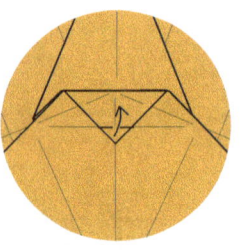

19. Valley fold up, so as to align with the crease behind.

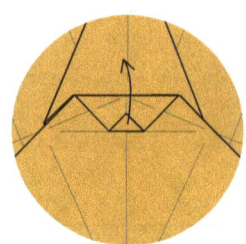

20. Unfold.

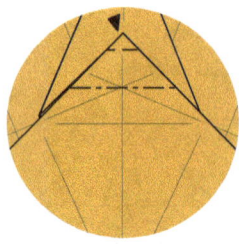

21. Double sink.

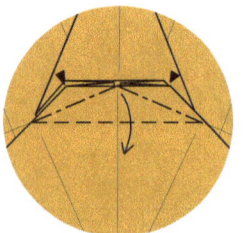

22. Spread squash.

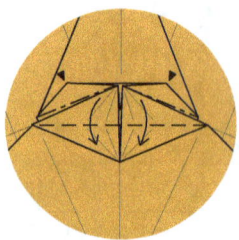

23. Spread squash again.

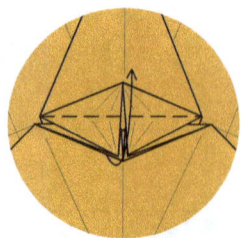

24. Bring the layers back up.

drummer

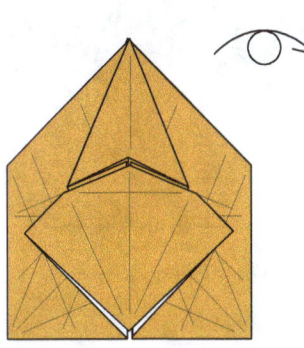

25. Turn over.

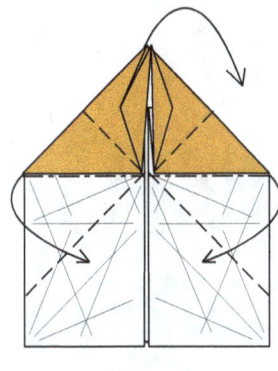

26. Form a waterbomb base at the top.

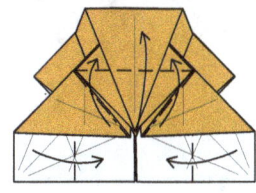

27. Fold the center layers up while bringing in the sides.

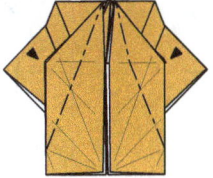

28. Sink along the existing creases.

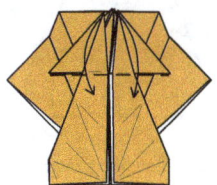

29. Swing down a flap at each side.

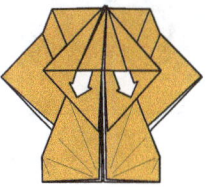

30. Pull out the two hidden points.

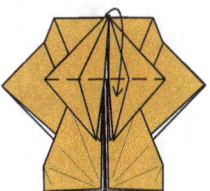

31. Valley fold down.

32. Swivel over the top layer.

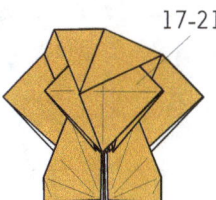

33. Repeat steps 17-21 on this flap.

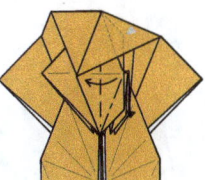

34. Spread squash. The resulting flap will fit into the top pocket.

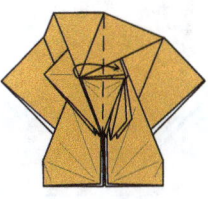

35. Valley fold over the thick double flap.

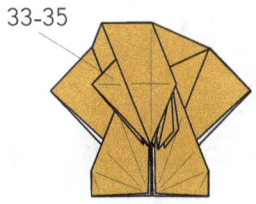

36. Repeat steps 33-35 in mirror image.

drummer

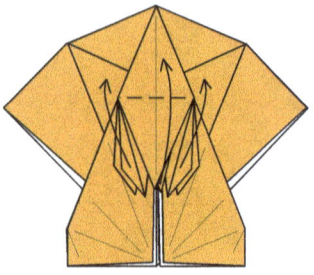

37. Swing the indicated flaps up.

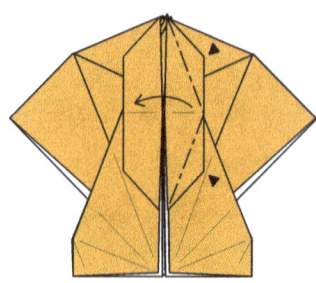

38. Spread squash over.

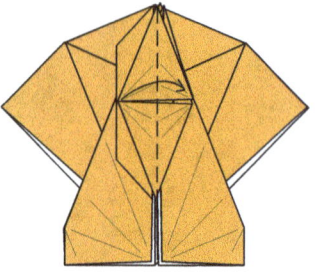

39. Valley fold back over.

40. Repeat steps 38-39 on the other side.

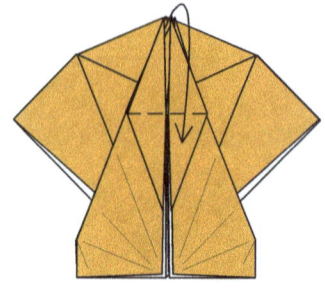

41. Swing all the flaps down.

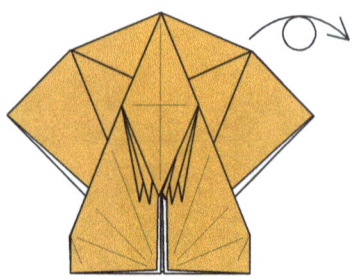

42. Turn over.

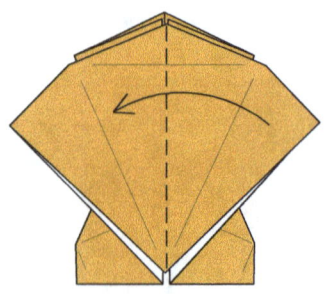

43. Swing over.

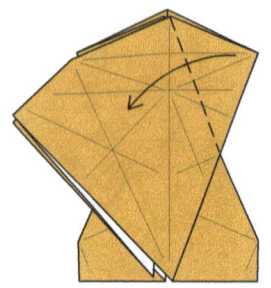

44. Valley fold over, so as to align with the edge behind.

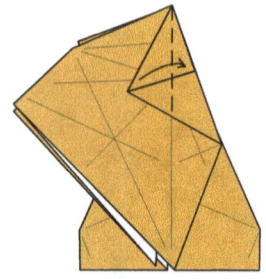

45. Valley fold over.

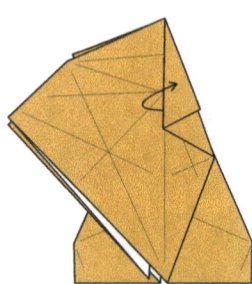

46. Bring the single layer to the surface (closed sink).

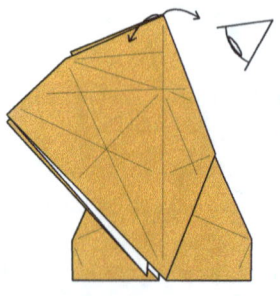

47. Pull apart the top cluster of layers, so as to reveal a web of paper.

48. Collapse back with reverse folds.

drummer

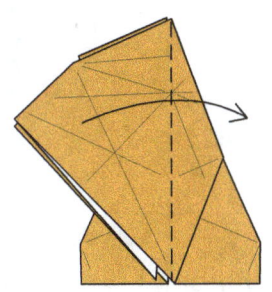

49. Swing back.

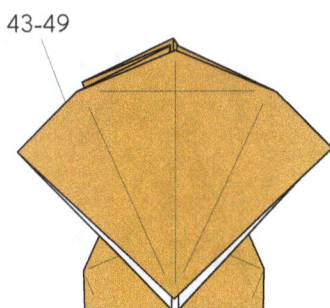

50. Repeat steps 43-49 on the other side.

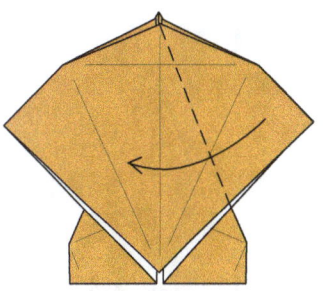

51. Valley fold over, so as to align with the edge behind.

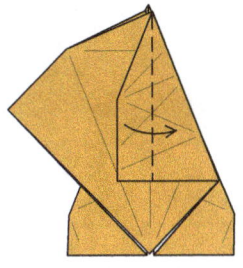

52. Valley fold over.

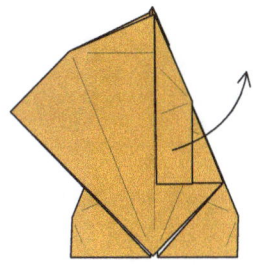

53. Swing up.

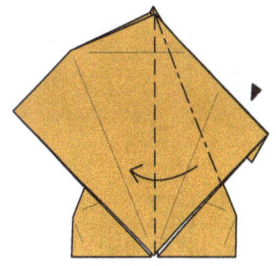

54. Squash fold.

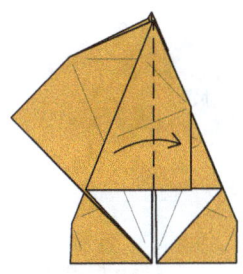

55. Valley fold over.

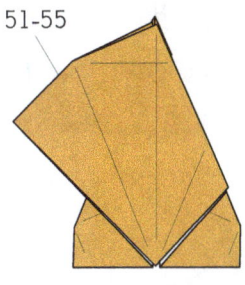

56. Repeat steps 51-55 on the other side.

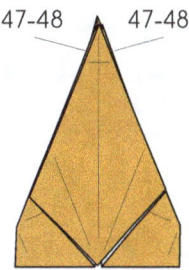

57. Repeat steps 47-48 on each side.

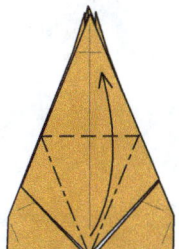

58. Petal fold.

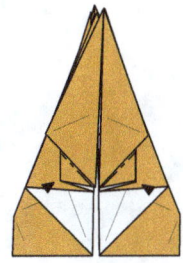

59. Reverse fold.

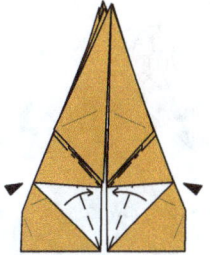

60. Reverse again.

drummer

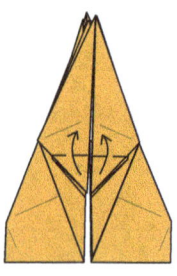

61. Valley fold up.

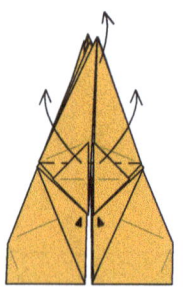

62. Stretch upwards.

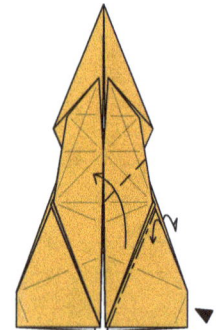

63. Spread squash.

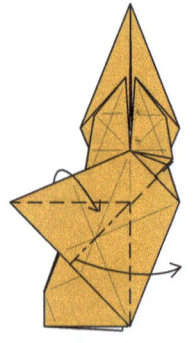

64. Swing down, while incorporating a reverse fold.

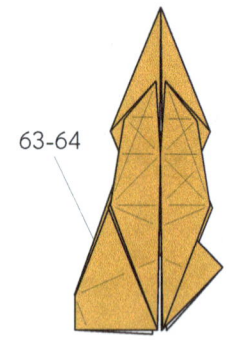

65. Repeat steps 63-64 at the left.

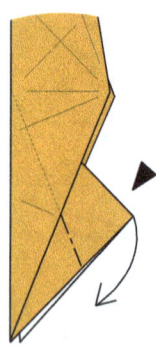

66. Detail of the bottom right flap. Reverse fold.

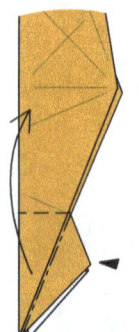

67. Petal fold upwards.

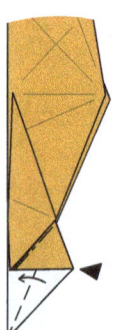

68. Reverse fold.

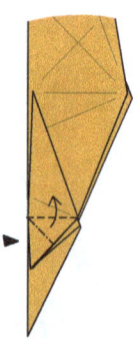

69. Squash.

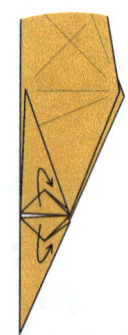

70. Wrap around a single layer.

drummer

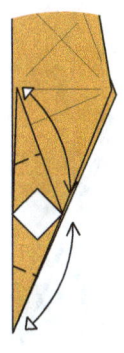

71. Valley fold the points to the center and unfold.

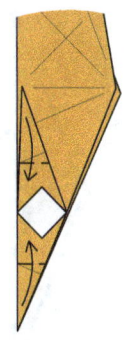

72. Valley fold.

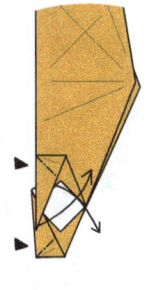

73. Squash fold.

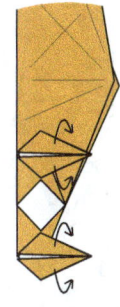

74. Wrap around all the layers.

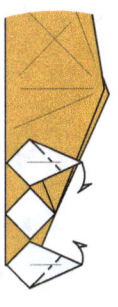

75. Mountain fold.

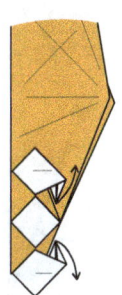

76. Unfold.

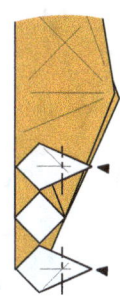

77. Sink.

78. Mountain fold.

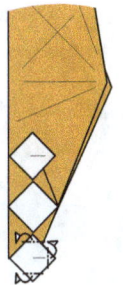

79. Mountain fold the corners about 1/3rd inwards.

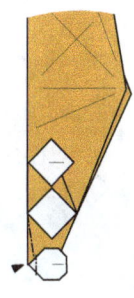

80. Sink the remaining corner to match.

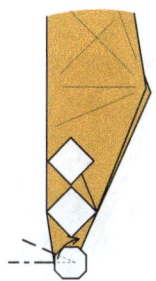

81. Crimp.

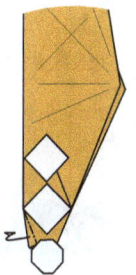

82. Mountain fold to match the other side.

drummer

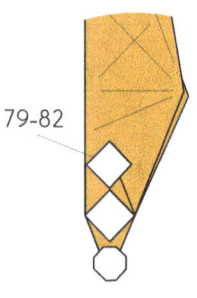

83. Repeat steps 79-82 on the other square.

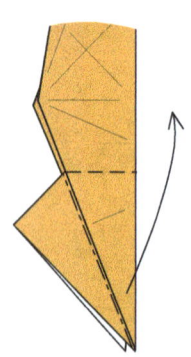

84. Detail of the bottom left flap. Stretch upwards.

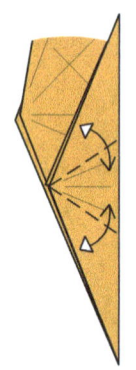

85. Precrease.

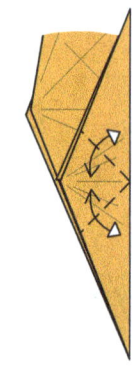

86. Precrease again.

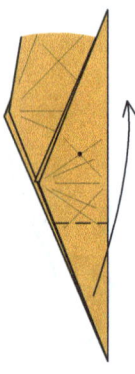

87. Valley fold up, so that edge passes through the intersection of creases.

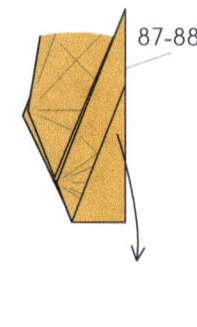

88. Unfold. Repeat steps 87-88 with the other flap.

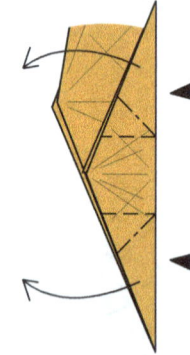

89. Squash the two flaps.

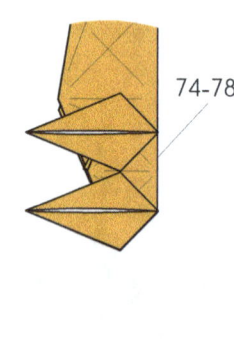

90. Repeat steps 74-78 on the two flaps.

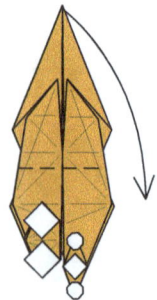

91. Swing down as far as possible.

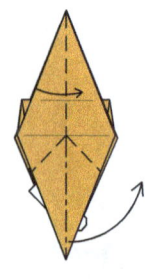

92. Swing over, while incorporating a reverse fold.

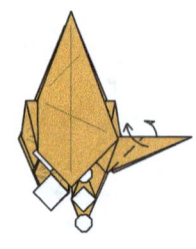

93. Outside reverse fold.

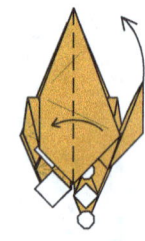

94. Swing over while pulling the flap up and flattening it.

drummer

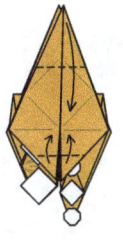

95. Valley fold the top flaps inward.

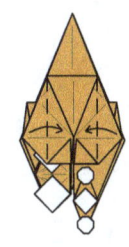

96. Valley fold again.

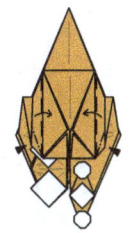

97. Valley fold over, spread squashing the corners.

98. Tuck underneath.

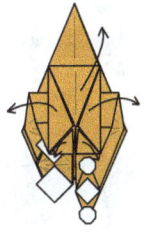

99. Unfold.

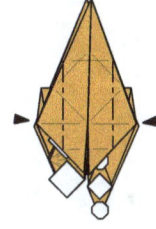

100. Sink.

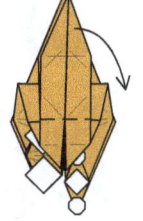

101. Swing the top flap down.

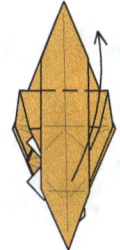

102. Swing up.

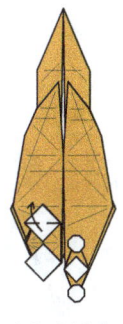

103. Lightly fold the square in half.

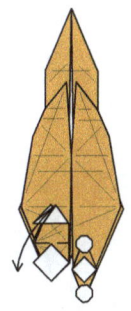

104. Lightly swing down.

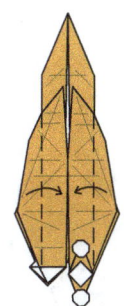

105. Valley fold the top layers.

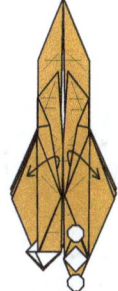

106. Bring the single layer to the surface (closed sink).

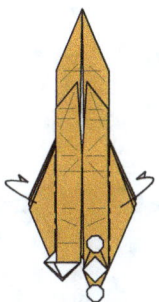

107. Mountain fold the next set of layers into the model.

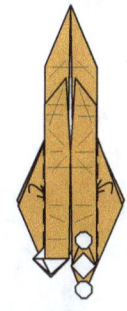

108. Valley fold the next set of layers into the model.

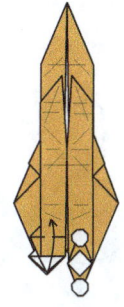

109. Swing back up.

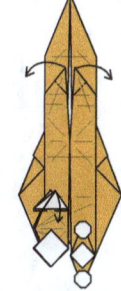

110. Unfold the square. Reverse fold at the top.

drummer

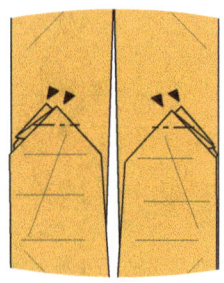

111. Reverse fold about 1/3 inward at each corner.

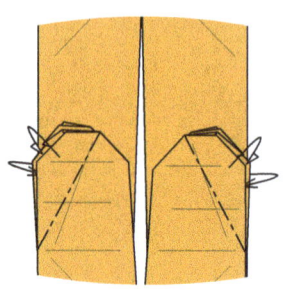

112. Swivel inwards.

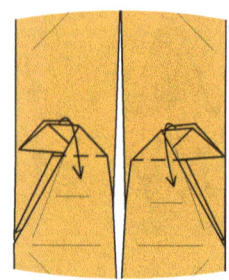

113. Swing down.

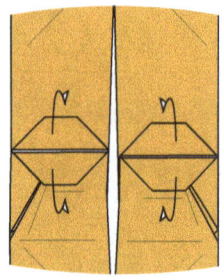

114. Wrap a layer around.

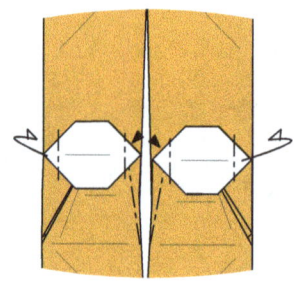

115. Sink and mountain fold to shape.

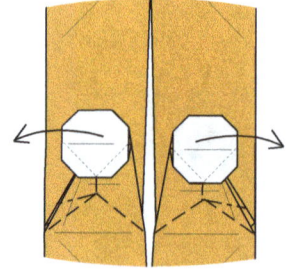

116. Rabbit ear outwards.

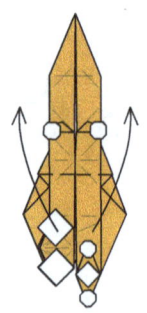

117. Swing upwards.

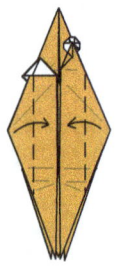

118. Valley fold inward.

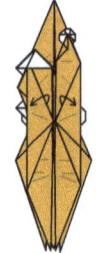

119. Bring the single layer to the surface (closed sink).

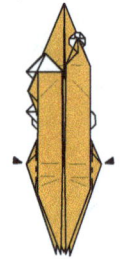

120. Sink.

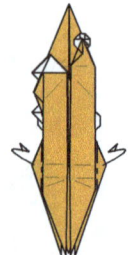

121. Mountain into the model.

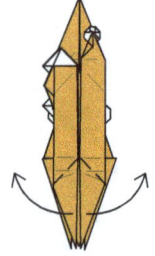

122. Valley fold outward.

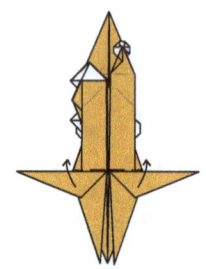

123. Swing upwards.

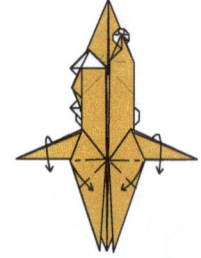

124. Swing back down, while reverse folding a layer down.

drummer

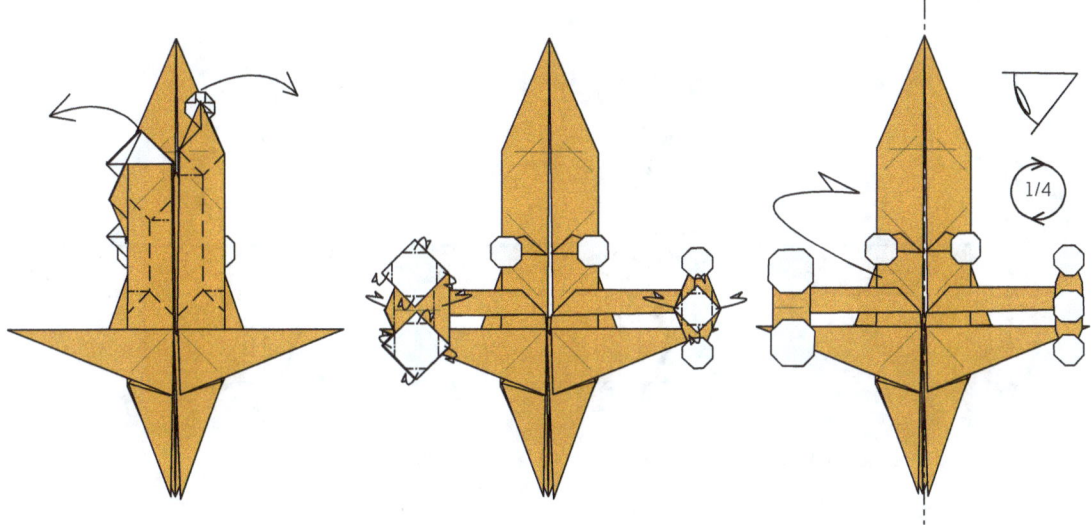

125. Rabbit ear outwards. The flaps should extend about as far as the outstretched flaps below.

126. Round off the corners of the drums with mountain folds.

127. Mountain fold the model in half. Rotate.

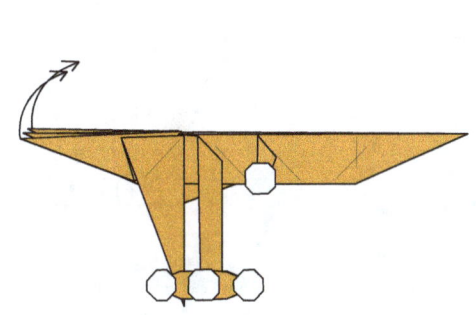

128. Pull the outer flaps upwards.

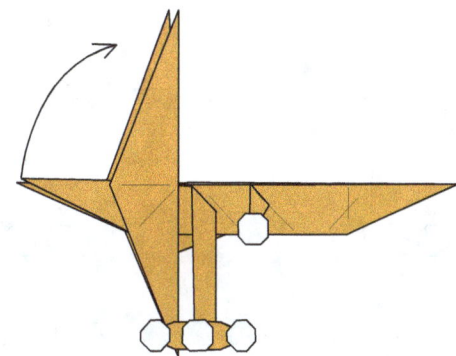

129. Pull upwards.

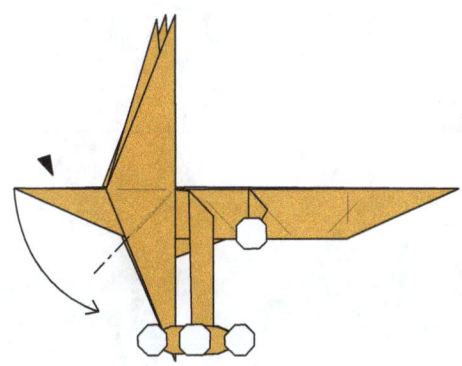

130. Reverse fold.

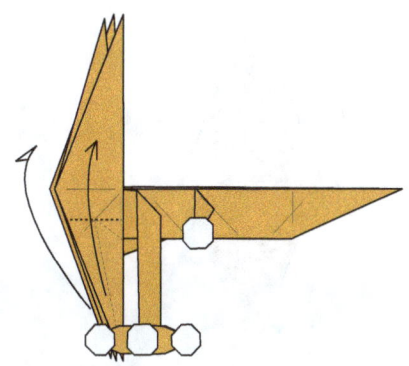

131. Bring the outer flaps upwards, allowing the inner layers of the flap to squash flat.

drummer

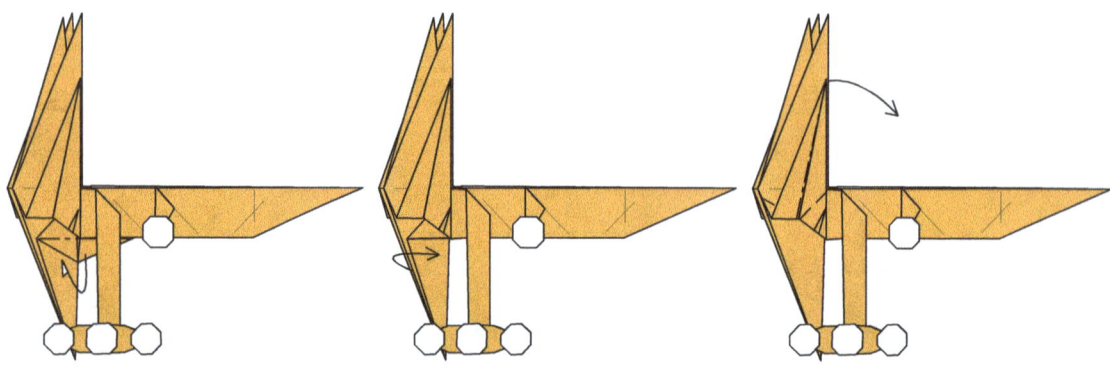

132. Tuck under. Repeat behind.

133. Pull the double layer to the surface (closed sink). Repeat behind.

134. Swivel the legs down.

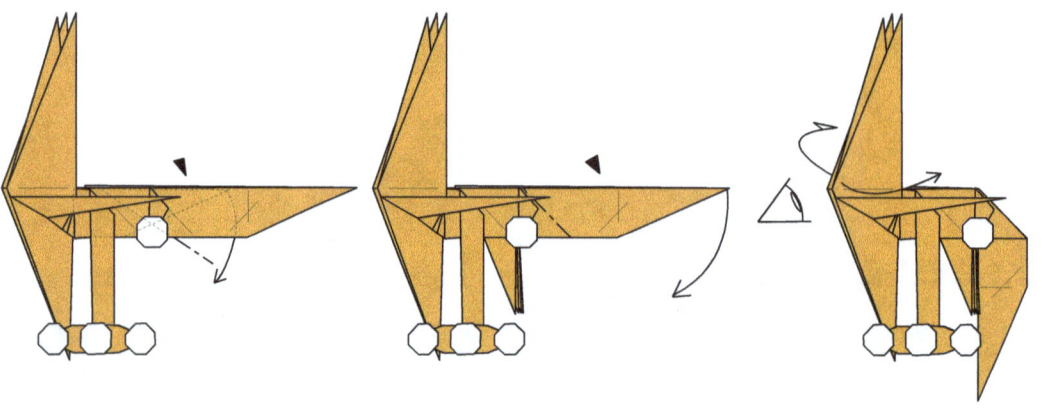

135. Reverse the hidden cluster of points down.

136. Reverse down along the existing creases.

137. Spread apart the cluster of layers evenly.

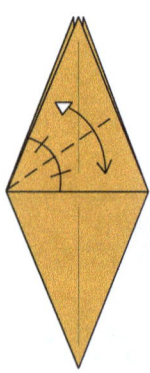 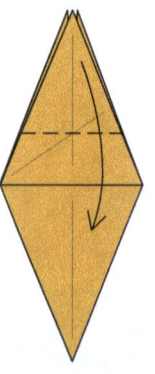 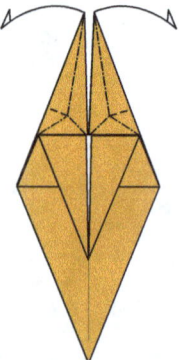

138. View from step 137. Precrease along angle bisector.

139. Valley fold down though the intersection of creases.

140. Rabbit ear outwards.

drummer

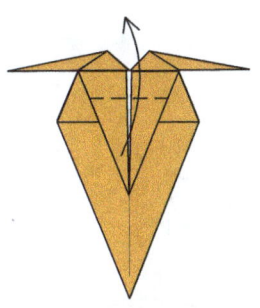

141. Valley fold up, so that the edges fall between the arms.

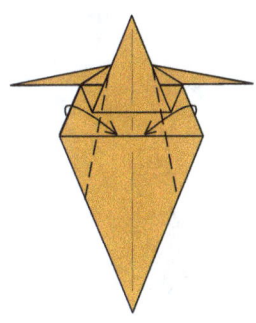

142. Valley fold to the center.

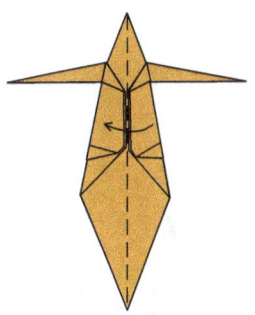

143. Valley fold in half.

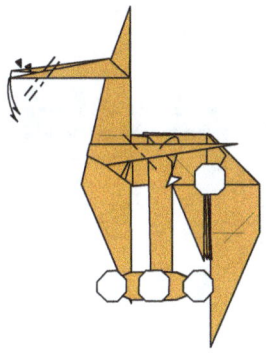

144. Mountain fold the legs. Reverse fold the arms, so as to reveal the white side.

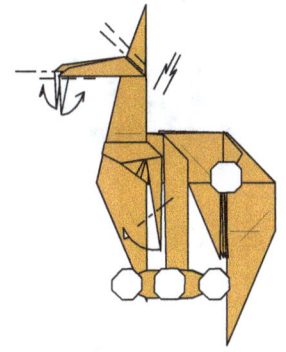

145. Crimp the head. Reverse fold the feet. Valley fold the drumsticks.

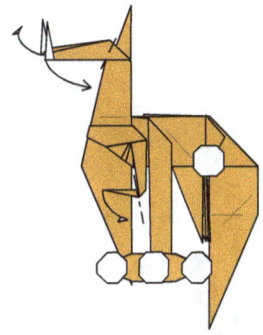

146. Valley fold the arms forward. Reverse fold the feet.

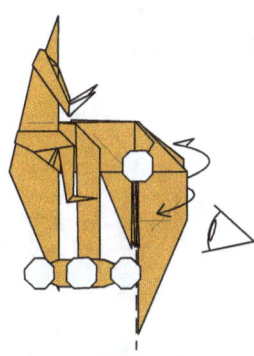

147. Spread apart the bass drum.

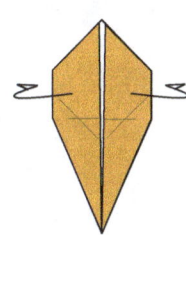

148. Detail of the bass drum. Wrap all the layers around.

149. Sink the point upwards.

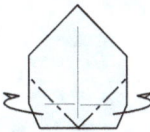

150. Mountain fold along existing creases.

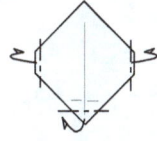

151. Round the corners with mountain folds.

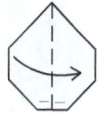

152. Fold back in half.

83

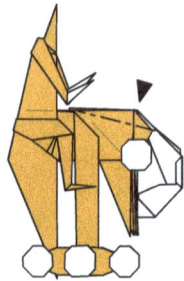

153. Sink.

154. Reverse fold the seat. Spread apart the outer and inner points of the drum stand.

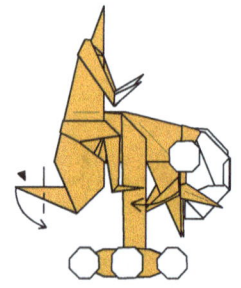

155. Reverse the base of the seat. Reposition the drum stand.

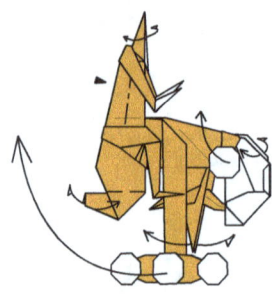

156. Open out the layers of the head. Shape the man. Open out the seat base. Spread the remaining two points of the drum stand. Open out the bass drum, and position the remaining drums to taste.

157. Completed *Drummer*.

Harpist

About

Conversations with award-winning Celtic harpist Jay Ansill provided the inspiration for this *Harpist*. The cover for his album *Origami* featured a two-piece harpist from paper which became the basis for the look of this single square version. To allow the harp to be more graceful, it was divided into two flaps. The longer and thinner flap could be more easily curved than had it been a single long thicker flap. The shorter flap comes from the center of the paper, so to create the color contrast, the remainder of the model had to be color changed. The player's appendages originate from the perimeter of the square, to facilitate such color changes. The only unusual one was for the head, which is turned inside out, and then reoriented via a twisted squash.

Tips

Note in step 20 that this is not the standard "sink halfway," but rather relies on specific reference points.

The squash in step 66 can sometimes be tricky if you do not pay special attention to hold the loose layers together while squashing.

To get the model to stand properly, the legs should be spread apart slightly. This way, together with the stool, the three appendages form a stable tripod.

harpist

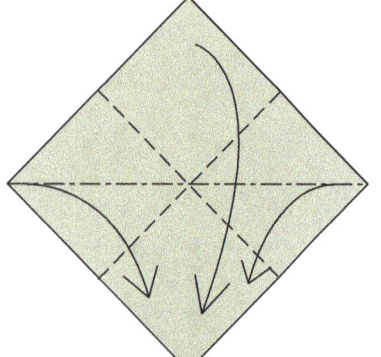
1. Form a preliminary base.

2. Valley fold up the top layer.

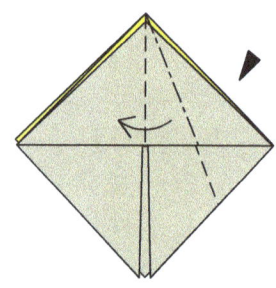
3. Squash fold.

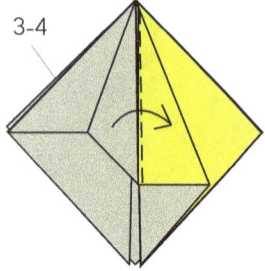
4. Valley fold over. Repeat steps 3-4 on the other side.

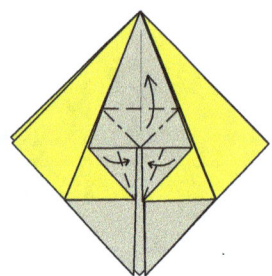
5. Petal fold.

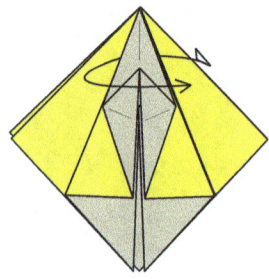
6. Unwrap the outer single layer of paper.

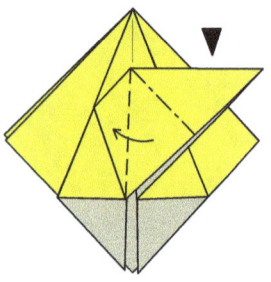
7. Squash fold.

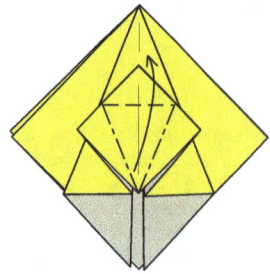
8. Petal fold.

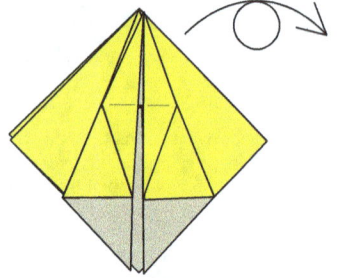
9. Turn over.

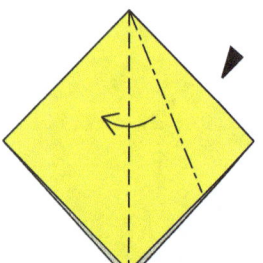
10. Squash fold.

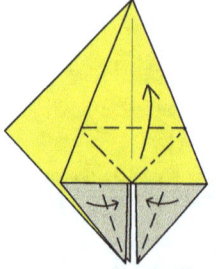
11. Petal fold.

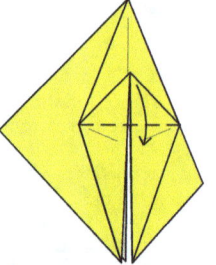
12. Valley fold down.

harpist

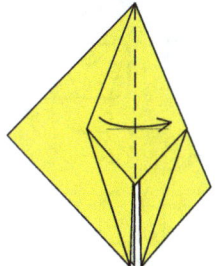

13. Valley fold over.

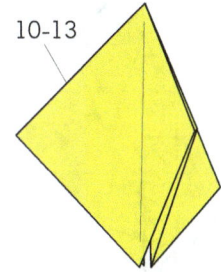

14. Repeat steps 10-13 on the other side.

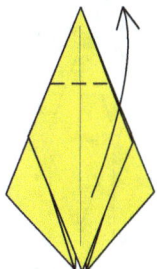

15. Stretch upwards.

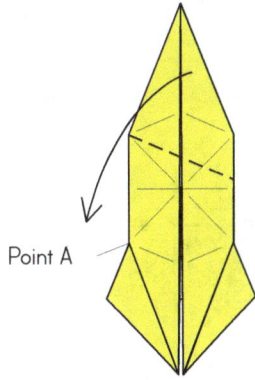

16. Valley fold, so that the edge hits point A.

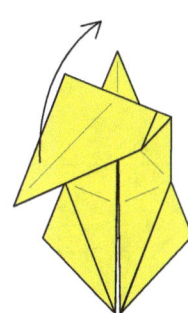

17. Unfold.

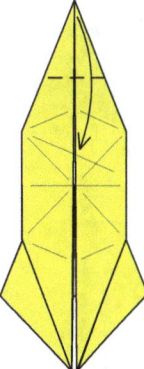

18. Valley fold to the crease.

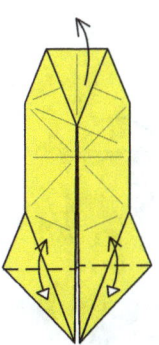

19. Unfold at the top. Precrease at the bottom.

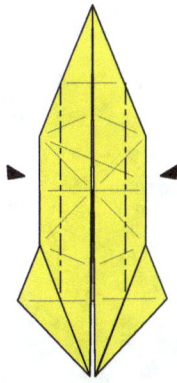

20. Closed sink the sides. These folds will meet with the creases from the previous steps.

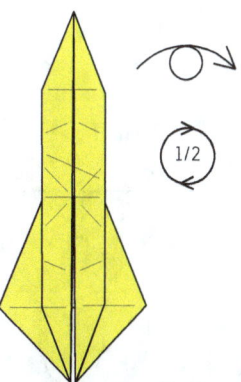

21. Turn over and rotate.

87

harpist

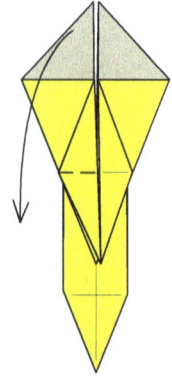

22. Valley fold down.

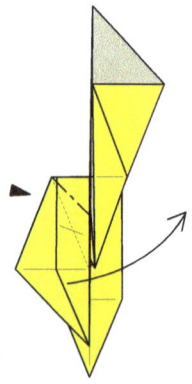

23. Squash asymmetrically.

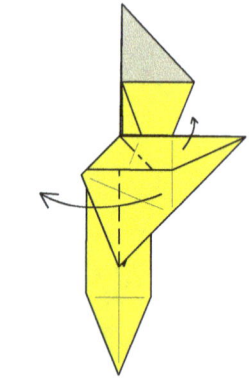

24. Valley fold over while pulling the hem upwards.

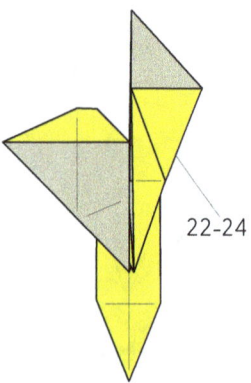

25. Repeat steps 22-24 in mirror image.

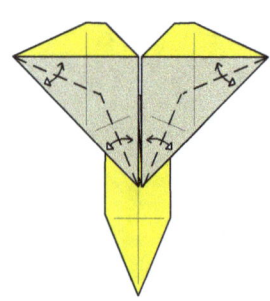

26. Precrease along the angle bisectors.

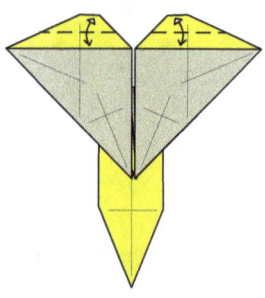

27. Precrease in half at the top.

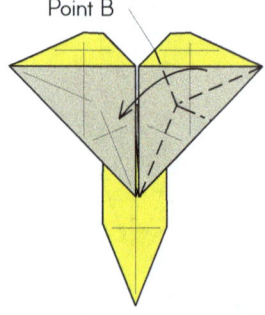

28. Form an offset rabbit ear, using point B as a guide.

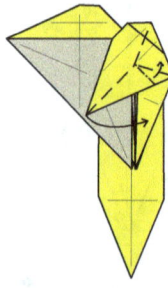

29. Rabbit ear again.

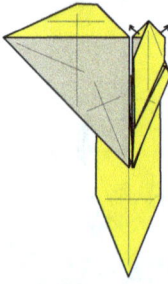

30. Pull out the single layer at the left and the double layer at the right.

harpist

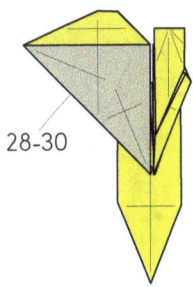
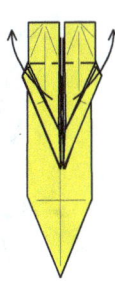
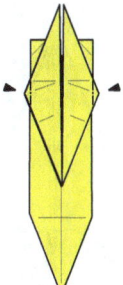

31. Repeat steps 28-30 at the left.

32. Swing the first set of flaps upwards.

33. Sink the sides, so that they are flush with the bottom edge.

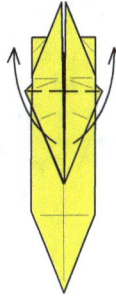
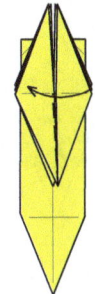
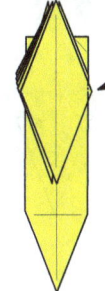

34. Swing the next set of flaps up.

35. Swing over two layers.

36. Sink.

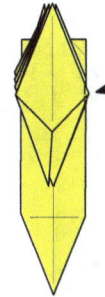
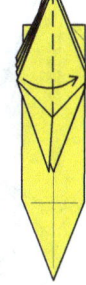

37. Swing over one layer.

38. Sink again.

39. Swing over.

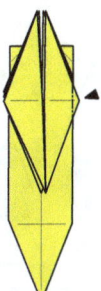
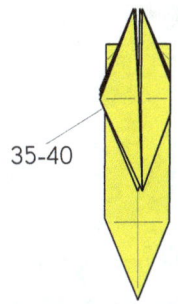
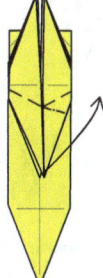

40. Sink.

41. Repeat steps 35-40 in mirror image.

42. Rabbit ear.

harpist

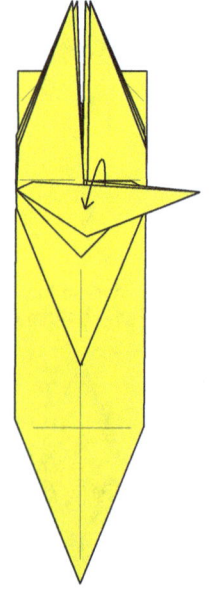

43. Wrap around a single layer.

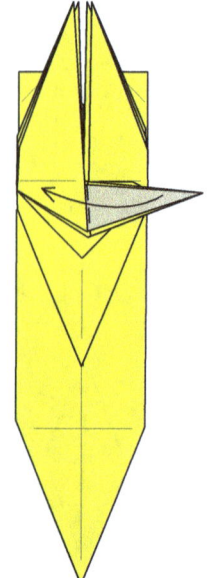

44. Swing the flap over.

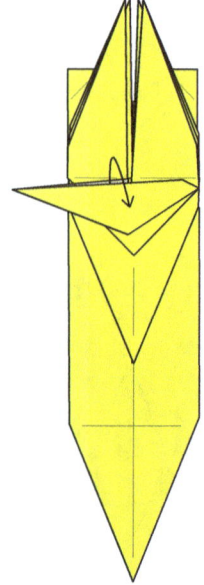

45. Wrap around a single layer.

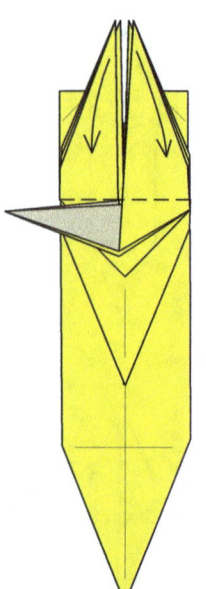

46. Valley fold the first set of flaps down.

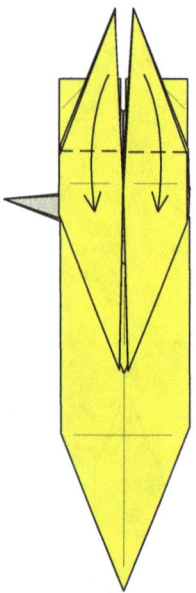

47. Valley fold the next set of flaps down.

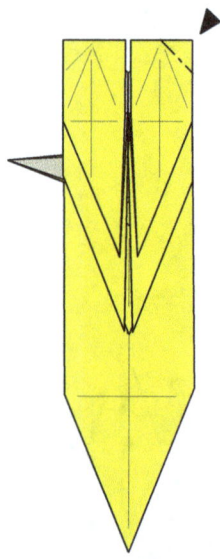

48. Reverse fold the corner along the existing crease.

harpist

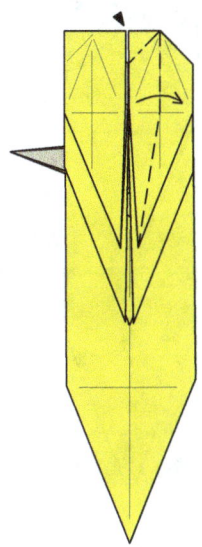

49. Squash the top layer. The flap will not lie flat.

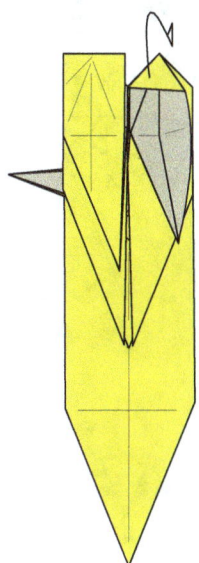

50. Wrap the single layer around.

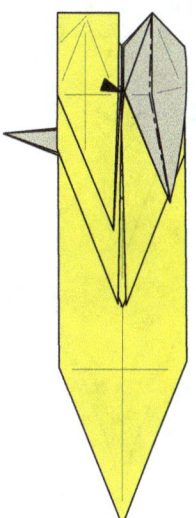

51. Sink.

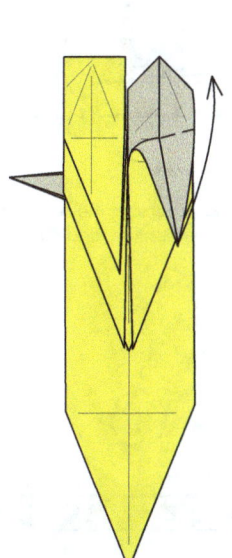

52. Swing up.

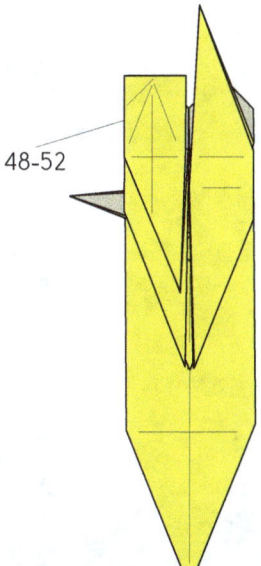

53. Repeat steps 48-52 on the other side.

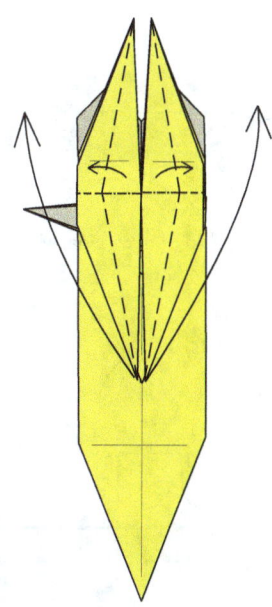

54. Swing the flaps up, while incorporating a reverse fold on the top layer.

harpist

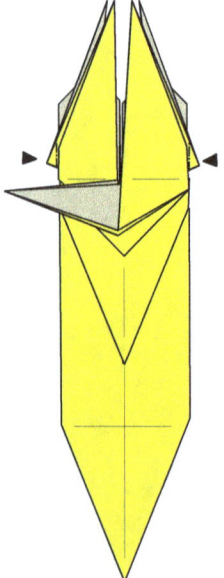 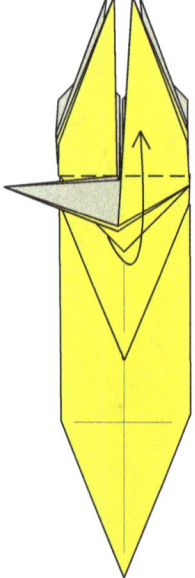 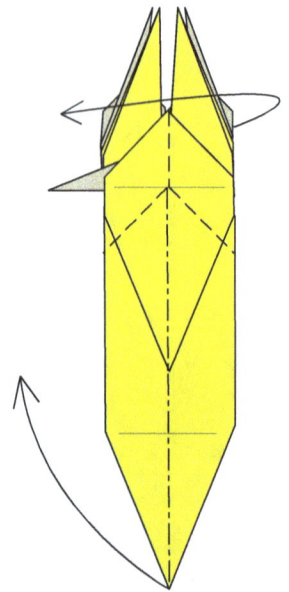

55. Reverse fold, to make flush with the side edges.

56. Swing up.

57. Fold in half while reverse folding through all layers.

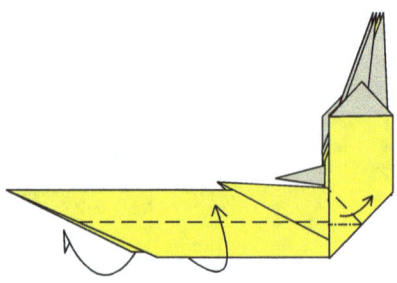 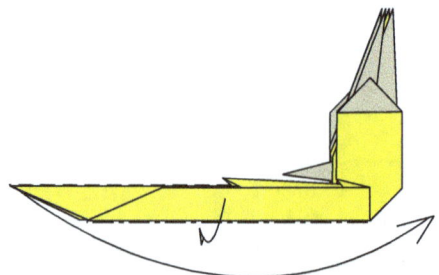

58. Valley fold at each side, while swiveling over.

59. Wrap the long point around, reversing the direction of creases (change valley to mountain, and change mountain to valley).

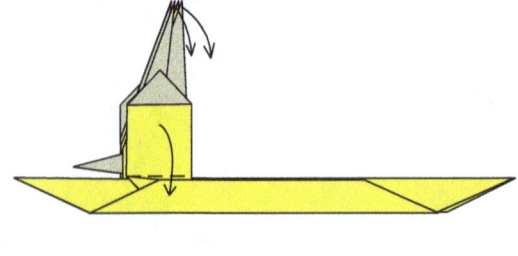 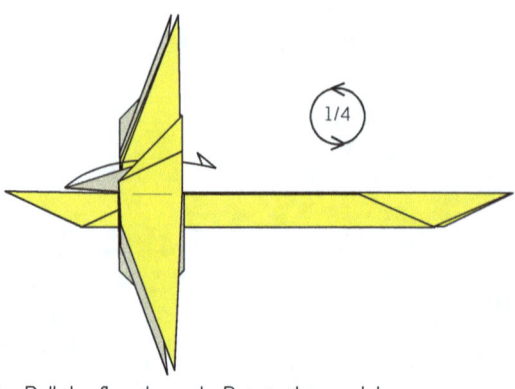

60. Swing the three connected points down.

61. Pull the flap through. Rotate the model.

harpist

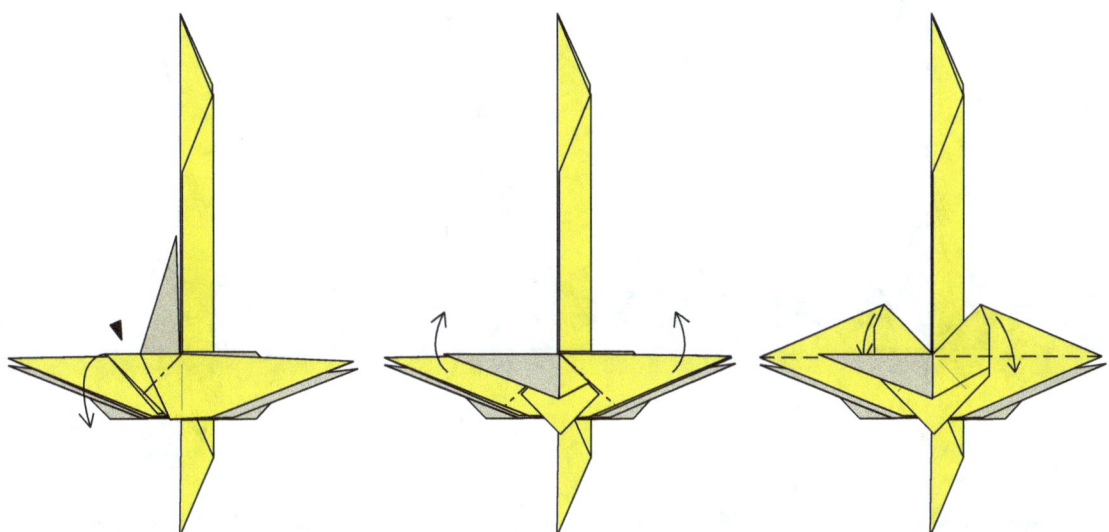

62. Squash the two flaps together.

63. Raise a layer at each side.

64. Valley fold down, leaving the center colored flap at the top.

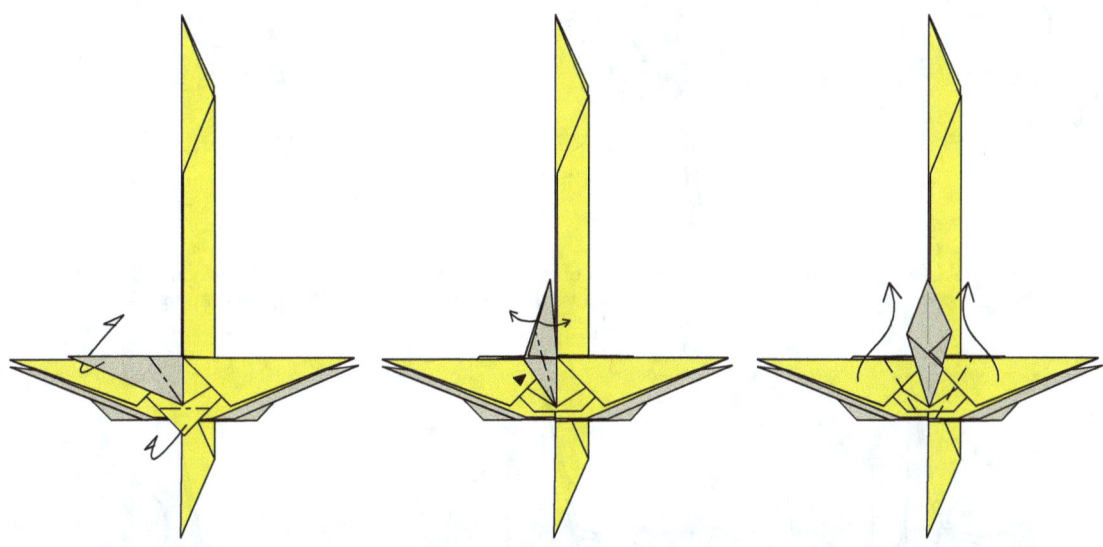

65. Mountain fold the center flap and the protruding bottom point.

66. Squash the center flap.

67. Valley fold the side flaps up and under the center flap.

harpist

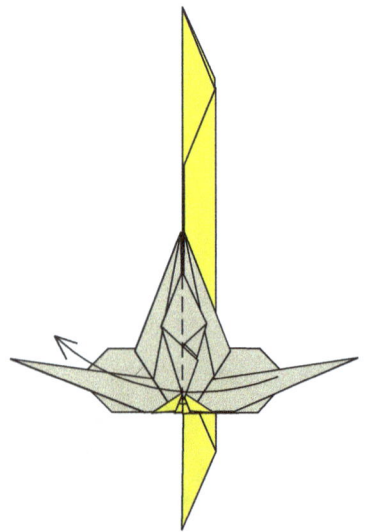

68. Fold in half.

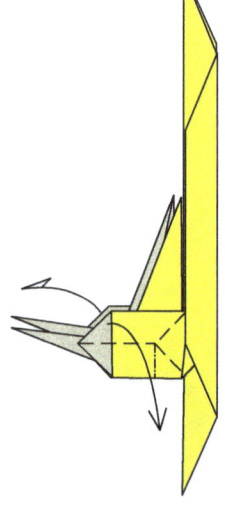

69. Rabbit ear the two points together. Repeat behind.

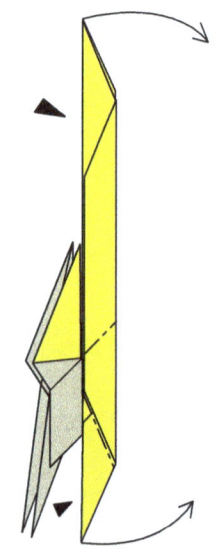

70. Reverse fold at the top and bottom.

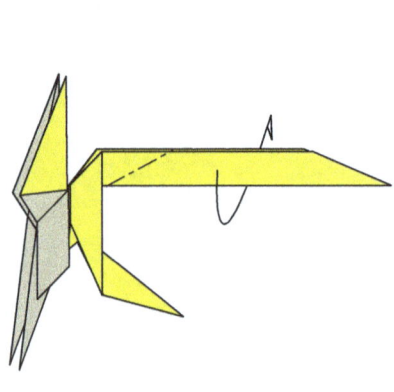

71. Mountain fold. Do not crease sharply.

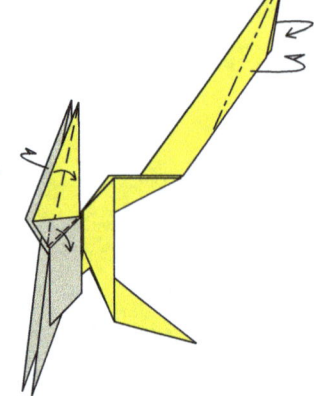

72. Thin the top of the harp with mountain folds. Thin the arms with swivel folds.

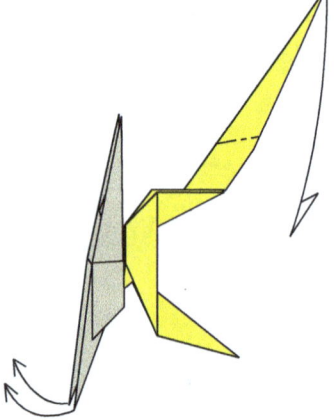

73. Pull the legs outwards. Curl the tip of the harp to the base.

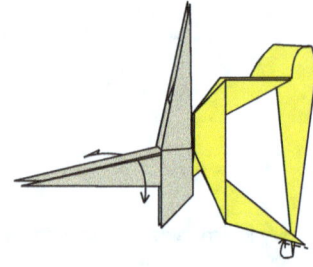

74. Tuck the tip of the harp into the base. Fold down two layers on each leg.

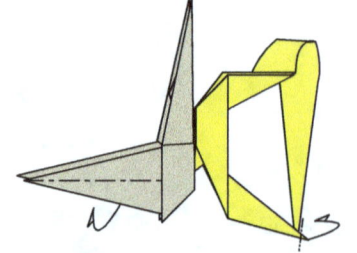

75. Mountain fold the leg layers upwards. Wrap around the base of the harp to lock.

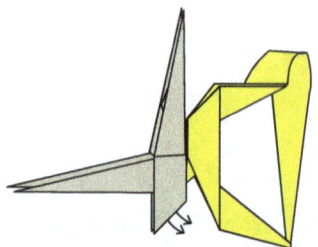

76. Pull out a single layer from each of the bottom points.

harpist

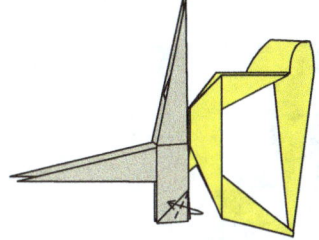 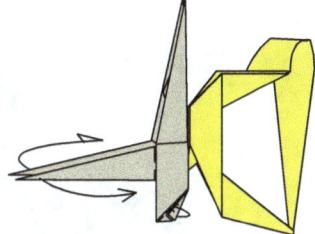 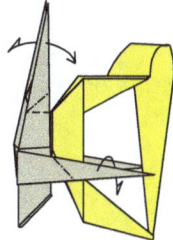

77. Valley fold both layers together.

78. Tuck the layers into the pocket to lock. Swing the legs forward.

79. Pleat the arms down. Mountain fold the legs.

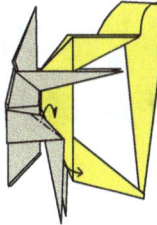 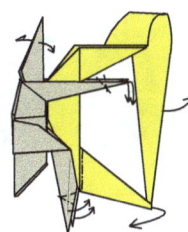

80. Swivel some material out from the side of the legs.

81. Pleat to form the feet. Squash the tips of the arms to form hands. Spread apart the layers of the head. Shape the harp and player to taste.

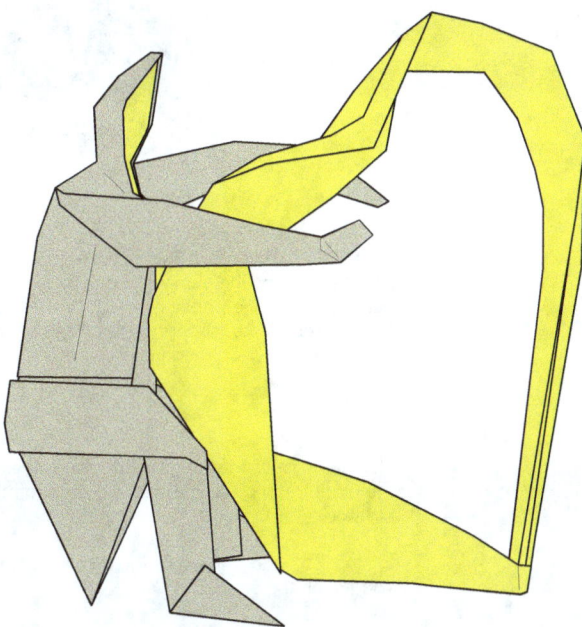

82. Completed *Harpist*.

Clarinetist

About

The clarinet in this model is from two pieces, each originating from the ends of the arms. This allows for a symmetrical model and reduces the length requirement for the clarinet appendage. Extra-long arms are needed to accommodate the paper needed for the clarinet. Effectively, this meant that the rest of the model's appendages needed to be shortened. Designing this *Clarinetist* became an exercise in inefficiency, while not being obvious about it.

Tips

Note the squash in step 20. This fold creates a "hem" that serves to shorten the model. You could theoretically chop off this hem, and the model would still work.

In step 25, ignore the valley fold at the center, as it will form naturally as you flatten the squash.

Step 60 features a "closed reverse fold" because the area to be reversed has a tiny extra corner that has to be inverted.

clarinetist

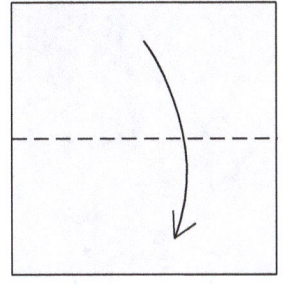

1. Valley fold down.

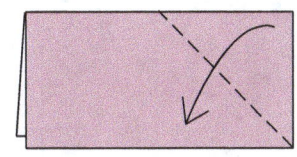

2. Valley fold the corner down.

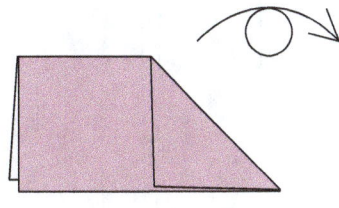

3. Turn over.

4. Rotate model counterclockwise one eighth turn.

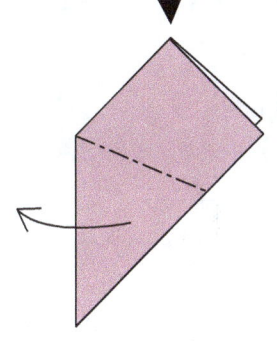

5. Squash.

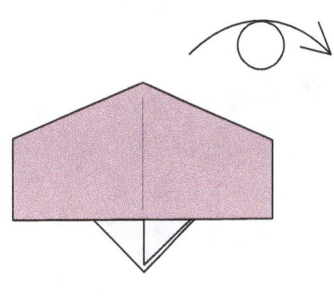

6. Turn over.

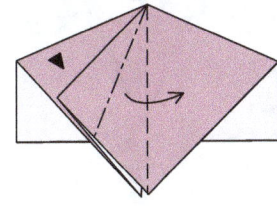

7. Squash the center flap.

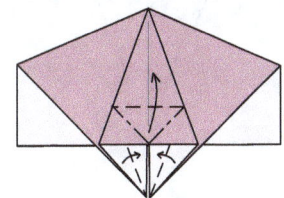

8. Petal fold.

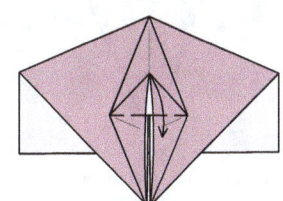

9. Valley fold down.

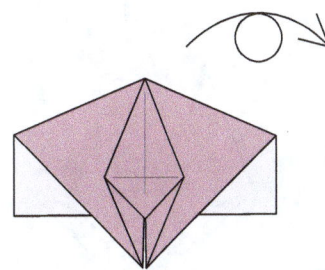

10. Turn over.

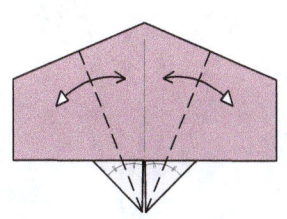

11. Precrease along the angle bisectors.

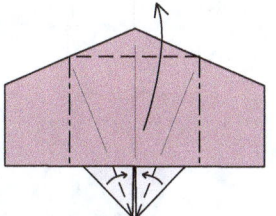

12. Petal fold up.

clarinetist

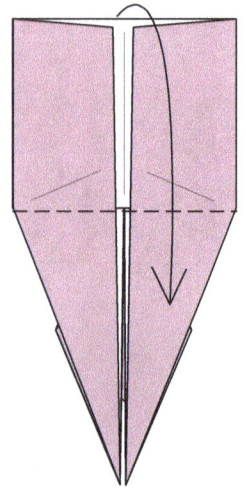
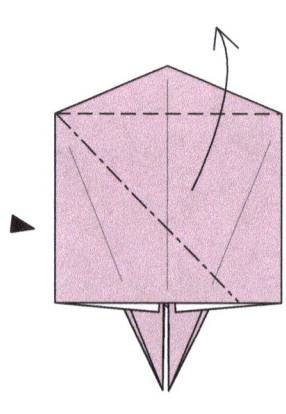
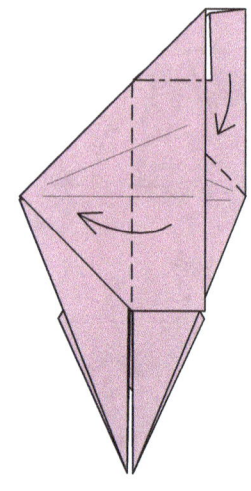

13. Valley fold down. 14. Squash. 15. Swivel over.

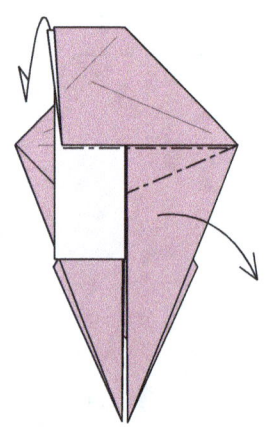
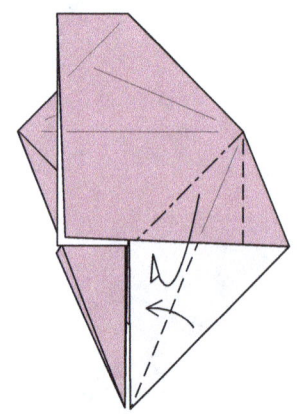
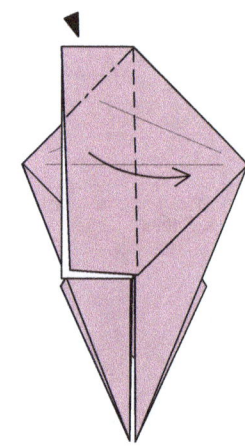

16. Open out the top layer. 17. Swivel under. 18. Squash.

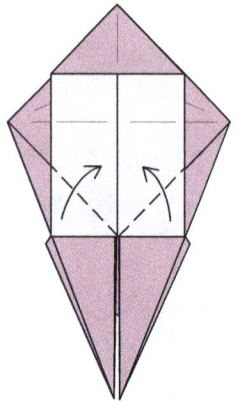
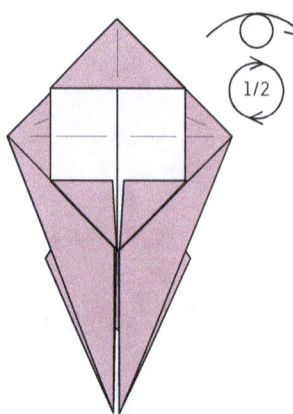
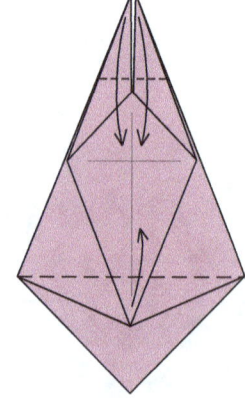

19. Valley fold the corners. 20. Turn over and rotate. 21. Form valley folds.

clarinetist

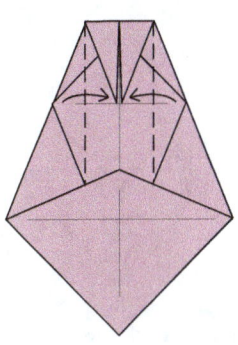

22. Valley fold to the center.

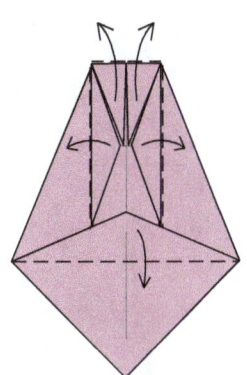

23. Unfold.

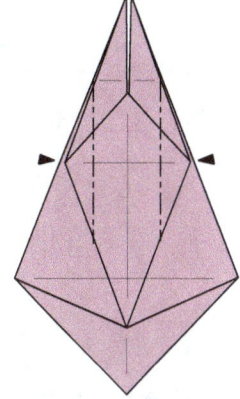

24. Sink along the existing creases.

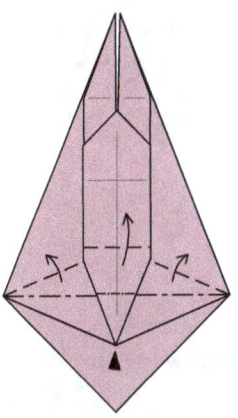

25. Spread squash upwards.

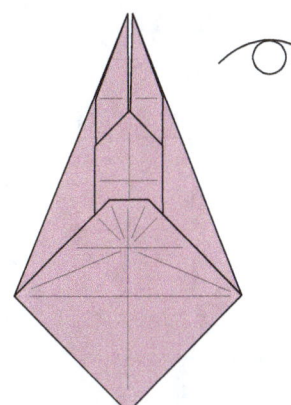

26. Turn over.

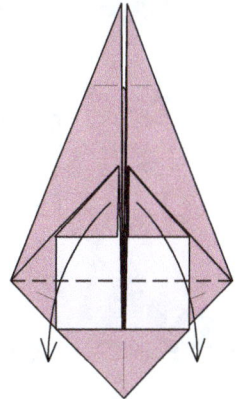

27. Valley fold down the bottom flaps.

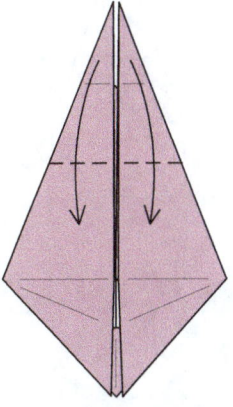

28. Valley fold down the upper flaps as far as possible.

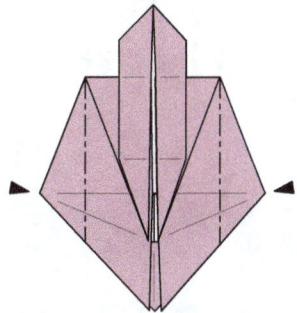

29. Sink triangularly.

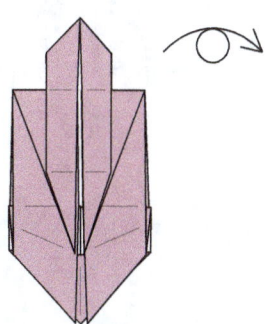

30. Turn over.

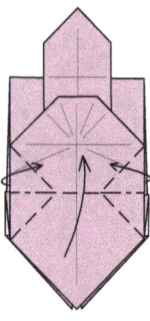
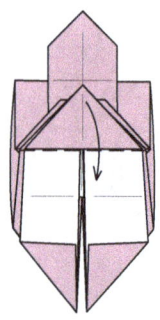
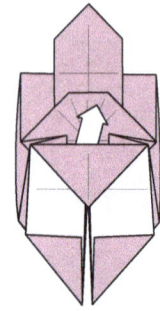

31. Valley fold up while reverse folding the sides in.

32. Valley fold down.

33. Unsink a single layer.

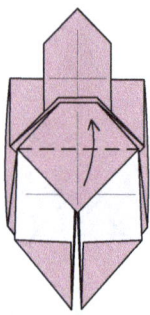
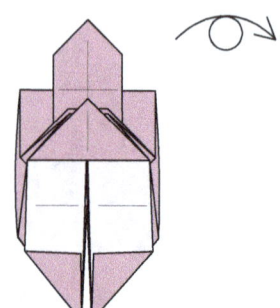
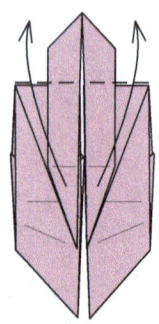

34. Valley fold up.

35. Turn over.

36. Swing the flaps up.

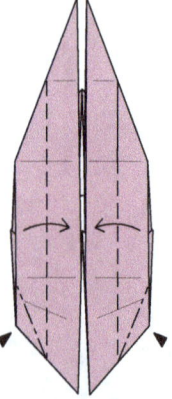
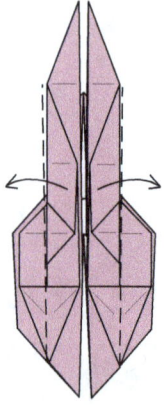
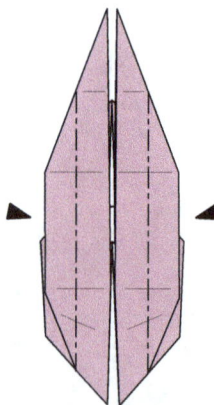

37. Valley fold the sides in, allowing spread squashes to form at the bottom.

38. Swing the sides back out.

39. Closed sink the sides.

clarinetist

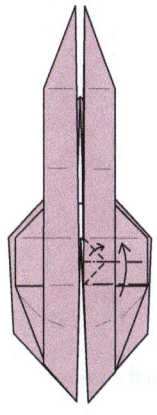

40. Pleat upwards while reverse folding through all layers.

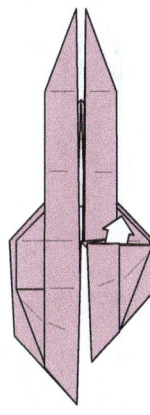

41. Unsink a single layer.

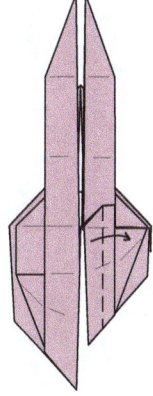

42. Valley fold over very lightly.

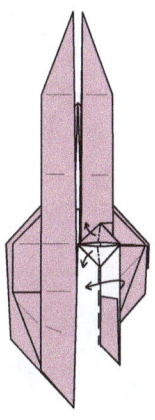

43. Swing back while pulling out the indicated layers.

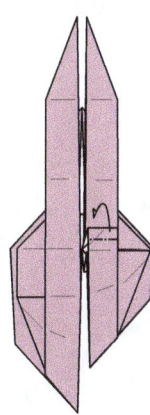

44. Mountain fold back halfway.

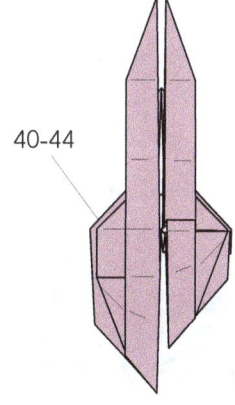

40-44

45. Repeat steps 40-44 on the other side.

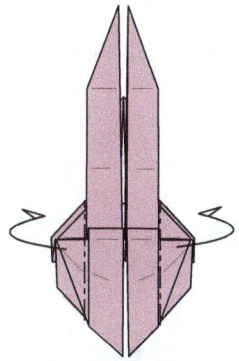

46. Mountain fold the sides behind.

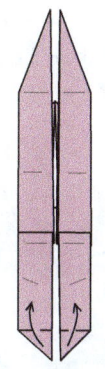

47. Valley fold the bottom points up.

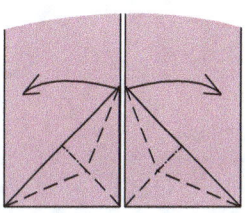

48. Rabbit ear the points outwards.

101

clarinetist

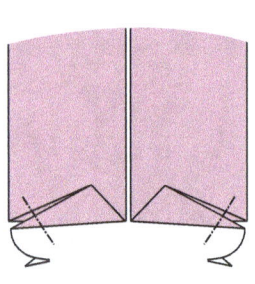 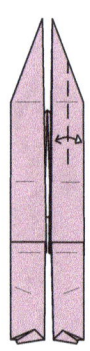 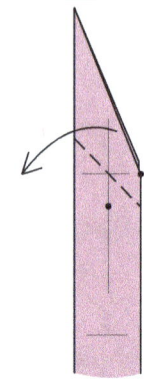

49. Reverse the tips of the feet.

50. Precrease the arm in half part way.

51. Detail of the arm. Valley fold through the intersection of creases.

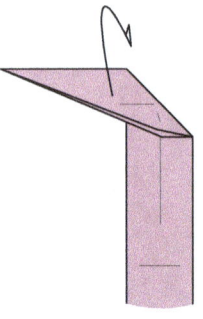 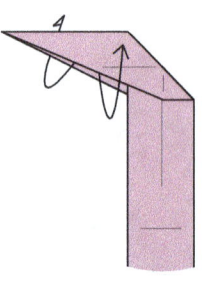 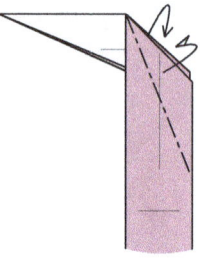

52. Wrap a layer around.

53. Pull out the single layers from the interior and wrap around to the exterior.

54. Thin the arm along the angle bisector.

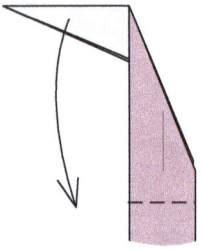 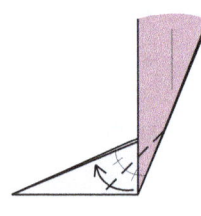 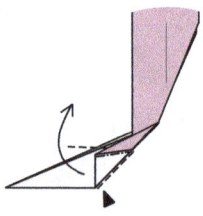

55. Swing the arm down lightly.

56. Valley fold along the angle bisector.

57. Reverse fold upwards.

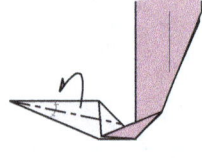 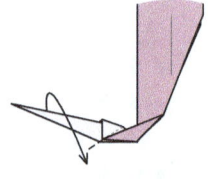 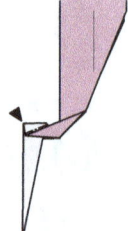

58. Mountain fold along the angle bisector.

59. Valley fold through.

60. Closed reverse fold.

clarinetist

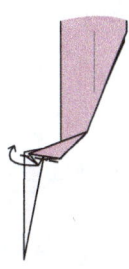

61. Reverse fold upwards.

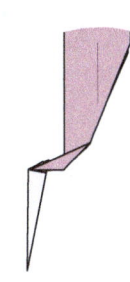

62. Complete.

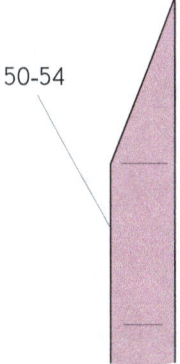

63. Repeat steps 50-54 on the other arm.

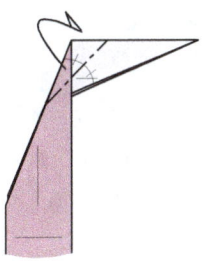

64. Mountain fold.

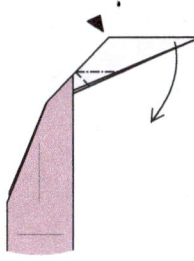

65. Swivel down. The mountain fold lies along an existing crease.

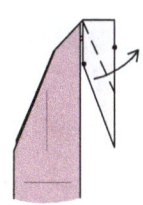

66. Valley fold the corner to lie along the right edge.

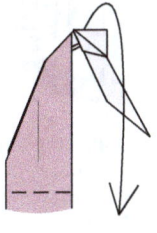

67. Swing down lightly.

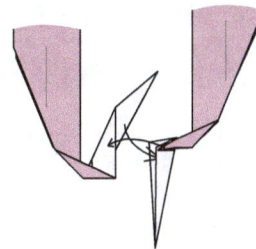

68. Interlock the layers of the clarinet.

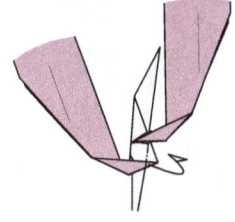

69

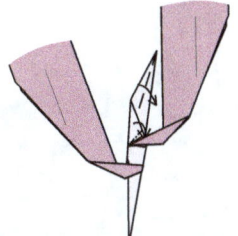

70. Thin the clarinet, swiveling the paper underneath the hand.

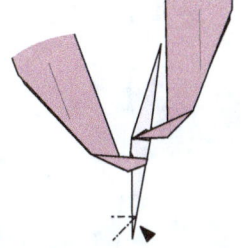

71. Squash the tip, distributing the layers evenly.

72. Squash again.

clarinetist

73. Spread apart the layers.

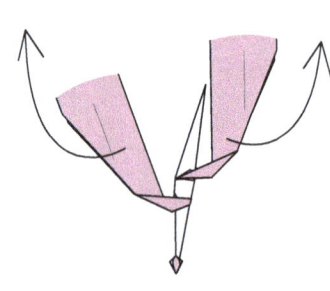

74. Undo the lock from steps 68-70.

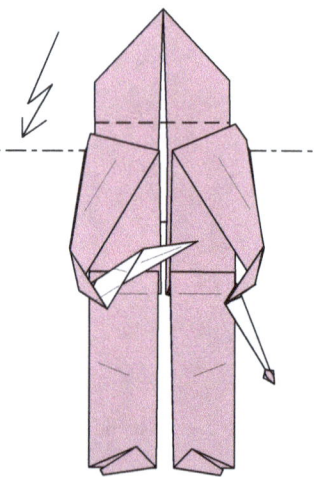

75. Pleat the head to taste.

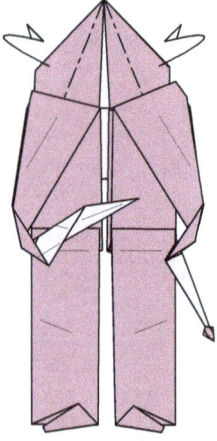

76. Thin the head. Squashes will form behind.

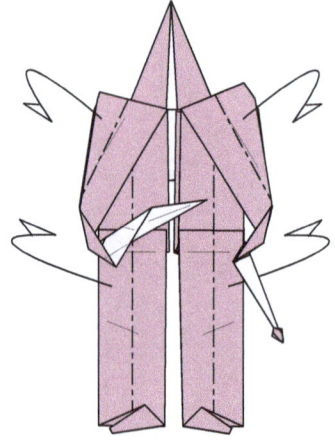

77. Thin the legs and body in half. Thin the arms along with it.

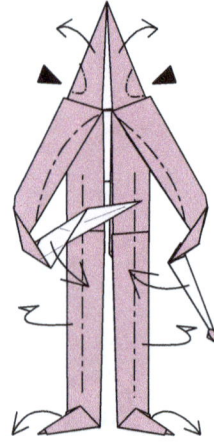

78. Open out the head and feet. Shape the body. Replace the lock from steps 68-70 while positioning the arms.

79. Completed *Clarinetist*.

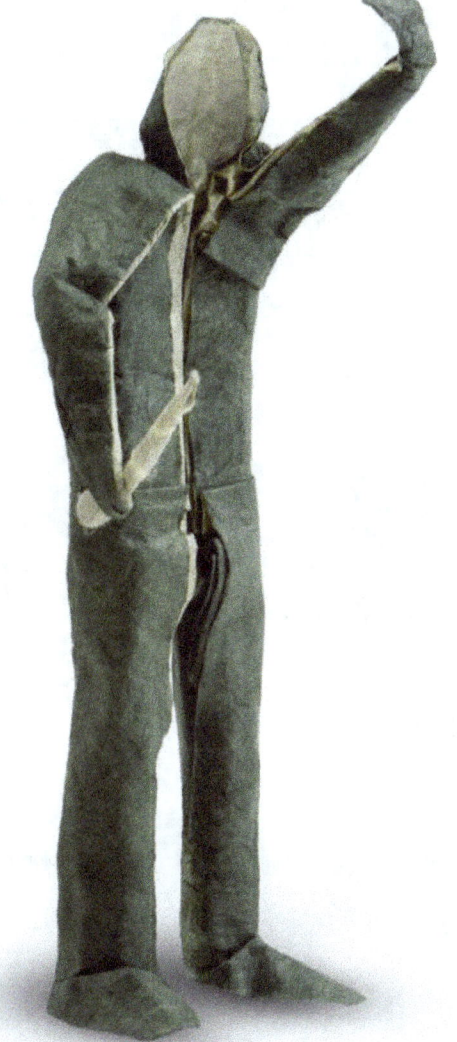

Conductor

About

This *Conductor* is an exercise in trying to match the symmetry of the square to a rather unsymmetrical subject. The trick was to think of the model as a symmetrical set of appendages. The baton and one arm became treated as one appendage, and the head and other arm as another long appendage. With that mindset, it was as if you were dealing with a symmetrical subject. Of course, each side of the model would have to get a different treatment, so this has resulted in an interesting folding sequence.

Tips

The strange looking lines at the side of step 42 represents a side view of the completed sink. These drawing are included to stress that these are both open sinks.

This model makes use of a lot of landmarks, so neatness really helps with this one. After you get a feel to where things are supposed to line up, you can be a bit more lax with the level of accuracy.

105

conductor

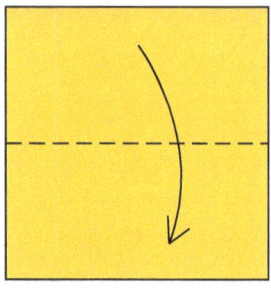

1. Valley fold down.

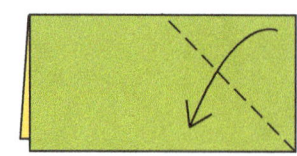

2. Valley fold the corner down.

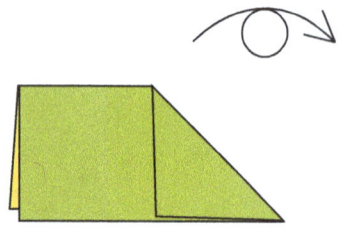

3. Turn over.

4. Rotate model counterclockwise one eighth turn.

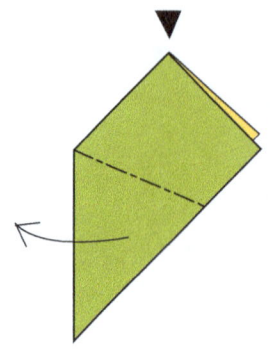

5. Squash fold.

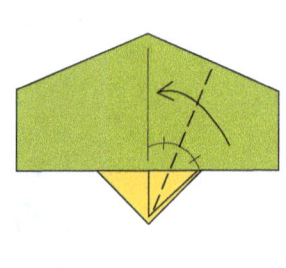

6. Valley fold along angle bisector.

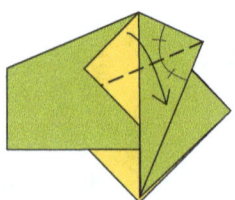

7. Valley fold along angle bisector.

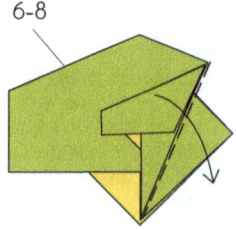

8. Swing down, leaving the last fold intact. Repeat steps 6-8 in mirror image.

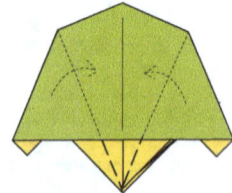

9. Valley fold along the existing creases. These folds extend underneath the top layer.

conductor

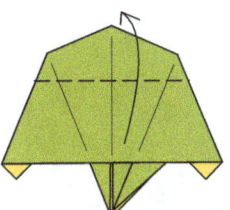 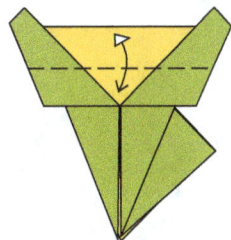 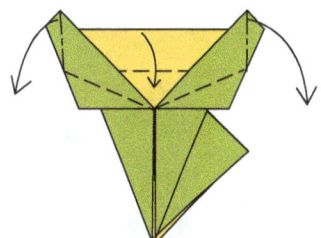

10. Valley fold up as far as possible.

11. Precrease the top layer in half.

12. Bring the top down, while stretching the two side points outwards.

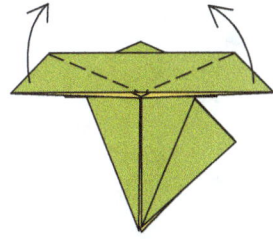 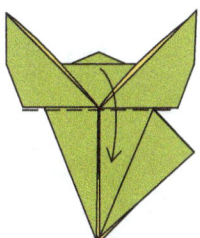 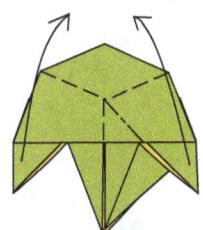

13. Swing the two points upwards.

14. Swing the top section down.

15. Rabbit ear the top section.

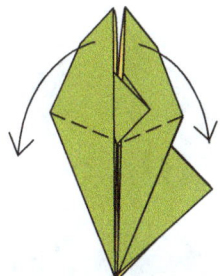 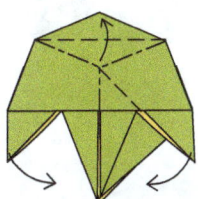 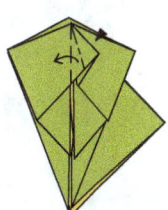

16. Undo the rabbit ear.

17. Reverse the direction of the previous rabbit ear. The side points will swing towards the center.

18. Squash the center flap.

conductor

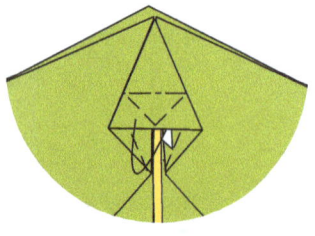
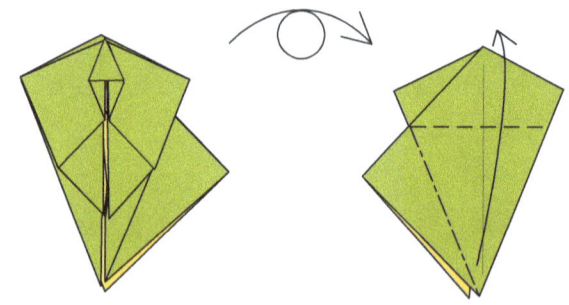

19. Petal fold under.
20. Turn over.
21. Petal fold.

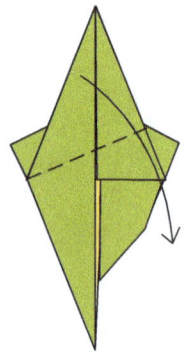
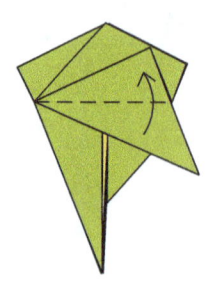
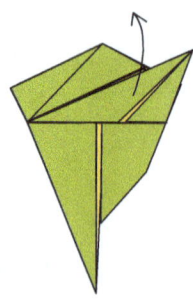

22. Valley fold down.
23. Valley fold up.
24. Open out.

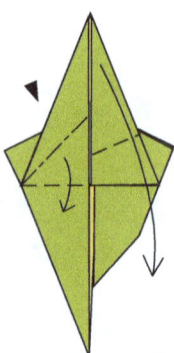
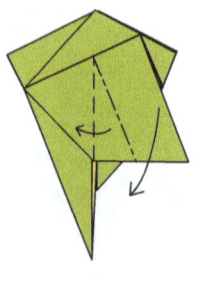
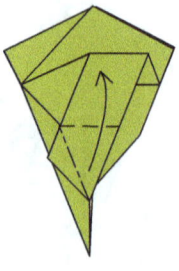

25. Squash asymmetrically
26. Swivel the lower right-hand point over to the center.
27. Petal fold up.

conductor

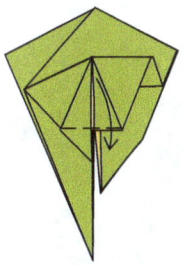 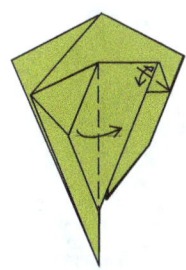 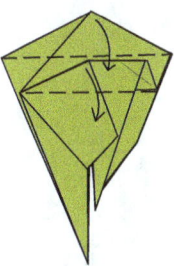

28. Swing down.

29. Precrease at the top. Swing over.

30. Valley fold down.

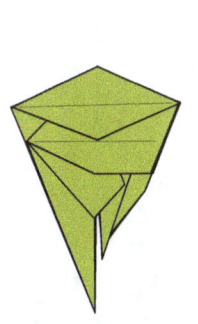  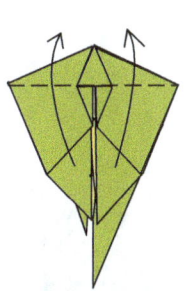 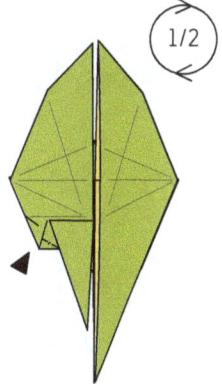

31. Turn over.

32. Bring the two large flaps up.

33. Reverse fold. Rotate the model.

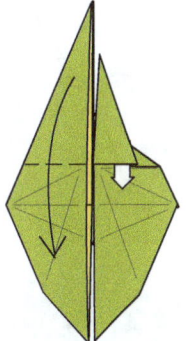 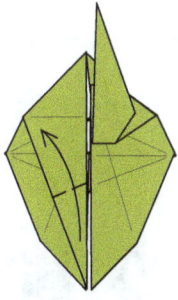 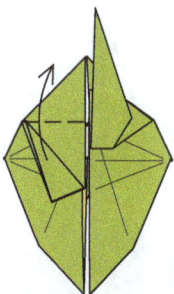

34. Valley fold the left flap down. Unsink at the right.

35. Valley fold to the corner.

36. Open out.

conductor

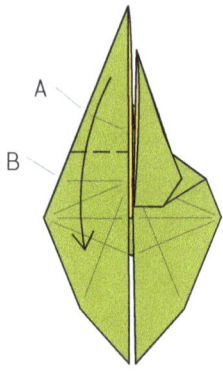
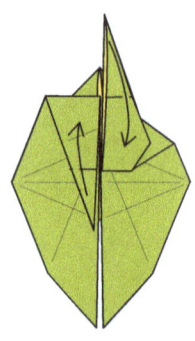
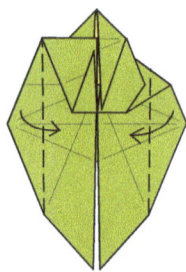

37. Valley fold down, so that A lies along the crease at point B.

38. Valley fold up to be flush with the adjacent edge. Valley fold down the right arm.

39. Valley fold in the sides, so that the edges lie along the internal creases.

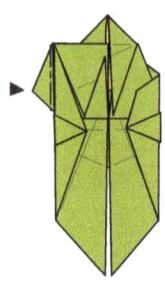
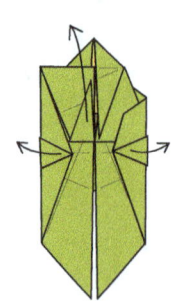
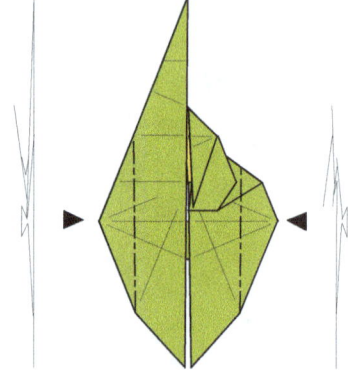

40. Open sink the protruding corner.

41. Open out.

42. Open sink the sides.

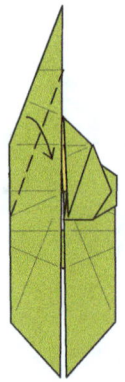
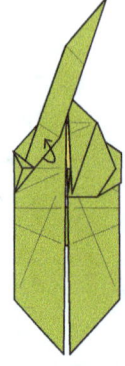
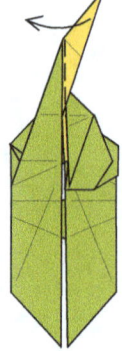

43. Valley fold, allowing a gusset to form at side of body.

44. Wrap a single layer around.

45. Valley fold over.

conductor

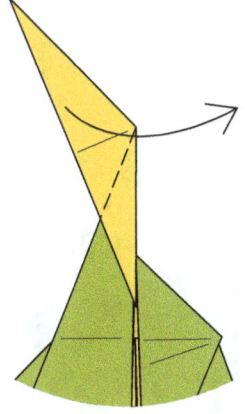

46. Valley fold over.

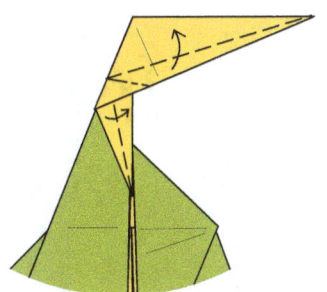

47. Swivel fold.

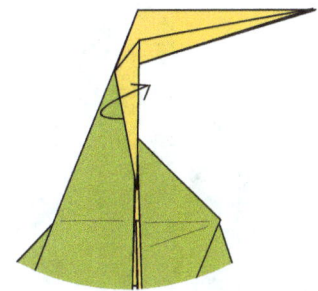

48. Bring a single layer to the surface.

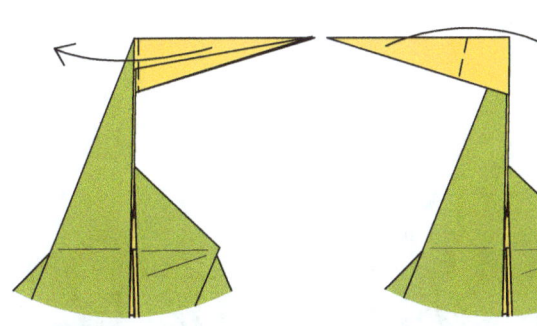

49. Valley fold over.

50. Valley fold over (there are no reference points).

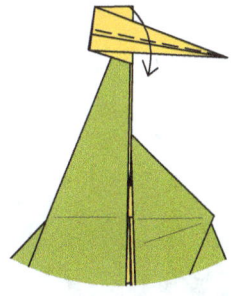

51. Valley fold in half.

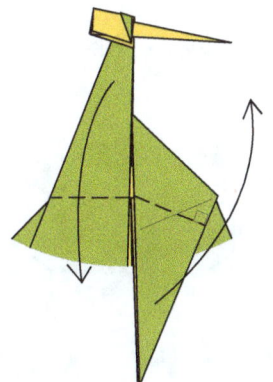

52. Valley fold the arms.

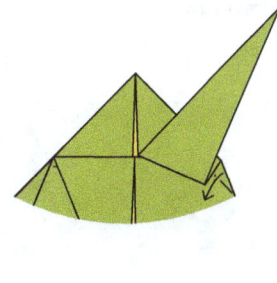

53. Reverse fold.

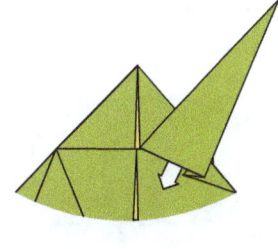

54. Unsink.

111

conductor

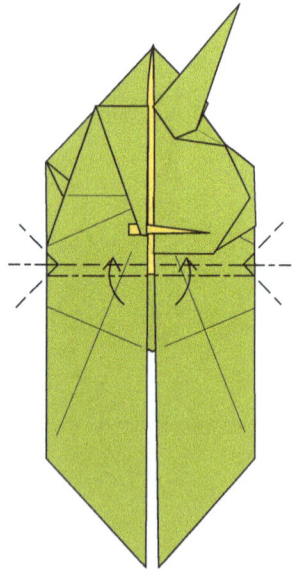

55. Pleat the legs while incorporating reverse folds.

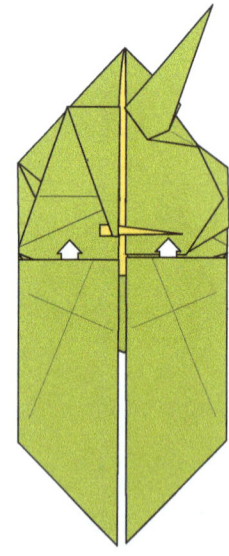

56. Unsink.

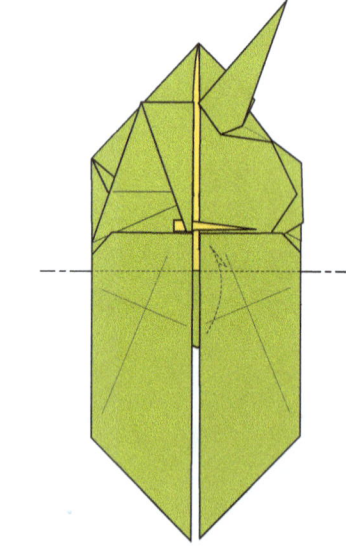

57. Swing the hidden flap upwards.

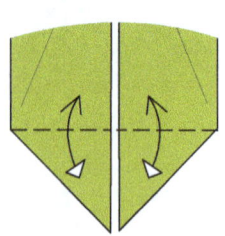

58. Precrease.

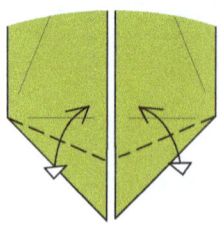

59. Precrease again.

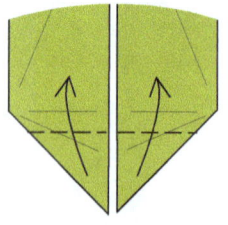

60. Valley fold up, so that the two creases meet.

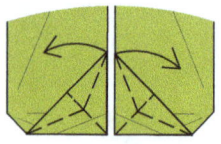

61. Rabbit ear outwards.

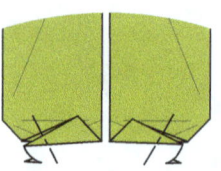

62. Reverse fold the tips inwards.

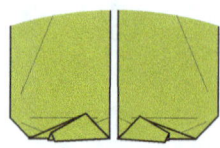

63. Completed feet.

conductor

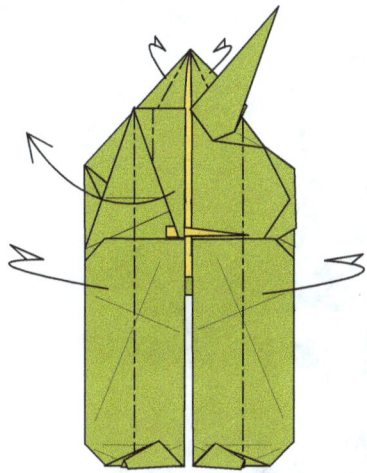

64. Mountain fold the body while narrowing the head and pulling out the arm.

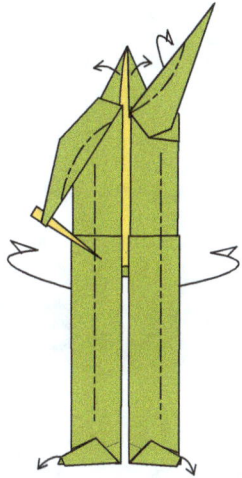

65. Round the body. Open out the head and the feet. Shape the arms.

66. Completed *Conductor*.

113

Dancing Couple

About

Fellow folder Ros Joyce thought it would be an interesting challenge to recreate Neal Elias' classic model of a dancing couple, *The Last Waltz*, from a square (Elias' model was from a 3x1 rectangle). The basic structure for this model is very simple but adding the necessary detail to create a graceful couple was a challenge.

Tips

Step 45 might look involved, but after forming the large mountain folds first, you are basically inserting a tiny reverse fold in the middle of this big collapse.

In step 52, the difficulty of this procedure is noted. By swinging the white section to the left, the wrap is reduced to a mere mountain fold. Viewing the sequence as a wrap puts the whole procedure in perspective.

The goal of step 81 is to make the dancers appear separate. By adding a different curve to the dress and to the man's leg, this effect can be achieved.

dancing couple

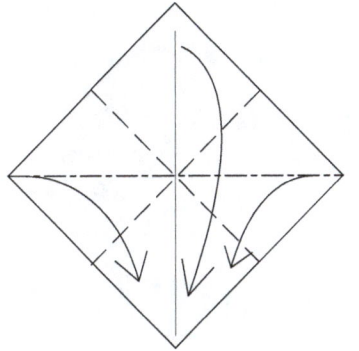
1. Form a preliminary base.

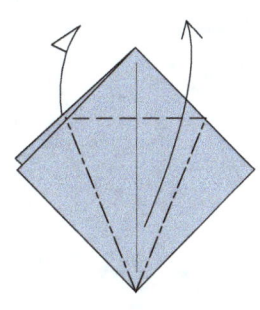
2. Petal fold both sides.

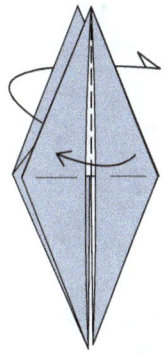
3. Swing over. Repeat behind.

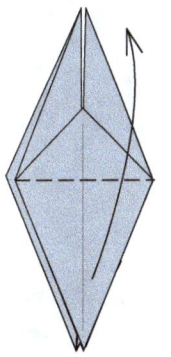
4. Valley fold up.

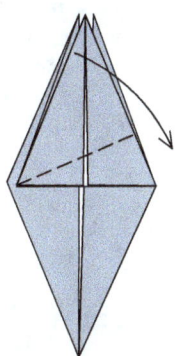
5. Valley fold over.

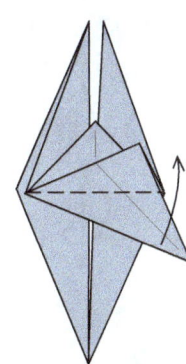
6. Valley fold up.

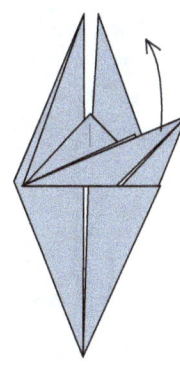
7. Unfold the pleat.

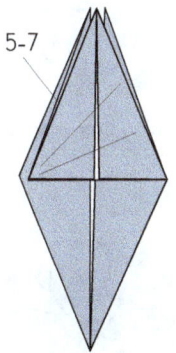
8. Repeat steps 5-7 in mirror image.

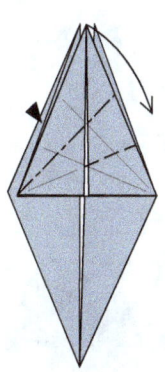
9. Asymmetrical squash.

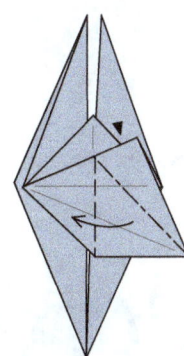
10. Squash again.

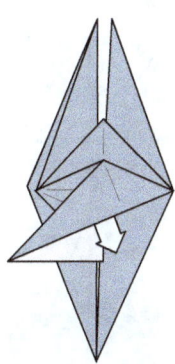
11. Pull out a single layer.

dancing couple

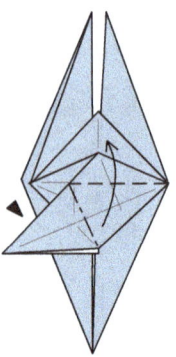
12. Squash fold.

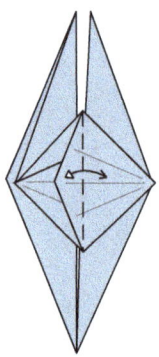
13. Precrease.

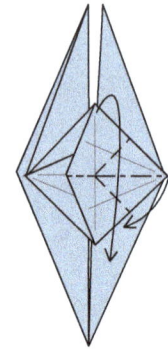
14. Swing down while reverse folding.

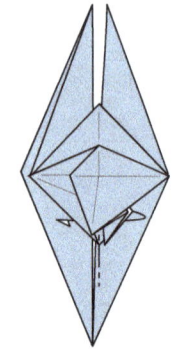
15. Swing the small white flap through.

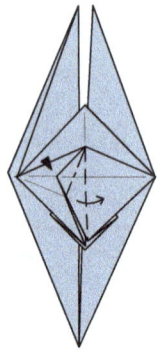
16. Spread squash.

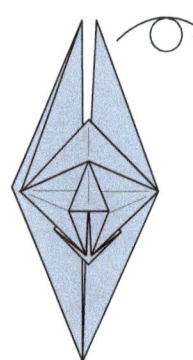
17. Turn over.

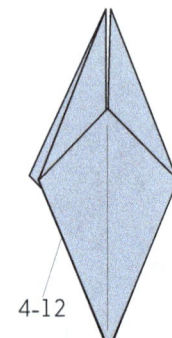
18. Repeat steps 4-12.

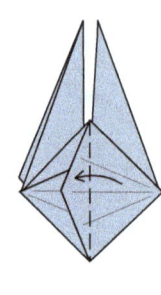
19. Valley fold over.

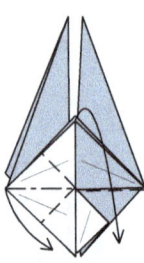
20. Swing down while reverse folding.

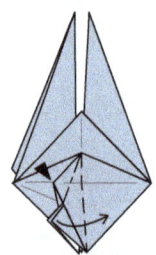
21. Swing over while spread squashing.

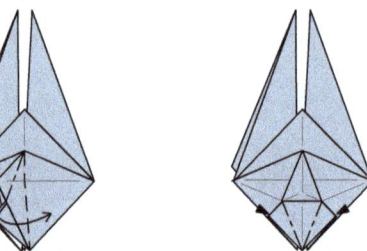
22. Reverse fold the sides.

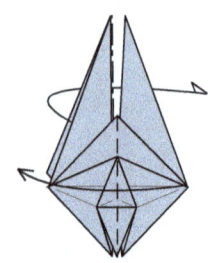
23. Swing over, front and back.

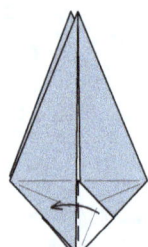
24. Swing over the small white flap.

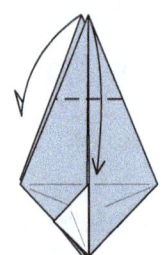
25. Valley fold the top points down.

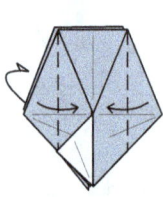
26. Valley fold the four side flaps inwards.

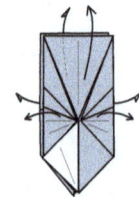
27. Unfold.

dancing couple

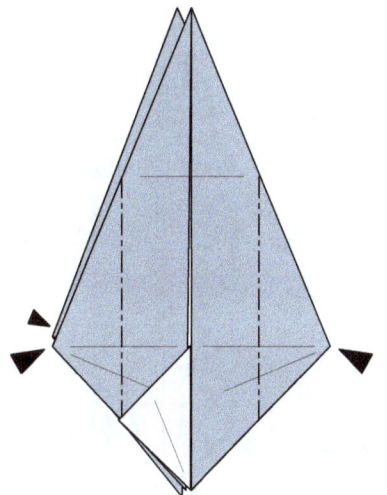

28. Closed sink at each of the four corners.

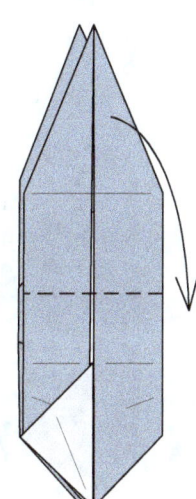

29. Valley fold down as far as possible.

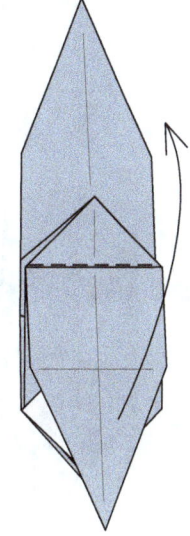

30. Swing back up.

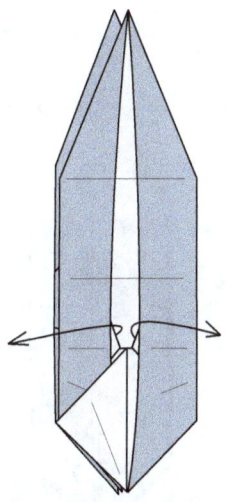

31. Open out the side layers. The model will not lie flat.

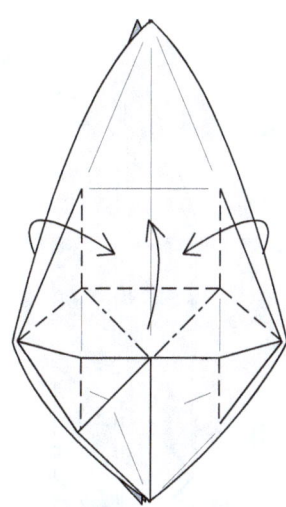

32. Close back up while incorporating a petal fold.

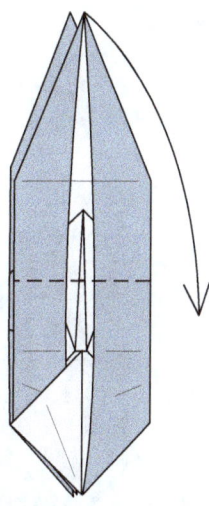

33. Swing back down.

dancing couple

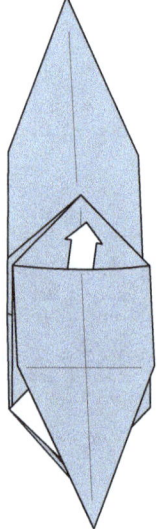

34. Unsink.

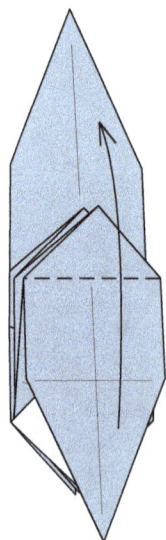

35. Swing up.

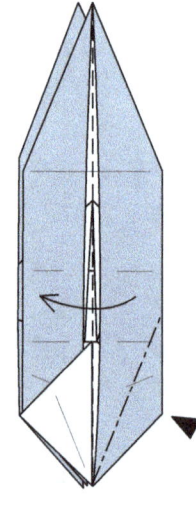

36. Valley fold over one layer, while spread squashing the corner.

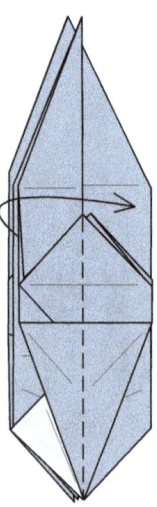

37. Swing back.

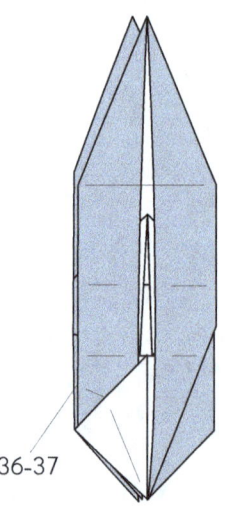

38. Repeat steps 36-37 on the other side.

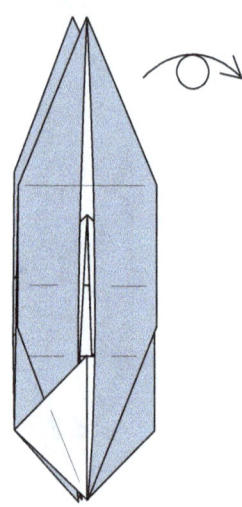

39. Turn over.

dancing couple

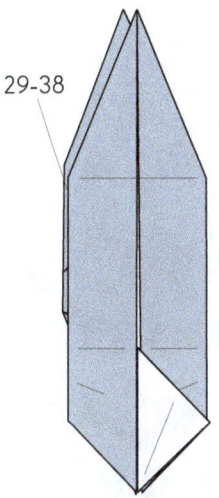 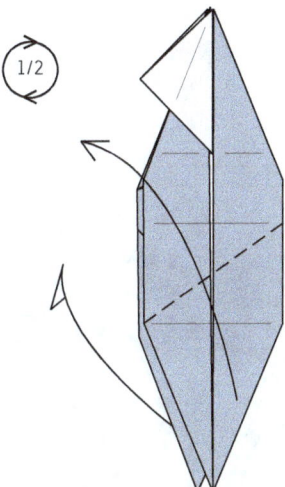 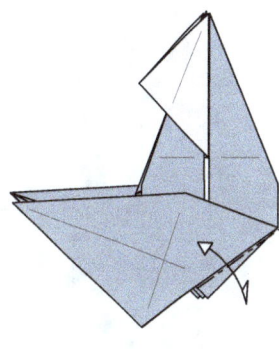

40. Repeat steps 29-38. Rotate the model.

41. Valley fold the bottom points up.

42. Precrease each of the three bottom triangles where they meet the folded edge.

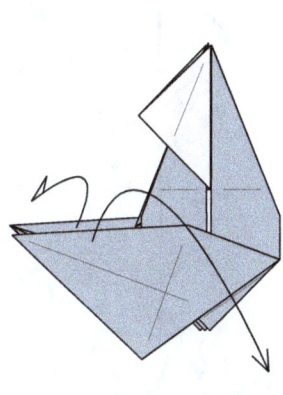 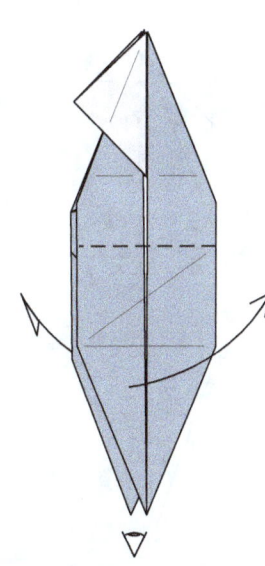 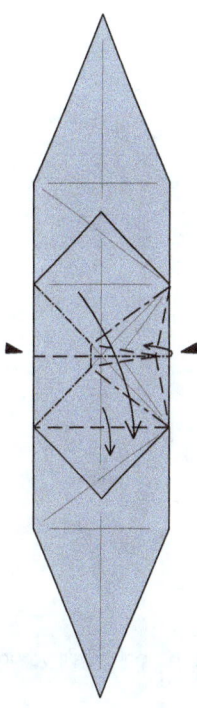

43. Swing back down.

44. Spread apart the bottom flaps, stretching the center triangle flat.

45. View from step 44. Reform the center triangle with the additional folds indicated. Form the mountain folds first.

dancing couple

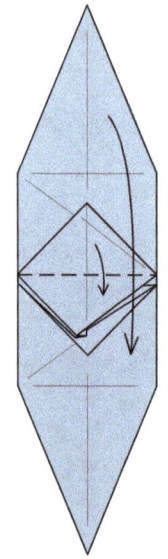

46. Swing down.

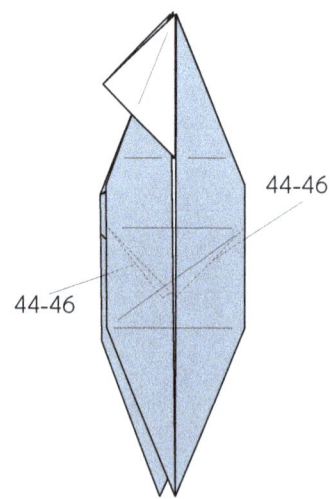

47. Repeat steps 44-46 on the other two triangles.

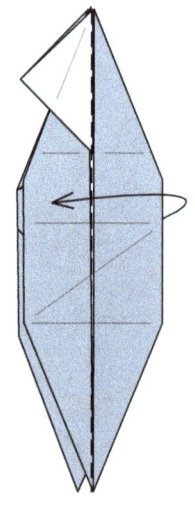

48. Swing over three flaps.

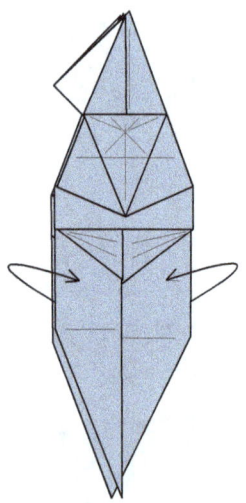

49. Wrap a single layer around at each side.

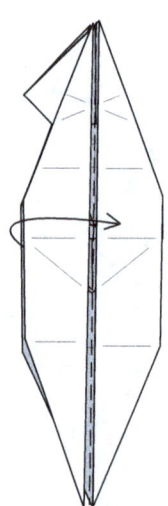

50. Swing back.

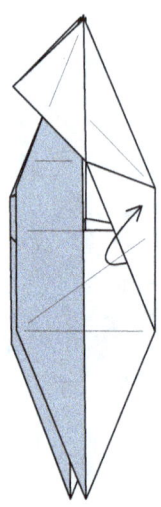

51. Unsink and wrap around.

dancing couple

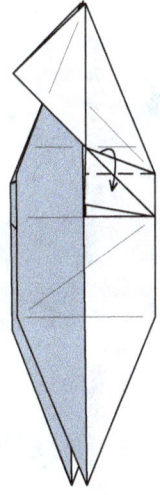

52. Wrap around (yes, this is very difficult).

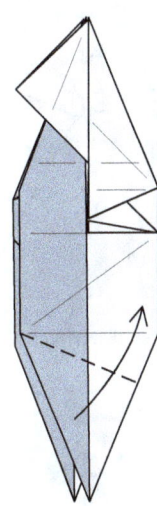

53. Valley fold up.

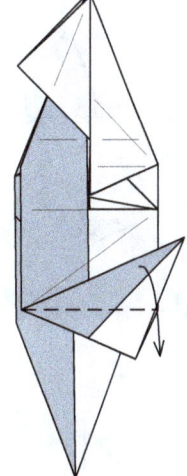

54. Valley fold down.

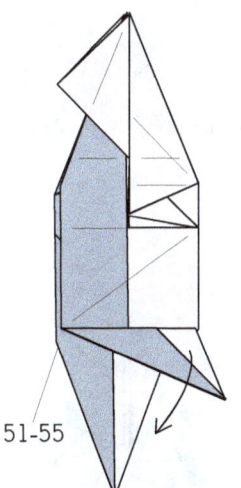

51-55

55. Unfold the pleat. Repeat steps 51-55 behind.

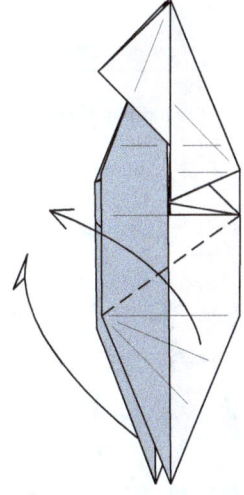

56. Valley fold the flaps upwards along the existing creases.

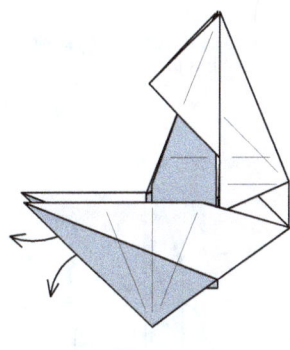

57. Swivel a single layer out from behind each flap. The new edge will lie along an existing crease.

dancing couple

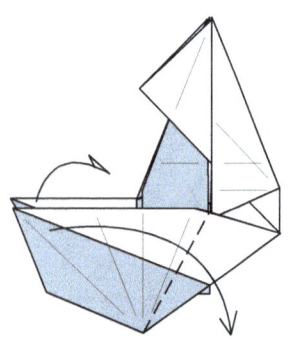

58. Swing the flaps down.

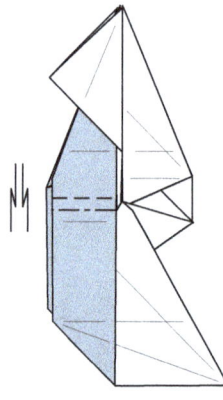

59. Form a shallow crimp.

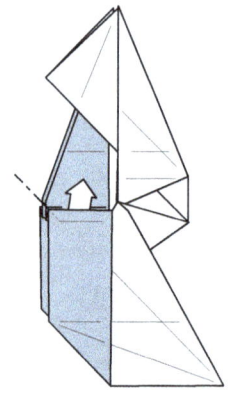

60. Unsink a single layer. Repeat behind.

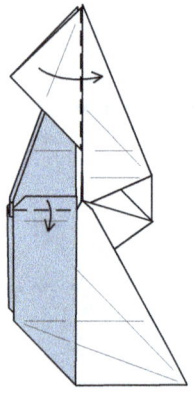

61. Swing the indicated flaps over. Repeat behind.

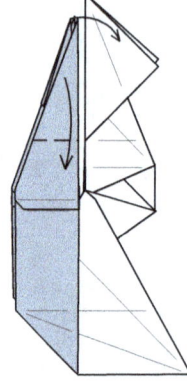

62. Valley fold the top flap down, stretching the center flap flat.

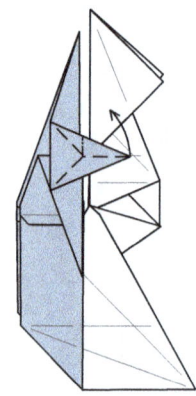

63. Rabbit ear the center flap up.

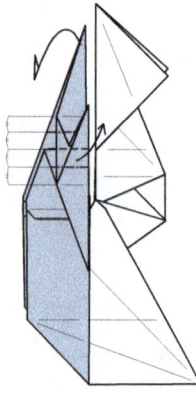

64. Pleat the arms as indicated.

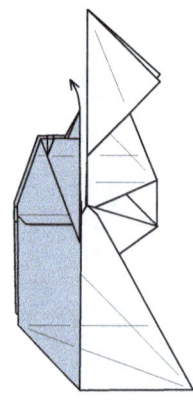

65. Stretch the center flap up as far as possible.

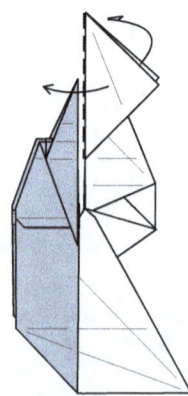

66. Swing the white flaps forward again.

dancing couple

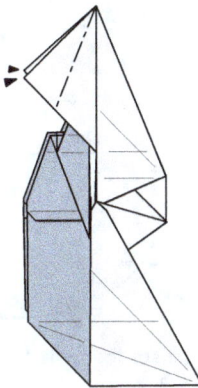

67. Reverse fold.

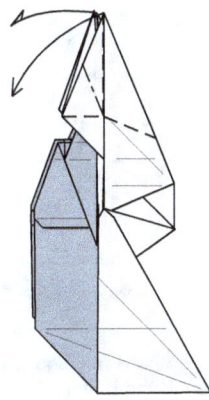

68. Rabbit ear the arms down.

69. Fold in the sides of the head. A swivel will form underneath the arms.

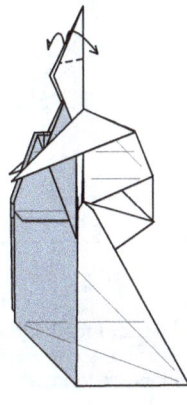

70. Outside reverse fold the head.

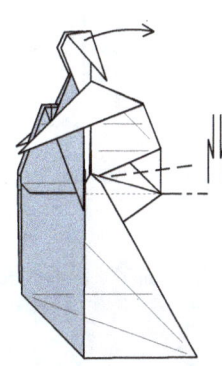

71. Crimp the body back at a slight angle.

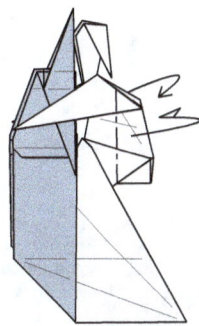

72. Fold in the sides of the body.

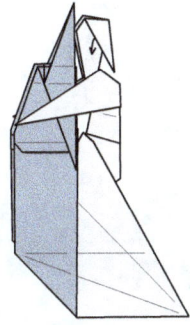

73. Pull out some paper to make the hair fuller.

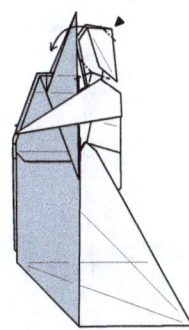

74. Shape the hair and crimp the neck to define the face.

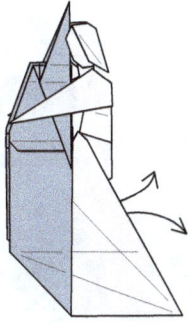

75. Pull out a single layer from each side. The dress will not lie flat anymore.

dancing couple

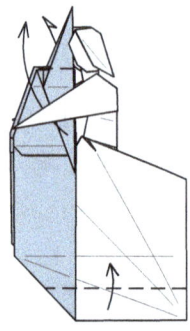

76. Swing the arms up. Valley fold the bottom edges of the dress up.

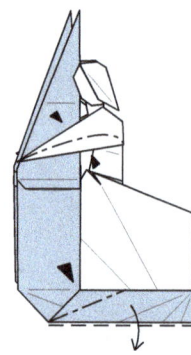

77. Shape the arms. Squash the edge at the bottom. Repeat behind.

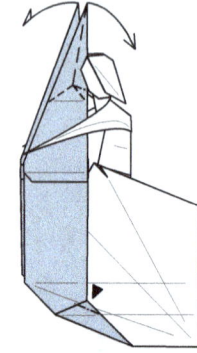

78. Rabbit ear the arms. Reverse fold the feet.

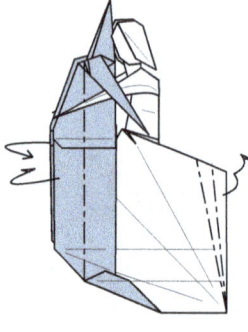

79. Mountain in the sides of the man. Roll over the edges of the dress together to lock.

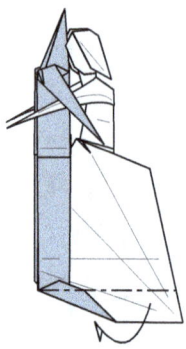

80. Mountain the bottom edges under.

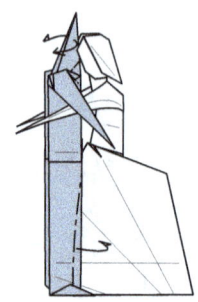

81. Taper the legs. Spread apart the layers of the head and shape. Shape and position the two dancers to taste.

82. Completed *Dancing Couple*.

Saxophonist

About

The structure of this *Saxophonist* is very standard, with the instrument appendage coming from the player's belly. Still, there are points of interest along the way, namely the sequence of steps that serve to lengthen the legs and make efficient usage of the material for the feet.

Tips

The pleat in step 44 should be as shallow as possible. Its purpose is to add a folded edge to define the player's waist.

Note in step 52 how the raw edges of the arm do not meet. The purpose of this step is to fix that, which will give the arms more freedom of movement.

In steps 60-63, feel free to alter the shaping of the saxophone to create a variety of related instruments.

saxophonist

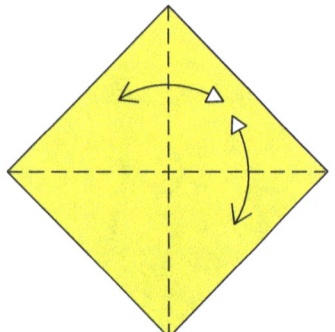

1. Precrease in half along the diagonals.

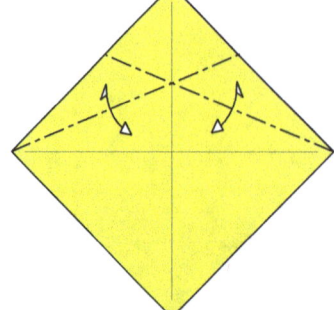

2. Precrease using mountain folds.

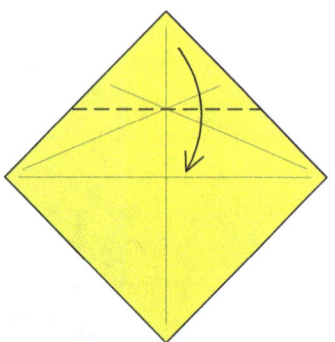

3. Valley fold through the intersection of creases.

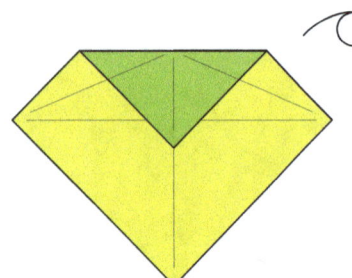

4. Turn over.

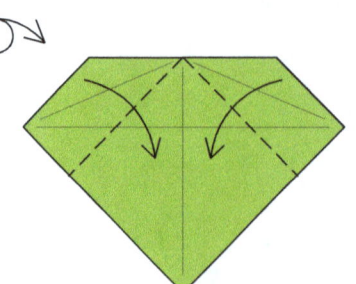

5. Valley fold to the center.

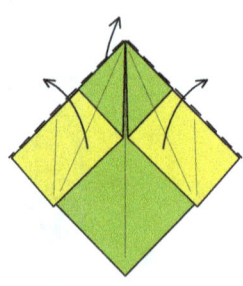

6. Unfold completely.

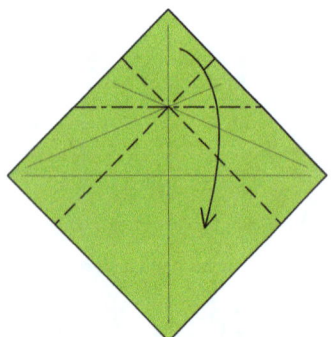

7. Form an offset preliminary base.

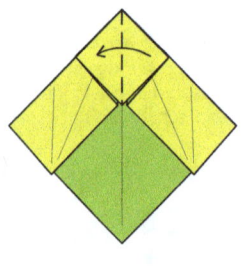

8. Swing one flap over.

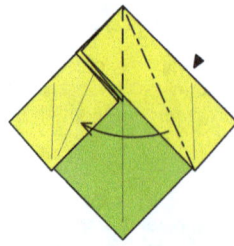

9. Squash.

saxophonist

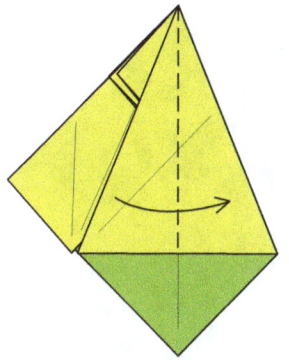
10. Valley fold over.

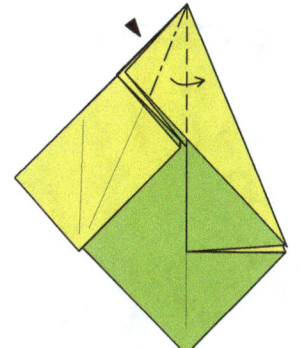
11. Squash fold.

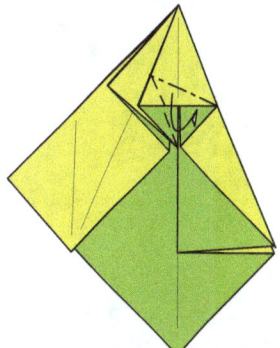
12. Swivel fold under.

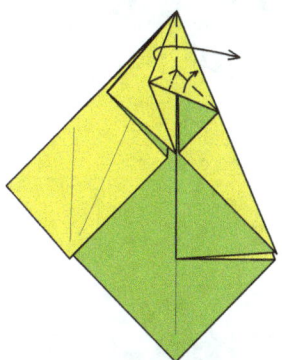
13. Swing over, while incorporating a reverse fold.

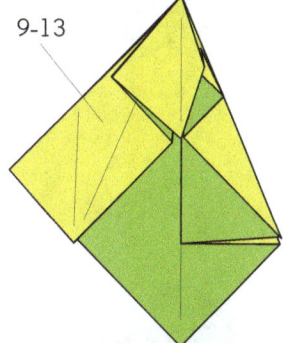
14. Repeat steps 9-13 in mirror image.

15. Turn over.

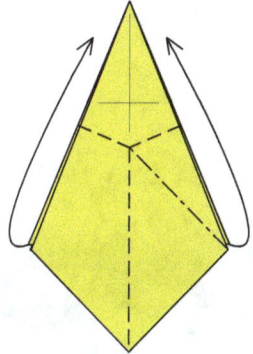
16. Rabbit ear all of the layers together.

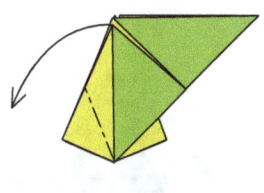
17. Pull out the top flap, allowing it to squash fold flat.

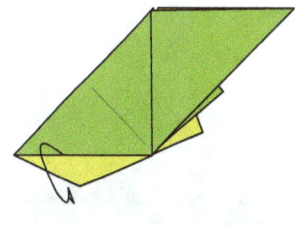
18. Wrap around a single layer.

127

saxophonist

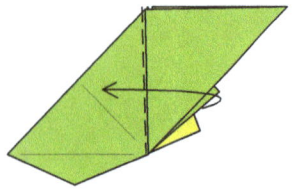

19. Swing two flaps over.

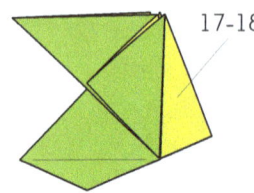

20. Repeat steps 17-18 in mirror image.

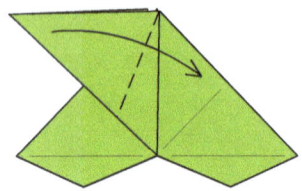

21. Valley fold over the center flap.

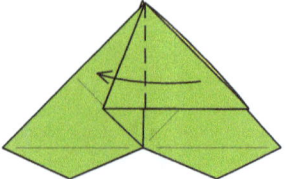

22. Valley fold over again.

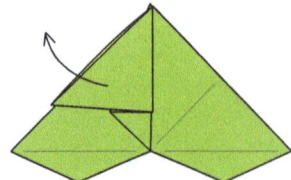

23. Unfold.

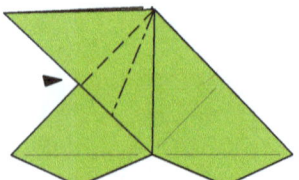

24. Reverse ifold n and out along the existing creases.

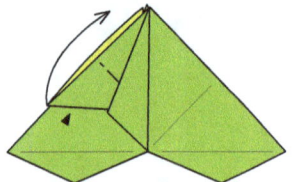

25. Reverse fold.

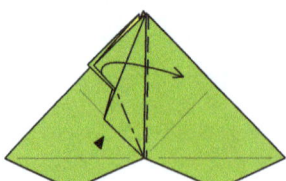

26. Spread apart the top flaps, allowing the bottom to squash flat.

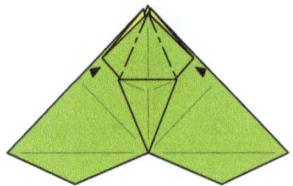

27. Reverse fold the sides.

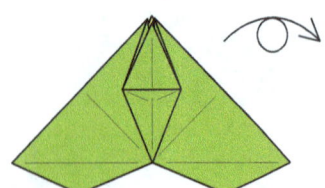

28. Turn over.

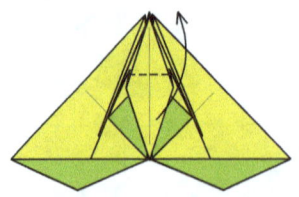

29. Lightly fold up the top flap as far as possible.

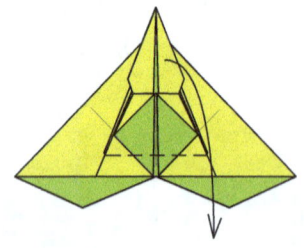

30. Valley fold down as far as possible.

saxophonist

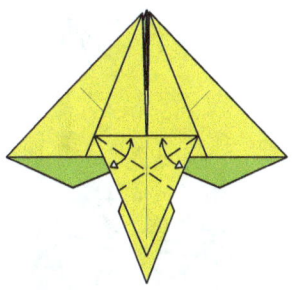

31. Precrease along the angle bisectors.

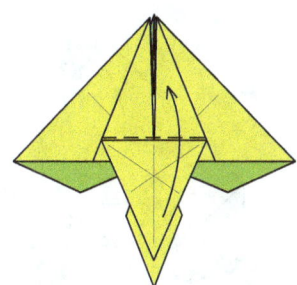

32. Swing back up.

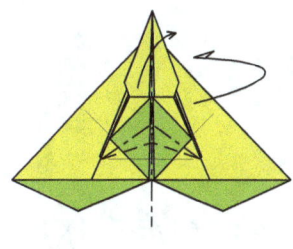

33. Crimp the center flap construction while folding the model in half.

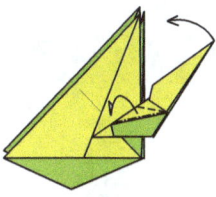

34. Inside crimp the center flap construction upwards.

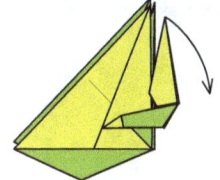

35. Unwrap the outer flap down.

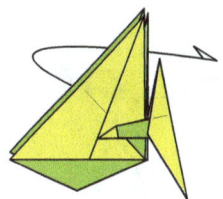

36. Distribute the back layers evenly.

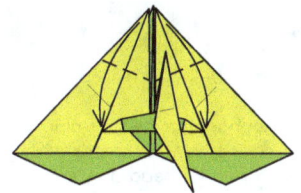

37. Valley fold down the top points to hit the intersection of folds.

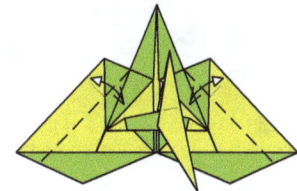

38. Precrease the outer edges to hit the colored flap.

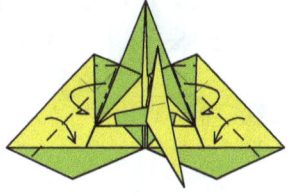

39. Reverse fold the sides using the existing creases.

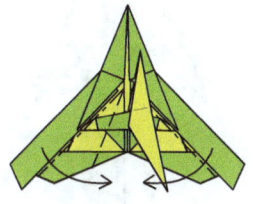

40. Pleat the sides inwards.

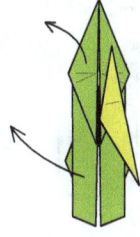

41. Open out one side.

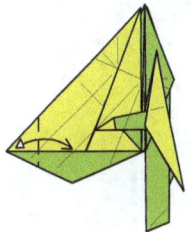

42. Precrease the corner to the second crease.

saxophonist

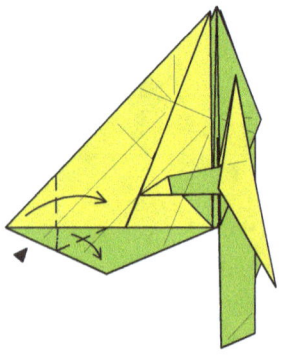

43. Squash fold.

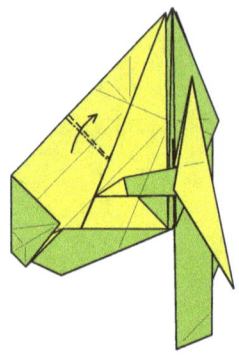

44. Insert a pleat along the single layer. The mountain fold lies along an existing crease.

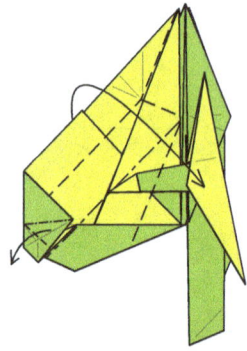

45. Collapse the side inward using the exiting folds.

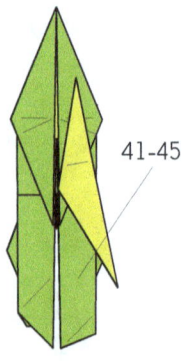

46. Repeat steps 41-45 in mirror image.

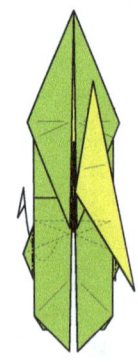

47. Petal fold behind, allowing the protruding points to fold inwards.

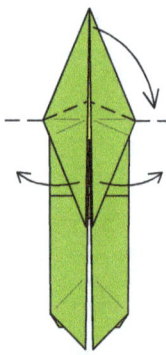

48. Saxophone omitted for clarity. Slide the arms outwards while swinging the head down.

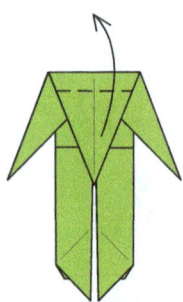

49. Valley fold up the head as far as possible.

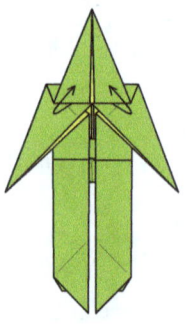

50. Bring the single layers of the arms to the surface.

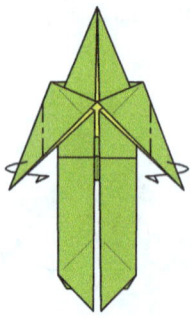

51. Mountain fold the arms inwards.

saxophonist

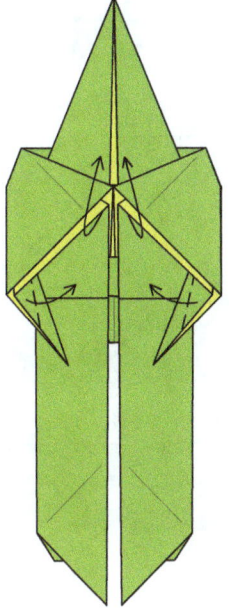 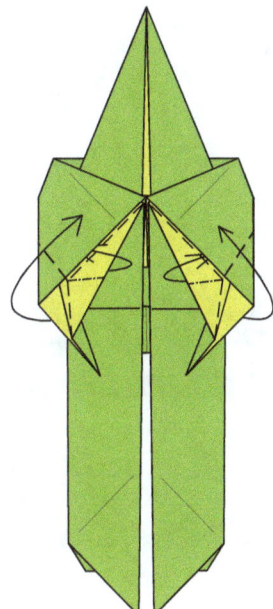 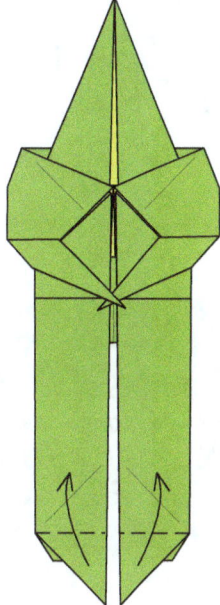

52. Pull the single layer up through the "armpits" allowing a layer to swivel outwards at the hands.

53. Rabbit ear, tucking the single layer into the arms.

54. Valley fold the feet up.

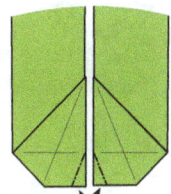 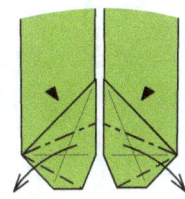 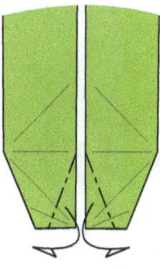

55. Detail of the feet. Reverse fold the interior corners.

56. Squash the feet down.

57. Mountain fold the interior edges.

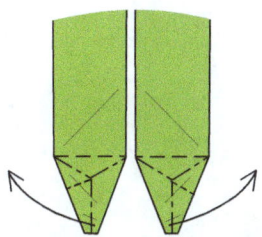 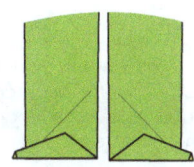 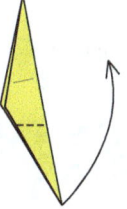

58. Rabbit ear the feet outwards.

59. Completed feet.

60. Detail of the saxophone. Outside reverse fold the bottom.

131

Saxophonist

61. Sink the lower corner and reverse fold the top.

62. Mountain fold the edges inward.

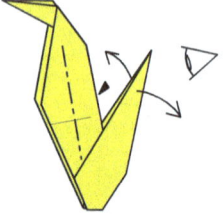

63. Round the body of the saxophone. Spread apart the layers at the tip.

64. View from the previous step. Completed saxophone.

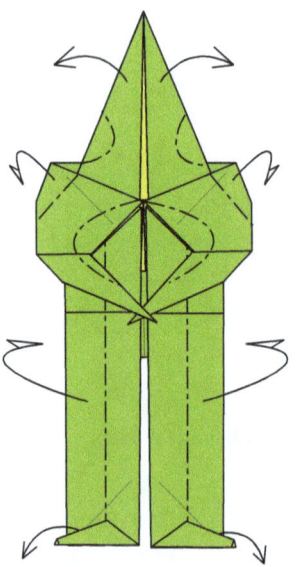

65. Thin the body, legs, and arms, and shape them with mountain folds. Open out the head and feet. Position the arms and saxophone into a playing position.

66. Completed *Saxophonist*.

Original Beatle

About

Fellow origami expert Jeremy Shafer was looking for origami puns at one of his design sessions, and this *Original Beatle* was born from that. The design is just splitting the appendages of the classic Bird Base, and since most of the flaps need to be thin, there is minimal shaping and detail folds.

Tips

This is one of the more straightforward models in this collection but choosing the right paper can be critical. The appendages can get very thick, so be sure to use material that is strong and thin.

Since there are a lot of flaps, using paper with a high contrast from front to back is important. This will help you make out the guitar amongst all the legs.

original beatle

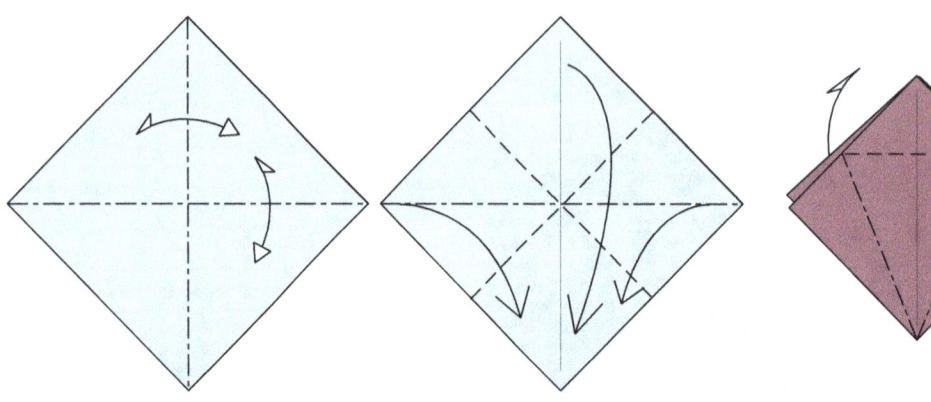

1. Precrease in half with mountain folds.

2. Collapse downwards.

3. Petal fold up. Repeat behind.

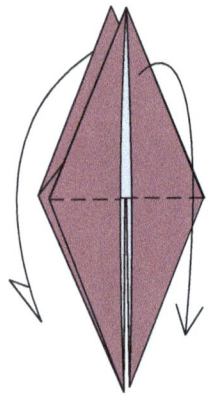 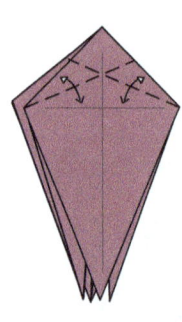 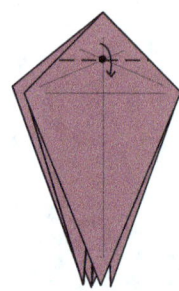 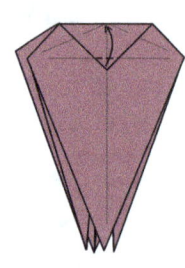

4. Valley fold the top flaps down.

5. Precrease along the angle bisectors.

6. Valley fold through the intersection of creases.

7. Valley fold to align with the crease below.

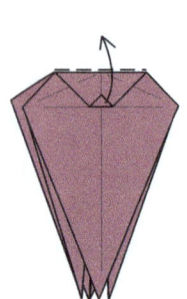 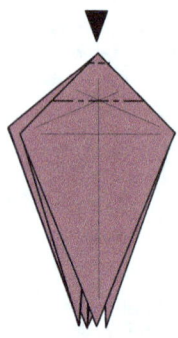 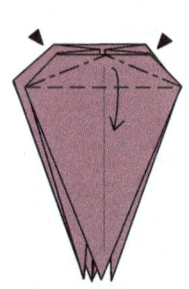 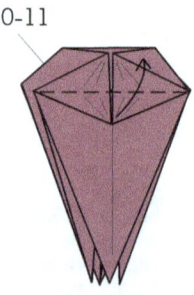

8. Unfold the pleat.

9. Sink along the existing creases.

10. Spread squash the corners.

11. Valley fold back up. Repeat steps 10-11 behind.

— original beatle —

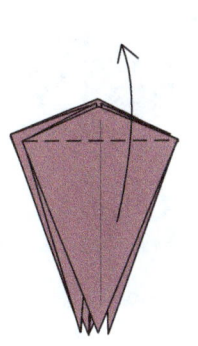
12. Valley fold up.

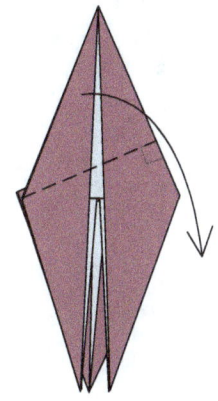
13. Valley fold down.

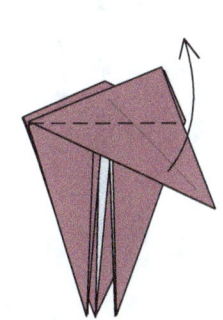
14. Valley fold up.

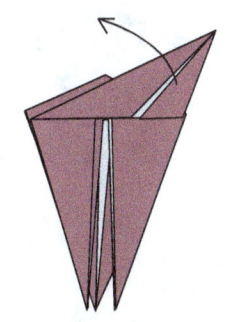
15. Unfold the pleat.

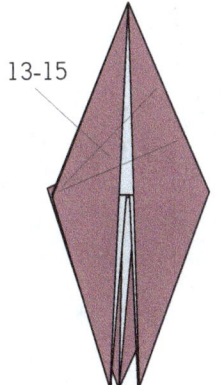
16. Repeat steps 13-15 in mirror image.

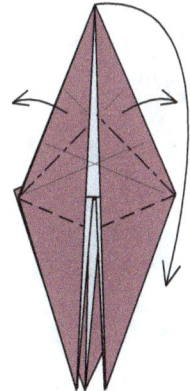
17. Spread apart the sides and squash down.

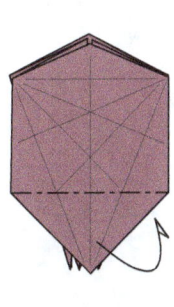
18. Mountain fold the corner.

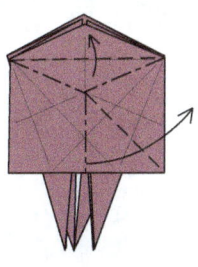
19. Rabbit ear the flap up.

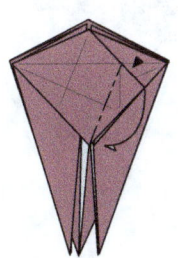
20. Reverse fold.

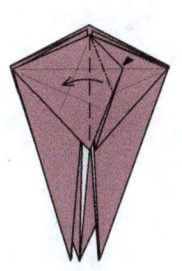
21. Spread squash.

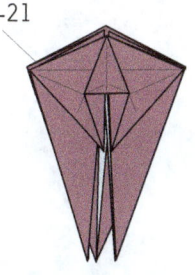
22. Repeat steps 12-21 behind.

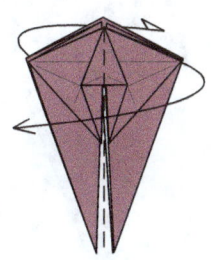
23. Swing a flap over at each side.

original beatle

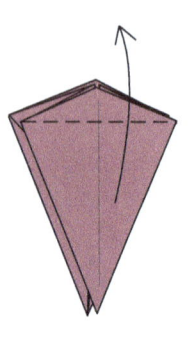
24. Swing the flap up.

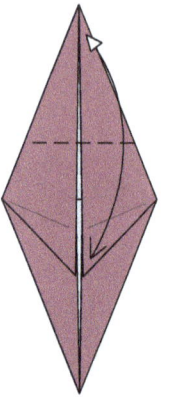
25. Valley fold down.

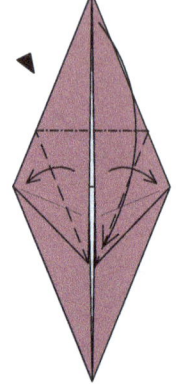
26. Squash the flap down.

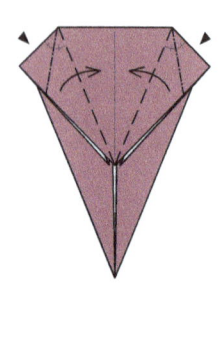
27. Squash fold the sides.

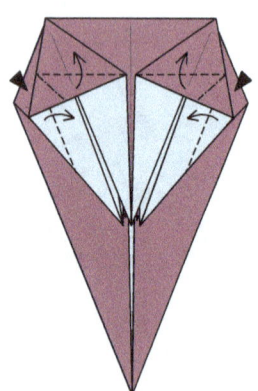
28. Swivel fold at each side.

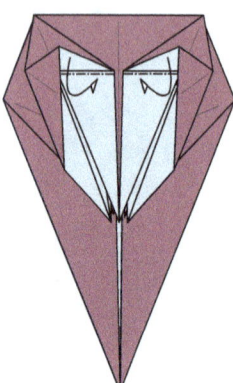
29. Wrap the flaps underneath.

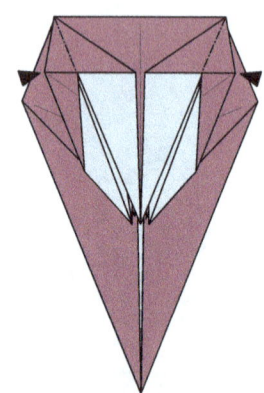
30. Closed sink the sides.

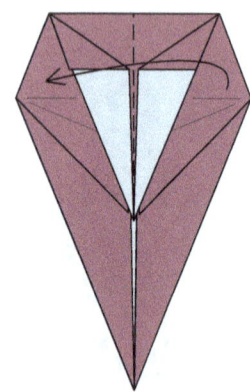
31. Swing over one flap.

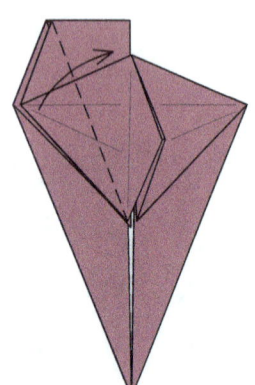
32. Valley fold.

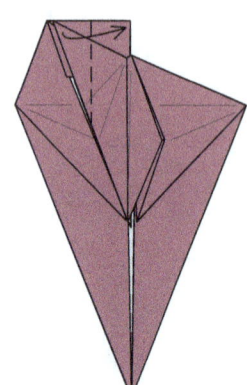
33. Valley fold.

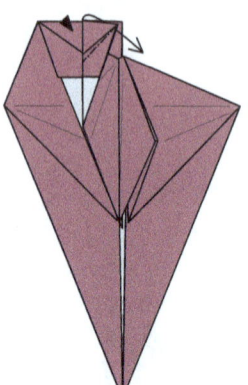
34. Reverse fold.

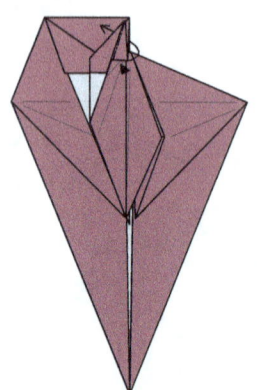
35. Reverse fold.

original beatle

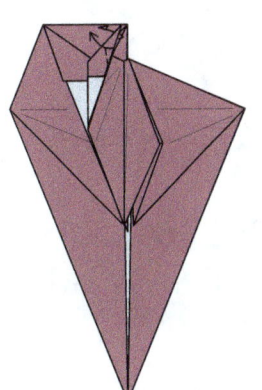
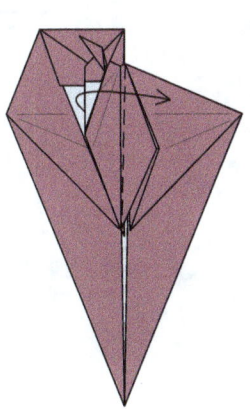
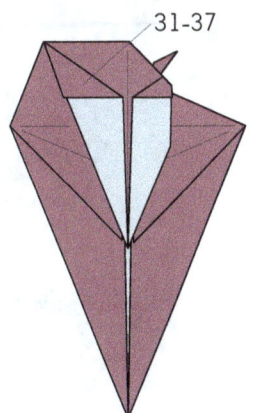
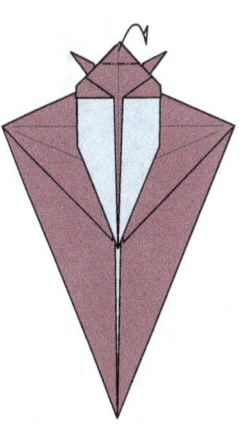

36. Outside reverse fold.
37. Swing the flap over.
38. Repeat steps 31-37 in mirror image.
39. Mountain fold.

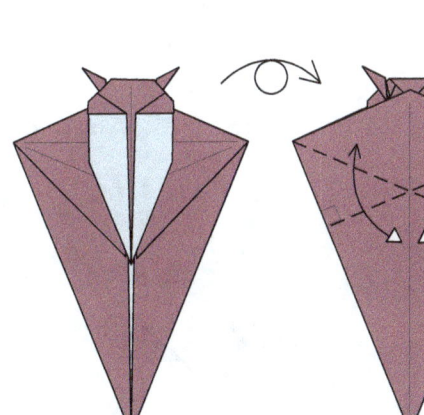
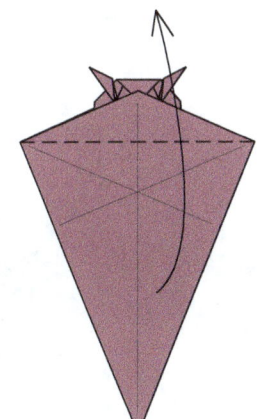
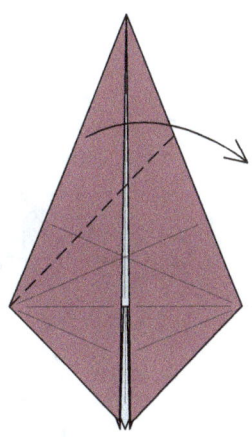

40. Turn over.
41. Precrease.
42. Swing the flap up.
43. Valley fold.

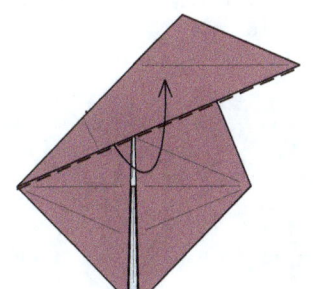
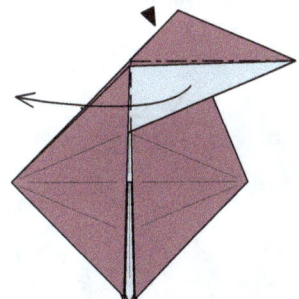
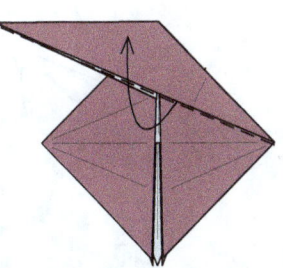

44. Wrap around a single layer.
45. Squash fold.
46. Wrap around a single layer.

137

original beatle

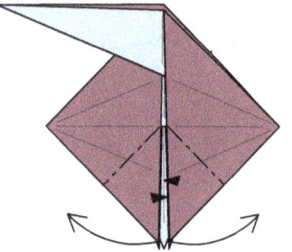

47. Reverse fold the flaps up.

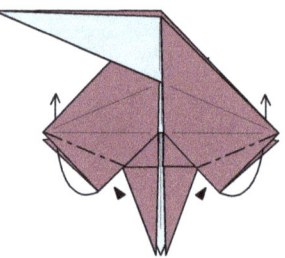

48. Reverse fold.

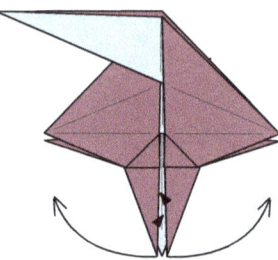

49. Reverse fold the next set of flaps up.

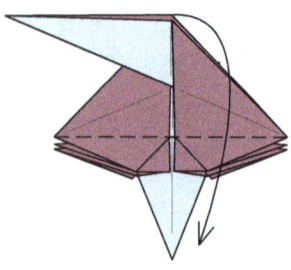

50. Swing down.

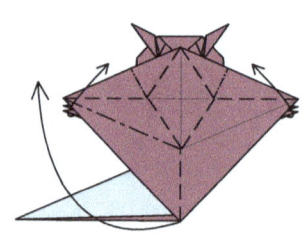

51. Collapse upwards with rabbit ears.

52. Rabbit ear the flaps outwards.

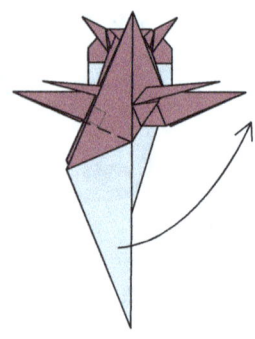

53. Valley fold up.

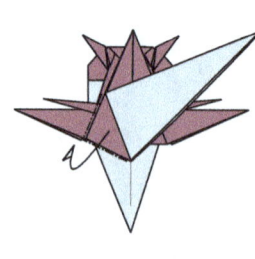

54. Wrap around a single layer.

55. Pull two layers over and squash flat.

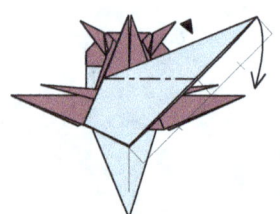

56. Reverse fold.

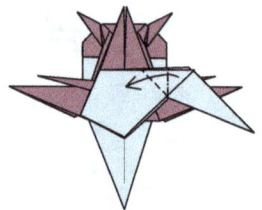

57. Pleat the flap over.

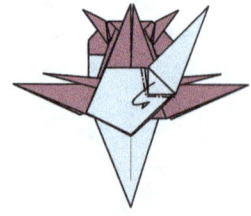

58. Wrap around a layer.

original beatle

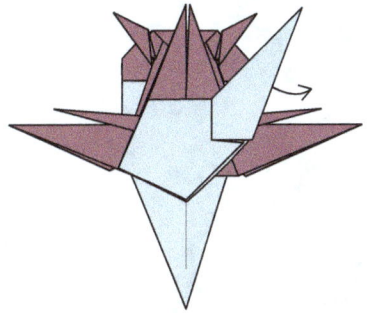

59. Slide out some paper.

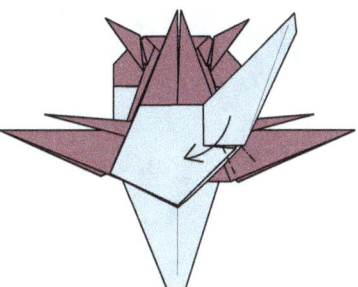

60. Pleat the flap down.

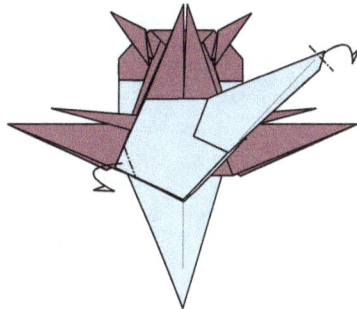

61. Mountain fold the corners.

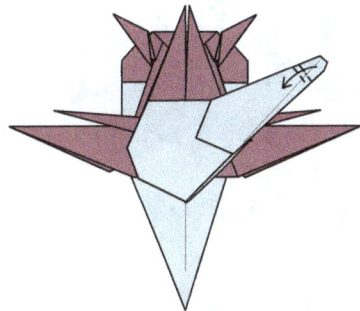

62. Pleat the tip of the flap.

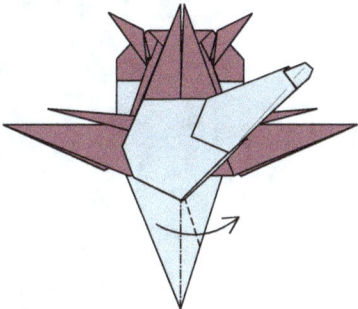

63. Form a pleat on the bottom flap, allowing the model to become concave.

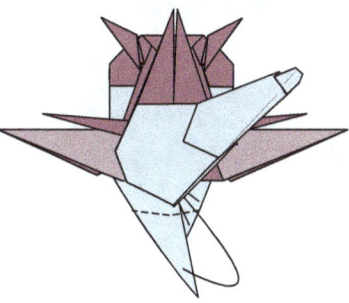

64. Tuck the flap into the model.

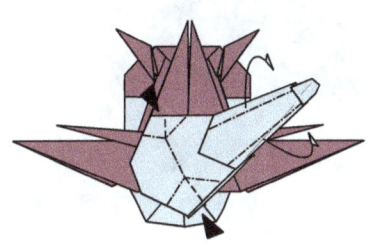

65. Shape the flap with partial reverse folds.

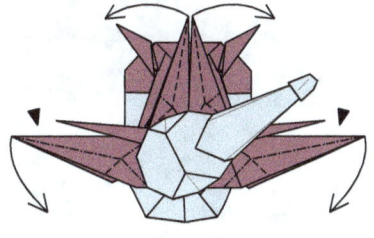

66. Rabbit ear the top flaps and double rabbit ear the bottom flaps.

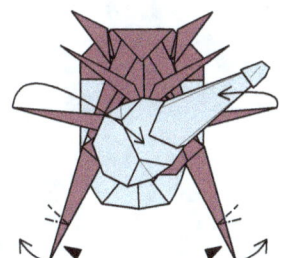

67. Squash fold the bottom points and position the flaps to taste.

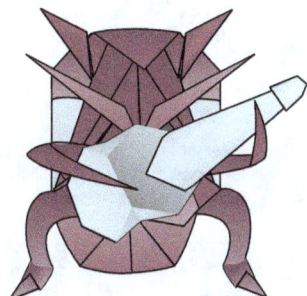

68. Completed *Original Beatle*.

Seated Guitarist

About

What does a biplane and a seated guitarist have in common? In terms of structure, quite a lot. An earlier airplane design became the starting point for this piece which was based on Neal Elias' classic *Andres Segovia*. The upper wings became the guitar and the tail turned into the bench. The remaining flaps became the player. Mr. Elias himself approved of this *Seated Guitarist*.

Tips

Every effort was made to have the sequence for the guitar early on. This is important, as you will likely have to do a lot of unfolding to gain access to complete the various closed sinks (step 52 in particular).

Technically, there is a small gap along the center of the model. It is okay to pull some material from the body layers for the final shaping to give the model a more closed look.

seated guitarist

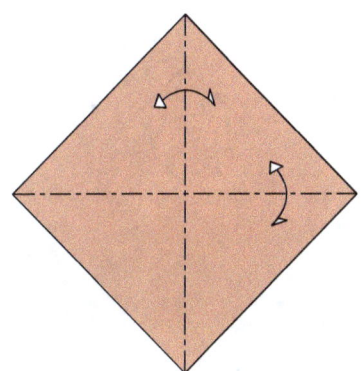

1. Precrease with mountain folds.

2. Precrease along the angle bisectors.

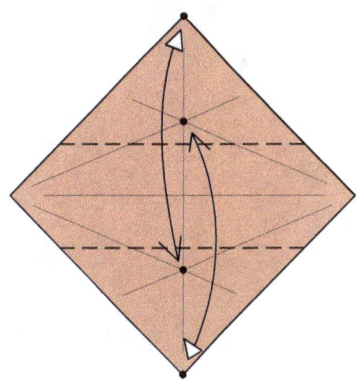

3. Valley fold the corners to the intersections of creases and unfold.

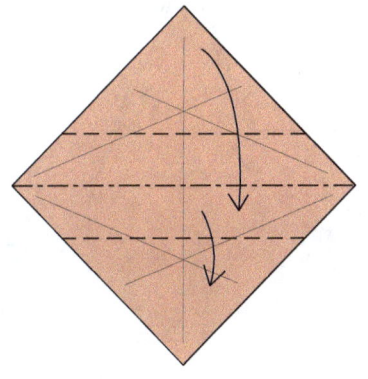

4. Pleat along the existing creases.

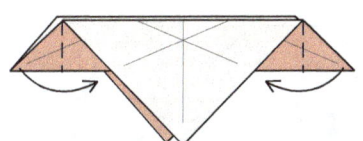

5. Valley fold the corners inwards.

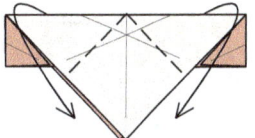

6. Valley fold the sides down.

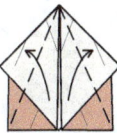

7. Valley fold towards the outer edge.

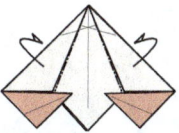

8. Mountain fold the sides.

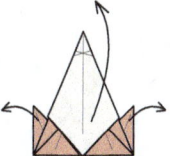

9. Unfold completely to the colored side.

141

seated guitarist

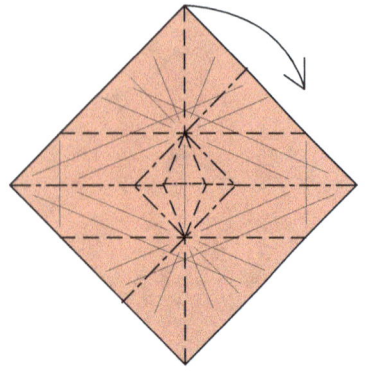

10. Collapse as indicated.

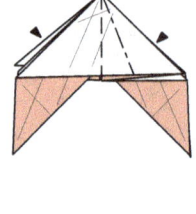

11. Squash fold. Repeat behind.

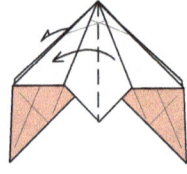

12. Swing a flap over at each side.

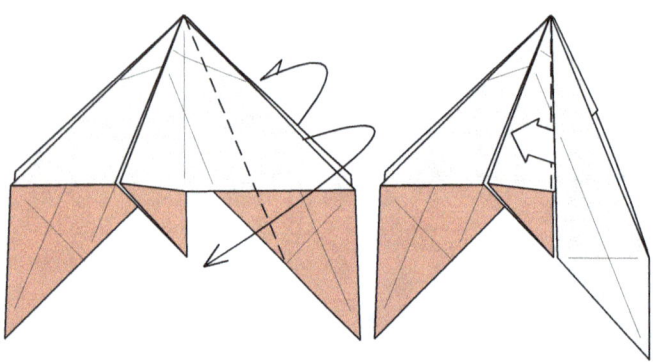

13. Outside reverse fold.

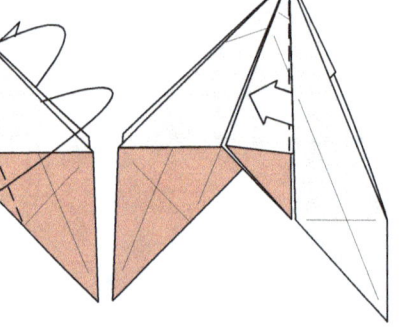

14. Pull out a single layer.

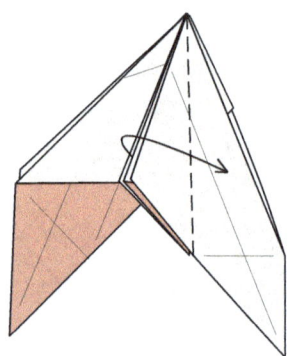

15. Swing over two flaps.

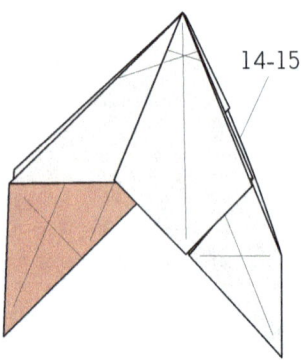

16. Repeat steps 14-15 behind.

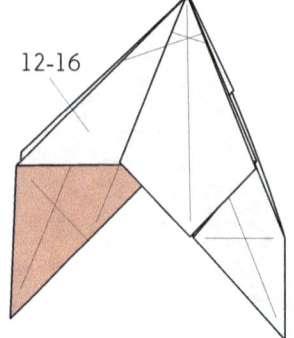

17. Repeat steps 12-16 in mirror image.

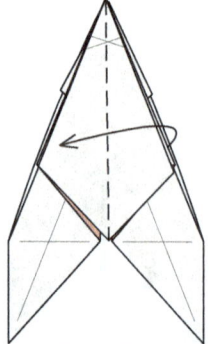

18. Swing over two flaps.

seated guitarist

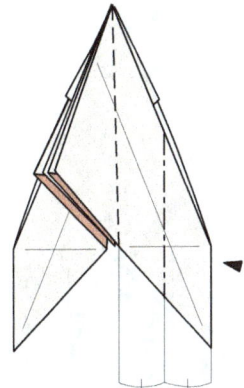
19. Spread squash.

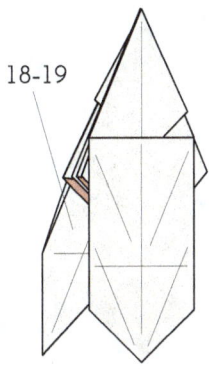
20. Repeat steps 18-19 behind.

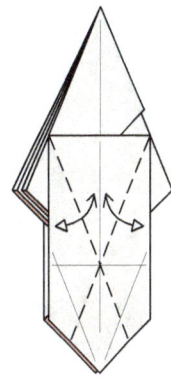
21. Precrease.

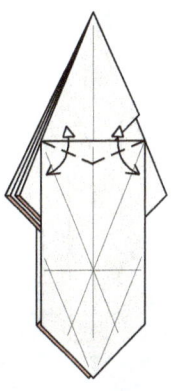
22. Precrease again.

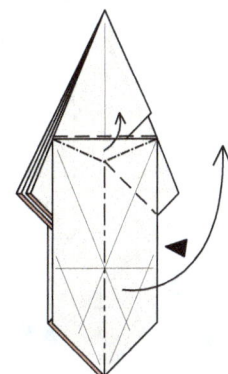
23. Collapse upwards.

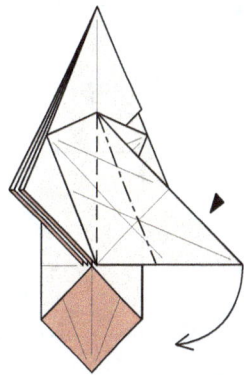
24. Squash fold the center flap.

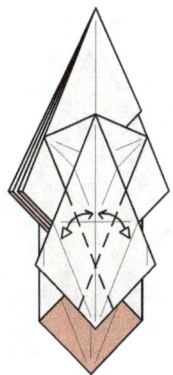
25. Precrease.

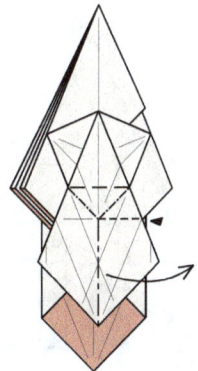
26. Collapse upwards.

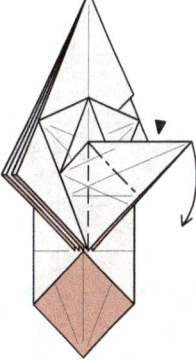
27. Squash fold the center flap.

seated guitarist

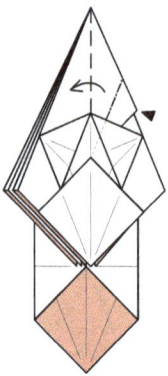 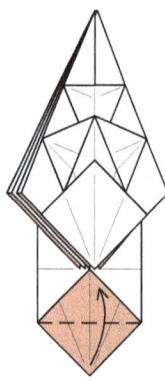 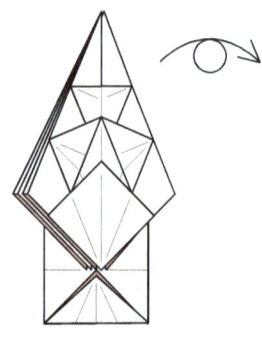

28. Spread squash the center flap.

29. Valley fold up the bottom corner.

30. Turn over.

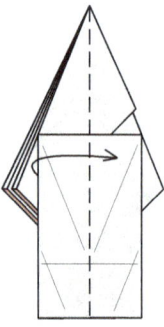 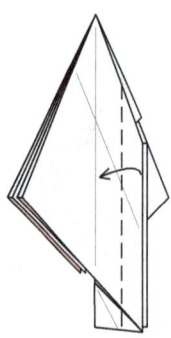 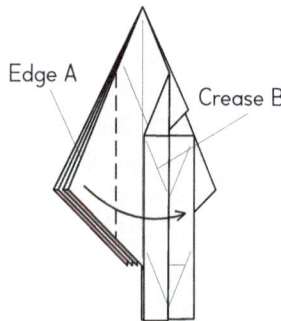

31. Swing over one flap.

32. Valley fold to the center.

33. Valley fold, such that edge A lies along crease B.

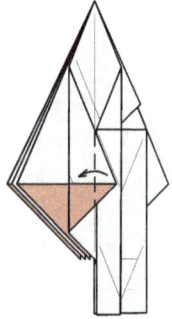 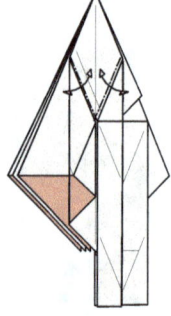 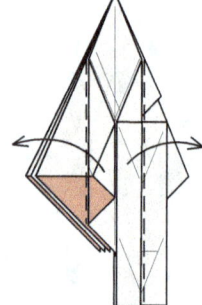

34. Valley fold over, such that the fold lies along the model's center.

35. Precrease with mountain folds on the top layer.

36. Open out.

seated guitarist

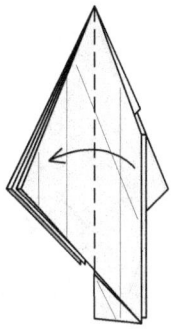

37. Swing over one flap.

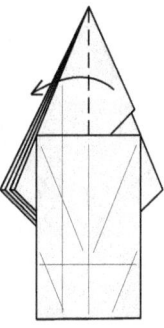

38. Swing over the center flap.

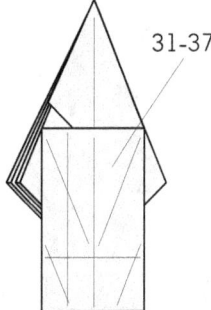

39. Repeat steps 31-37 in mirror image.

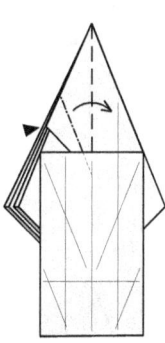

40. Spread squash the center flap.

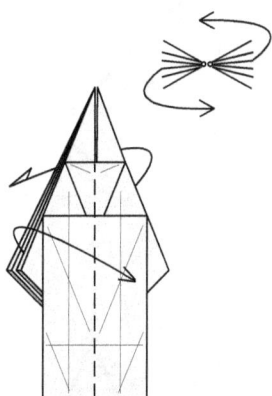

41. Swing over three large flaps at each side.

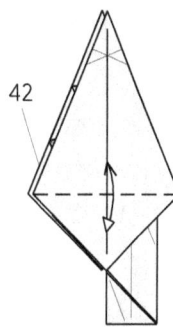

42. Precrease. Repeat behind.

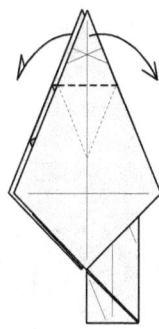

43. Valley fold down the top flaps to align with the hidden folded edge.

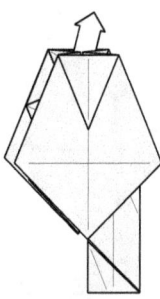

44. Unsink the center.

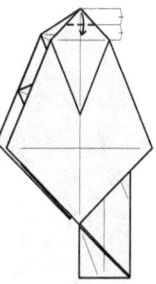

45. Valley fold the tip.

145

seated guitarist

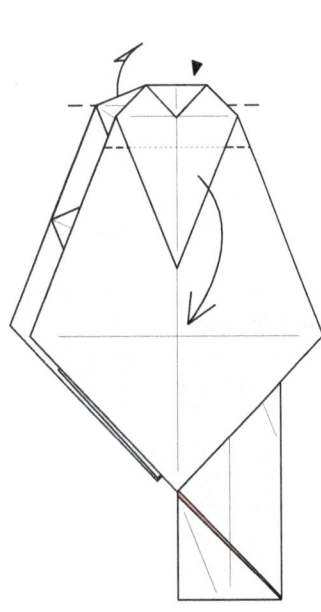

46. Stretch the front flap down, while pulling the back flap up.

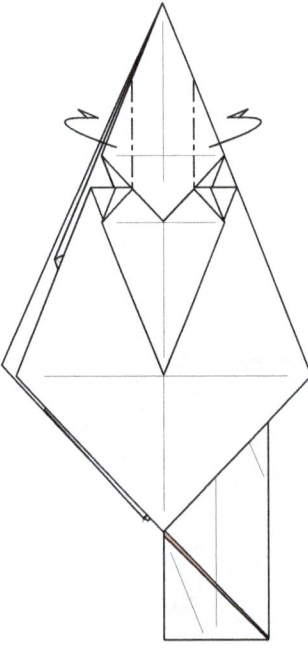

47. Mountain fold the top layer halfway.

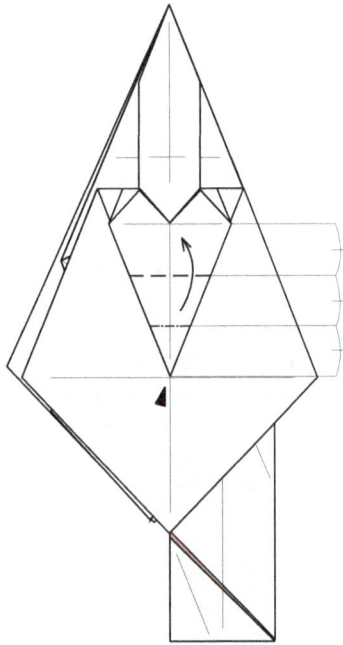

48. Spread squash.

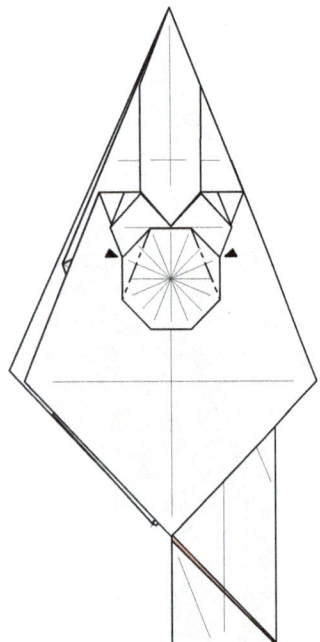

49. Closed sink the corners.

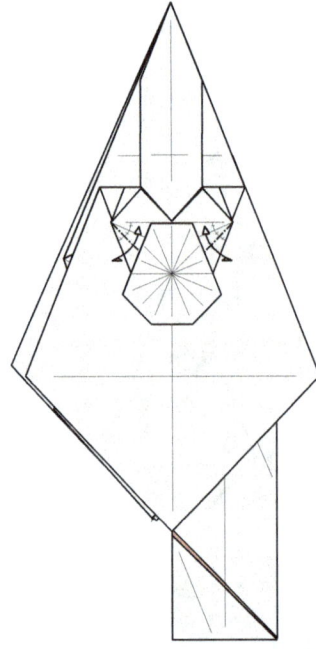

50. Precrease with mountain folds (two layers only).

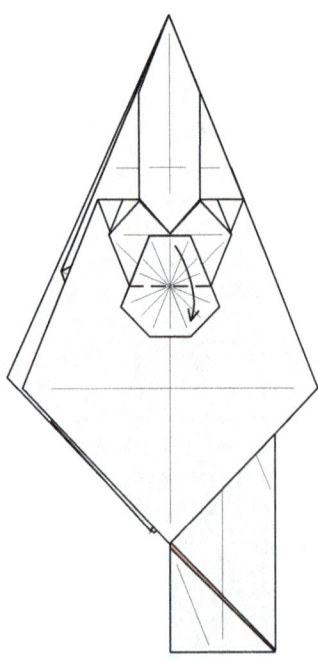

51. Swing the flap down.

seated guitarist

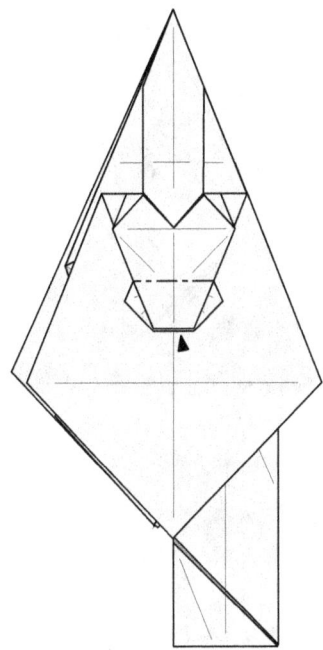

52. Closed sink the flap (good luck).

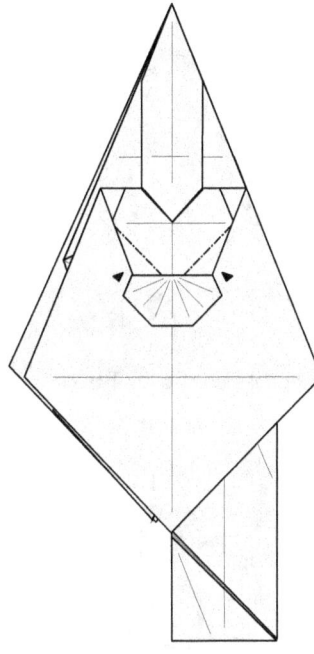

53. Open sink the trapped corners.

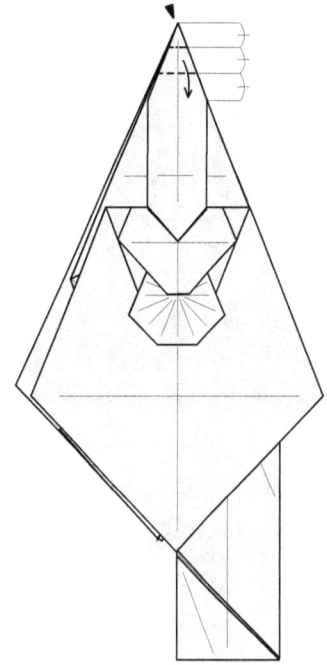

54. Spread squash the top point.

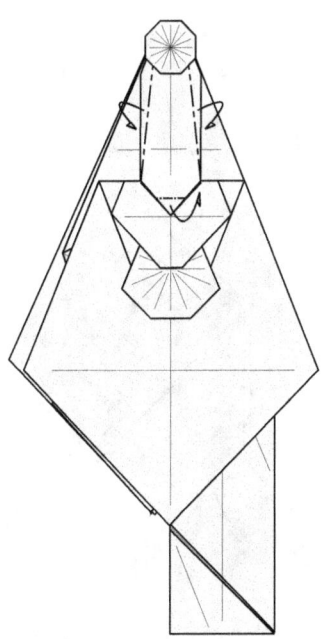

55. Shape with mountain folds.

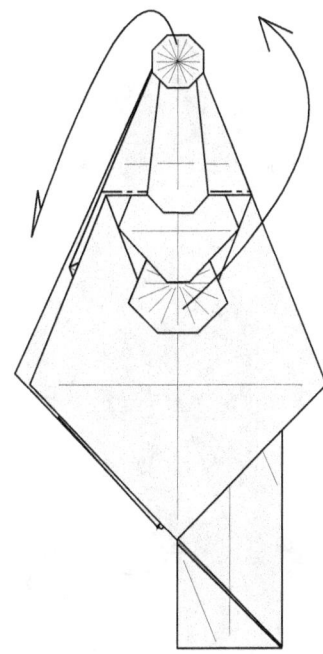

56. Flip the top section.

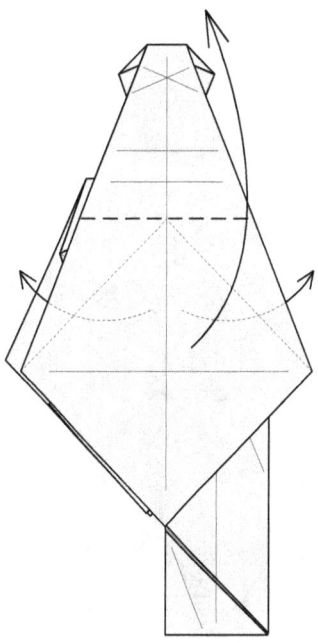

57. Raise the top flap, while allowing the sides to squash flat.

seated guitarist

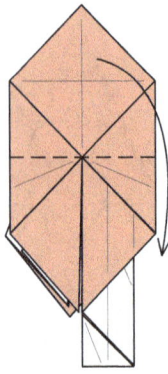

58. Swing the top flap down.

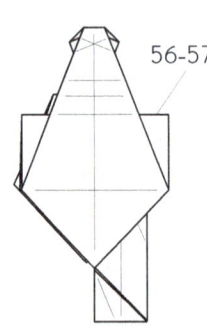

59. Repeat steps 56-57 behind.

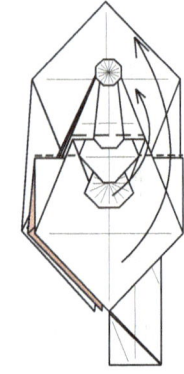

60. Swing two flaps up.

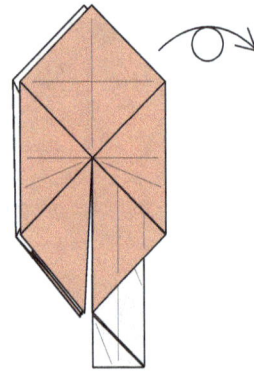

61. Turn over.

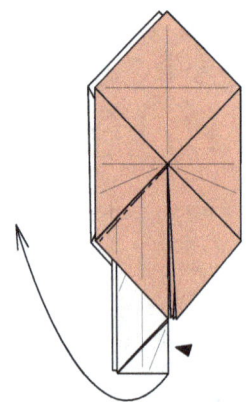

62. Reverse fold.

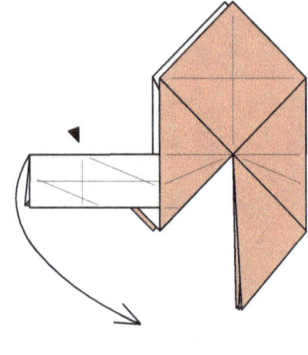

63. Undo the reverse-fold.

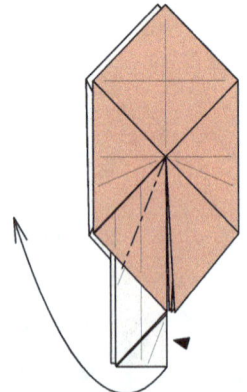

64. Reverse fold along the angle bisector.

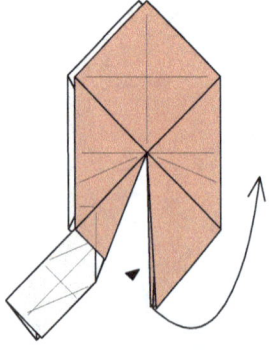

65. Reverse fold the set of flaps up evenly.

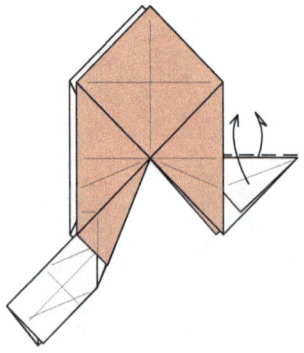

66. Swing the two side flaps up.

seated guitarist

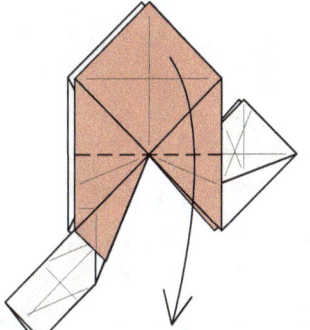

67. Swing down.

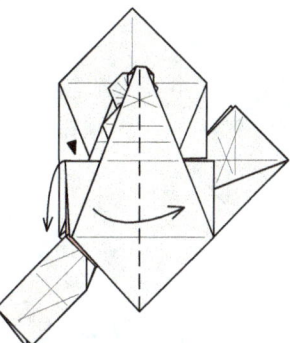

68. Swing over, undoing the side reverse fold. The top will not lie flat.

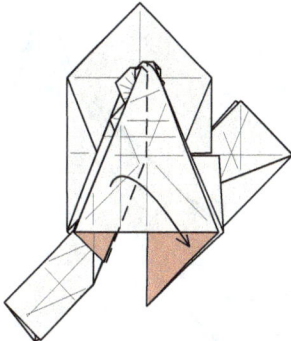

69. Swing down. The top will be less flat.

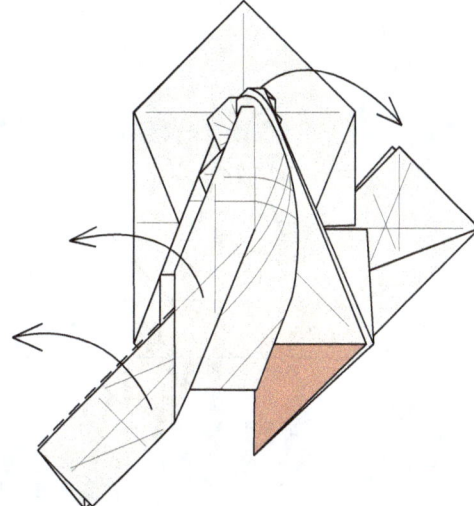

70. Open out the flap. The structure will flatten a little.

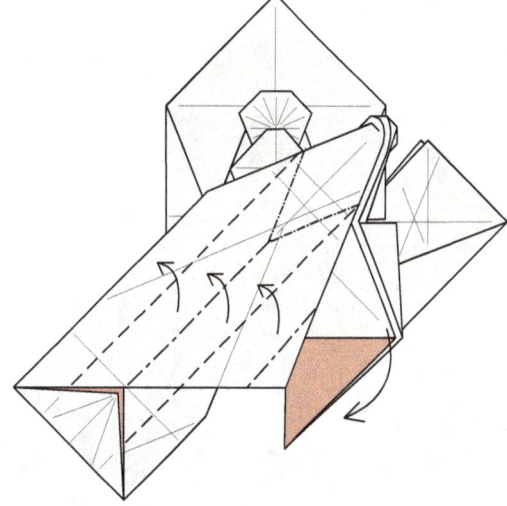

71. Pleat the top layer upwards, allowing a ridge to form at the top.

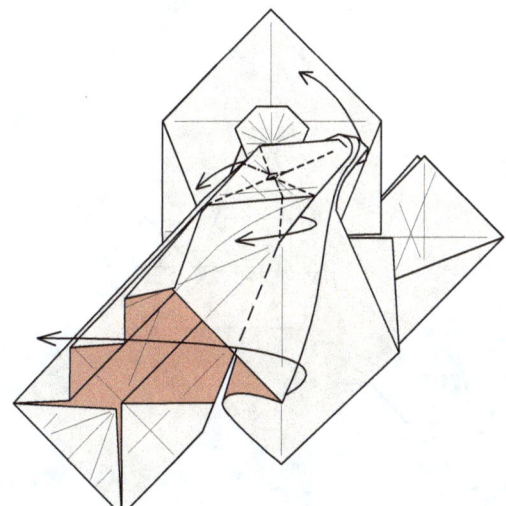

72. Collapse the ridge over, allowing the model to flatten.

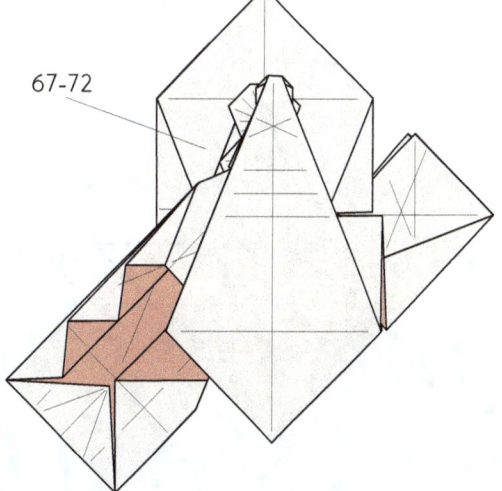

73. Repeat steps 67-72 behind.

149

seated guitarist

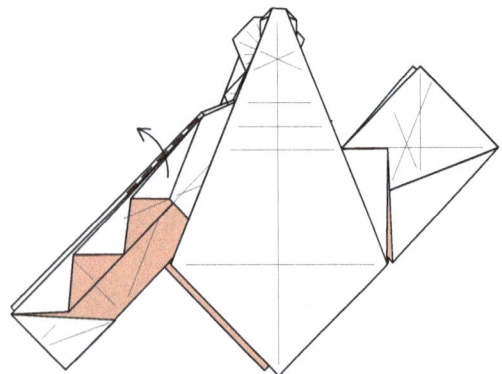

74. Swing the flap up.

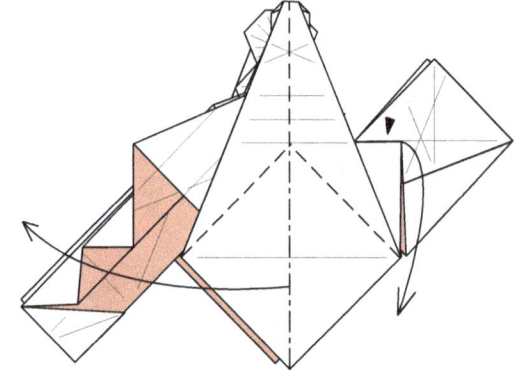

75. Swing over, undoing the side reverse fold. The model will not lie flat.

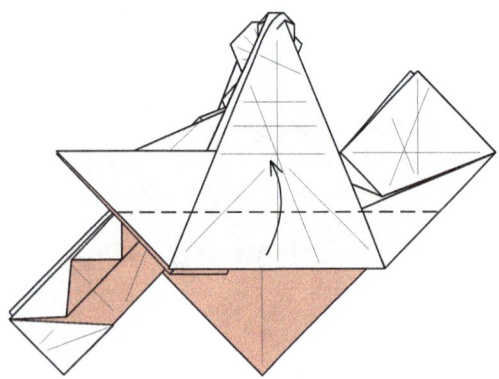

76. Valley fold up.

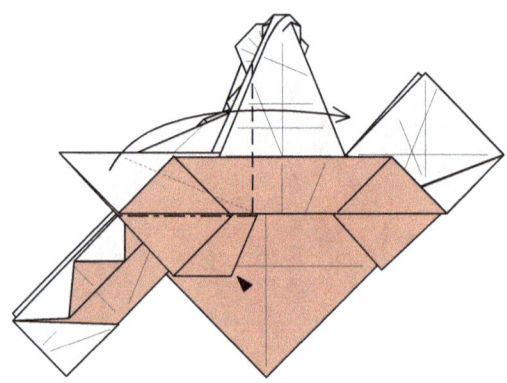

77. Valley fold over, allowing a squash fold to form.

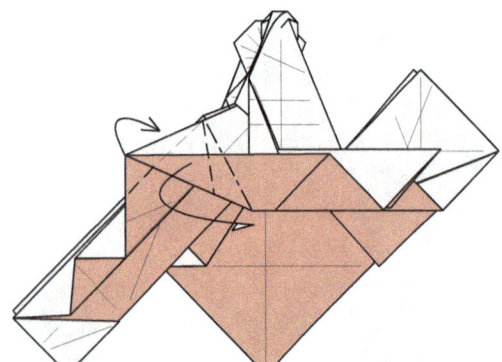

78. Valley fold down, while swiveling under.

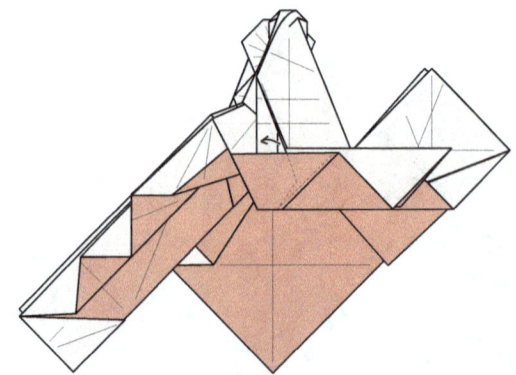

79. Swivel fold over.

seated guitarist

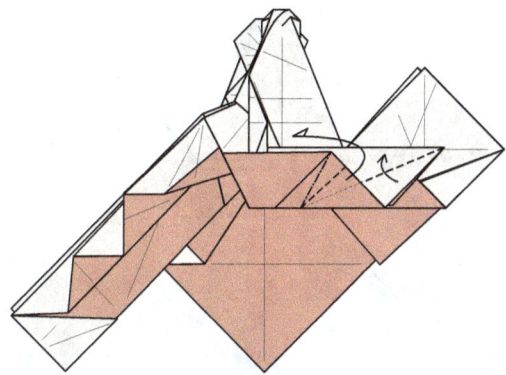

80. Swivel in one layer along the angle bisector.

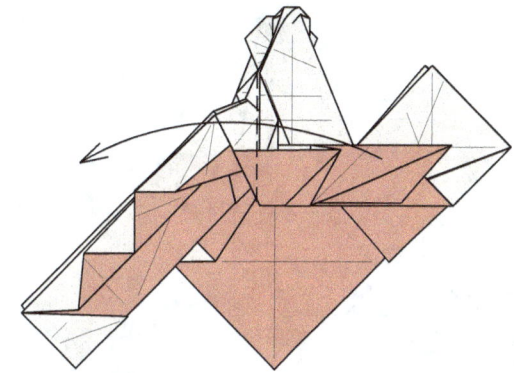

81. Swing the flap back over.

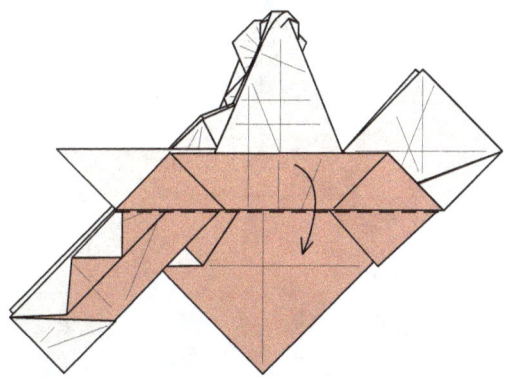

82. Swing down one layer.

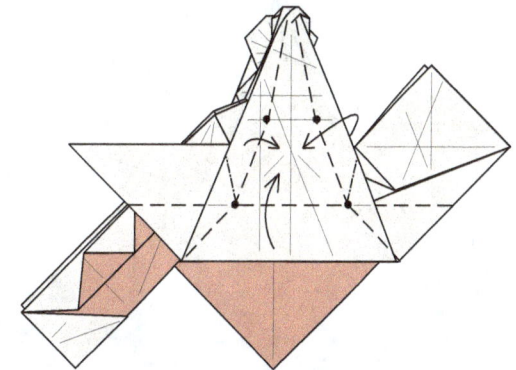

83. Valley fold the flap back up, while swiveling in the sides (1 layer at the left and 2 at the right). The flap will curl towards you.

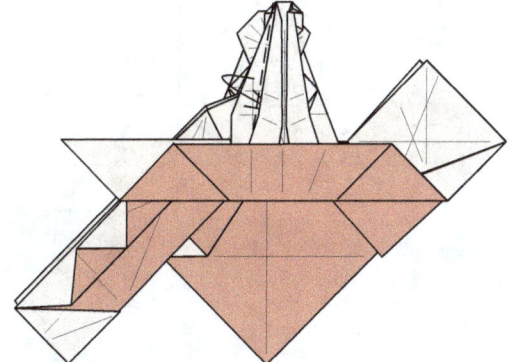

84. Tuck in one layer.

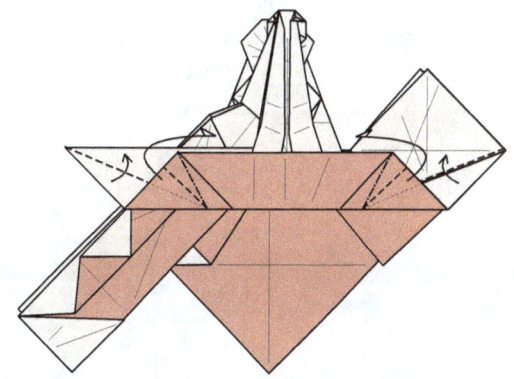

85. Swivel in both sides along the angle bisector.

seated guitarist

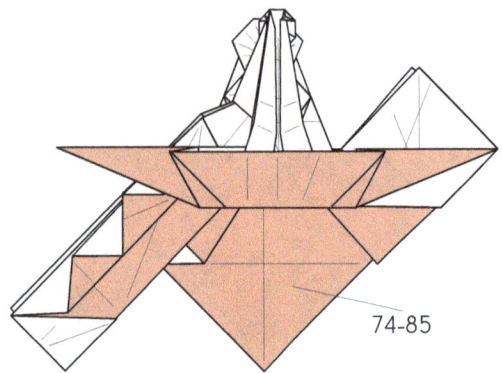

86. Repeat steps 74-85 behind.

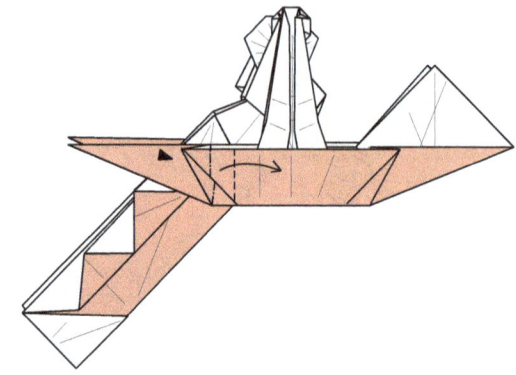

87. Spread squash the small point.

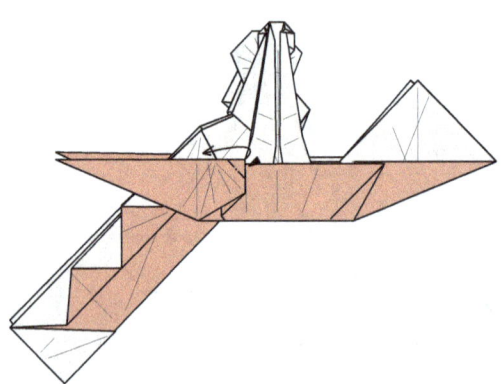

88. Form a small reverse fold.

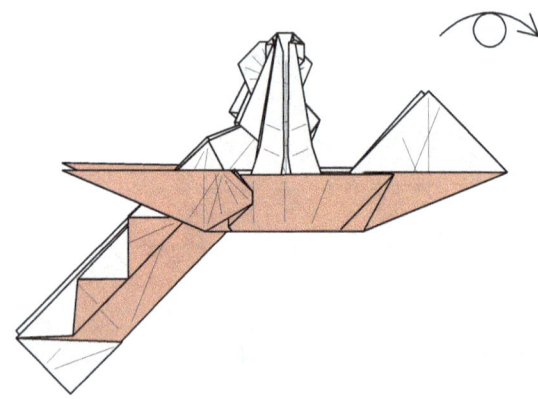

89. Turn over.

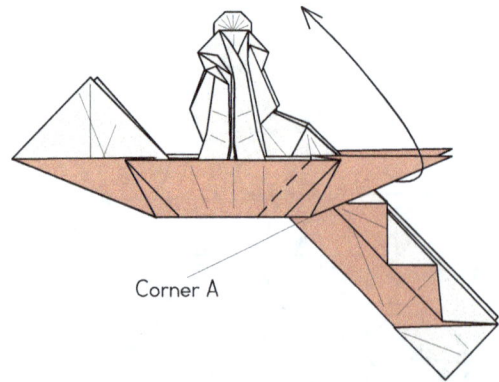

90. Valley fold up at a 45° angle, such that corner A hits the edge.

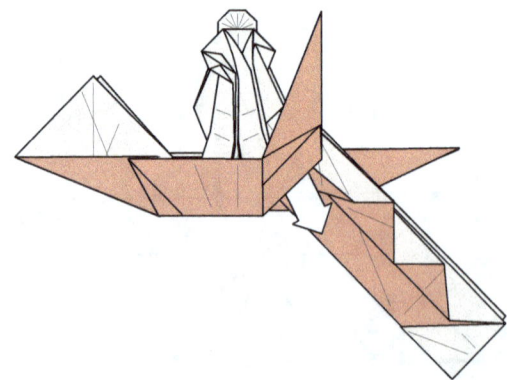

91. Pull out a bit of the single layer.

seated guitarist

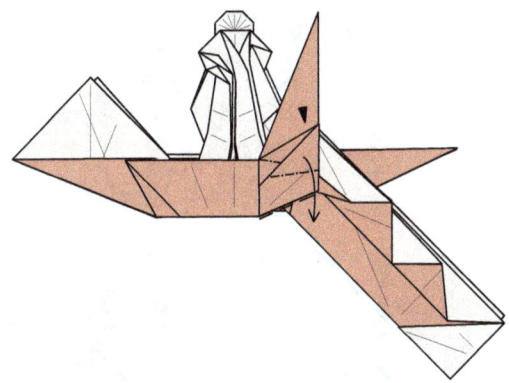

92. Spread squash the small point down.

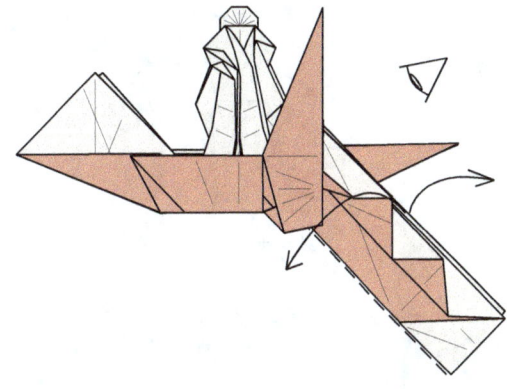

93. Spread apart the sides. The model will not lie flat.

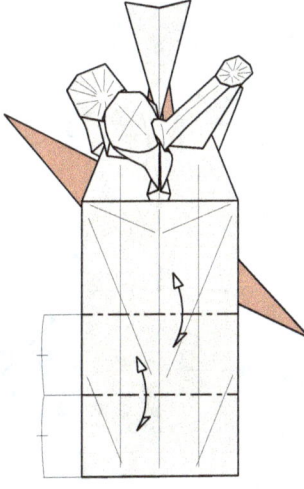

94. Precrease with mountain folds. The lower fold is along an existing crease.

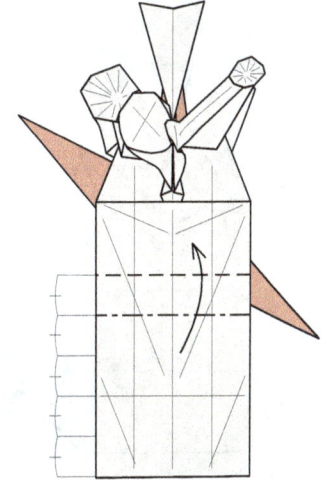

95. Pleat upwards.

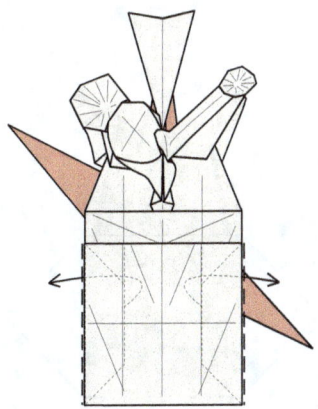

96. Swivel out the sides.

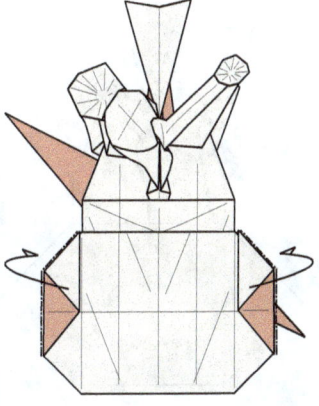

97. Wrap around a single layer at each side.

153

seated guitarist

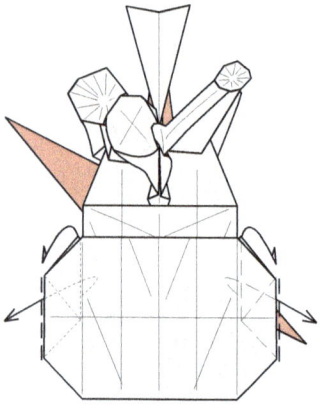

98. Pull out the sides from behind, allowing paper to swivel downwards.

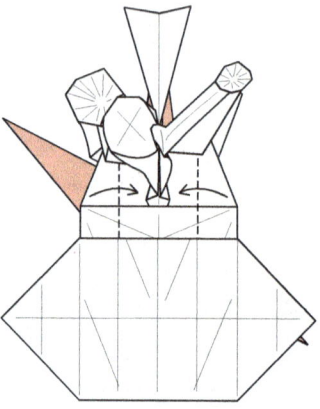

99. Swivel in the top layer on each side.

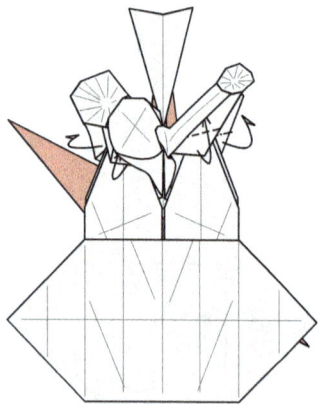

100. Tuck the indicated flaps into their respective pockets.

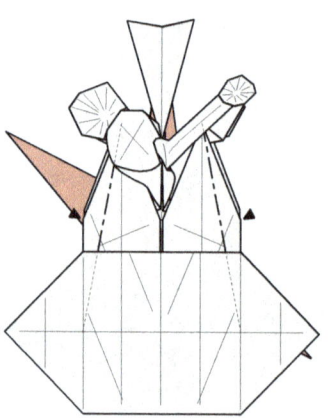

101. Sink the top flap at each side.

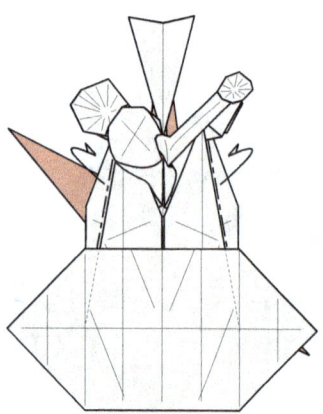

102. Mountain fold the side flaps.

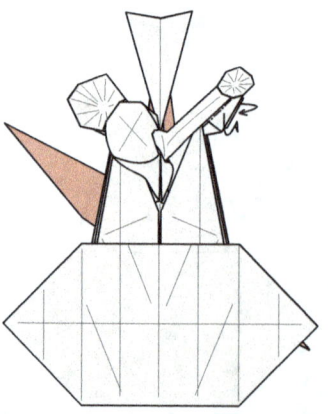

103. Tuck the protruding flaps inward.

seated guitarist

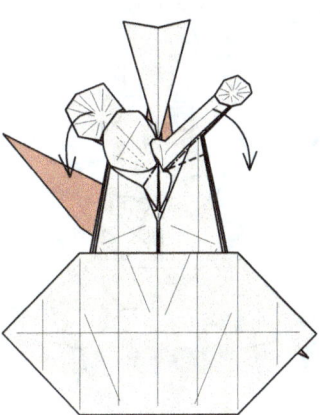

104. Pleat the side flaps down. They will still not be flush with the base of the model.

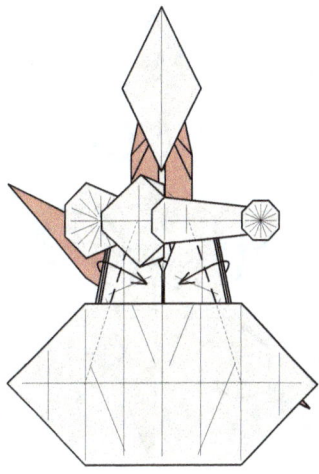

105. Swivel in the sides as far as possible.

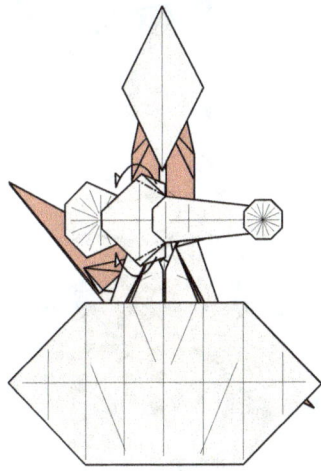

106. Reverse fold the two corners.

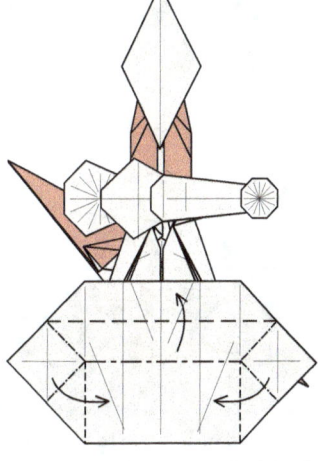

107. Collapse upwards. The long valley fold should not be creased sharply.

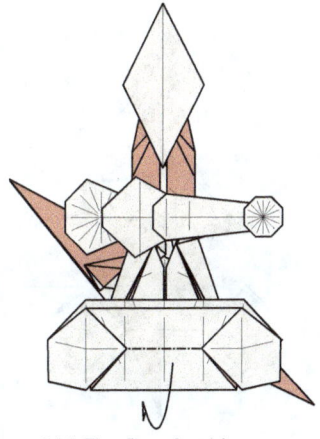

108. Mountain fold. The flap should not wrap around any layers.

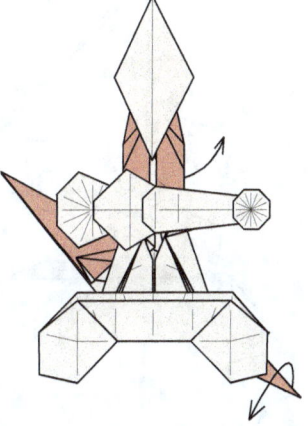

109. Swing the side section out to lie straight.

seated guitarist

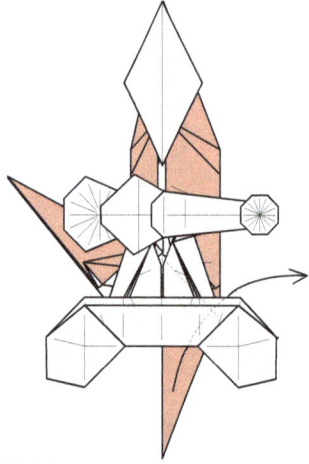

110. Valley fold the point outwards as far as possible.

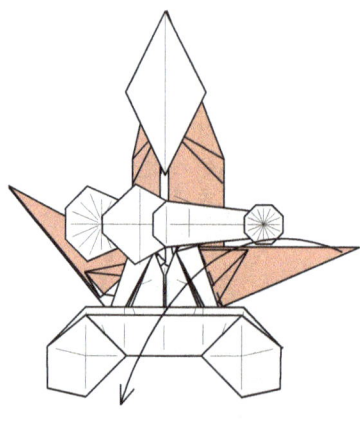

111. Valley fold the point around, allowing the top single layer to be on the surface.

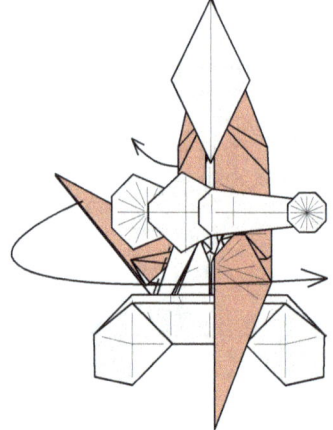

112. Swing the side section out to lie straight, while pulling the side point through.

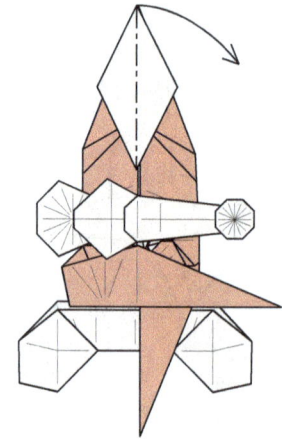

113. Pull out the center flap.

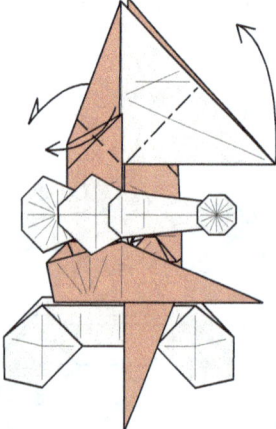

114. Carefully outside reverse fold. The center flap will rotate.

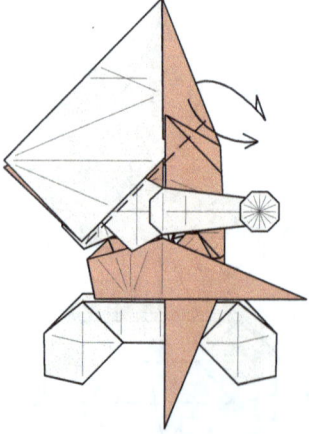

115. Outside reverse fold the other side.

156

seated guitarist

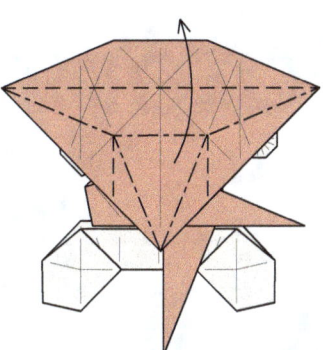

116. Collapse upwards.

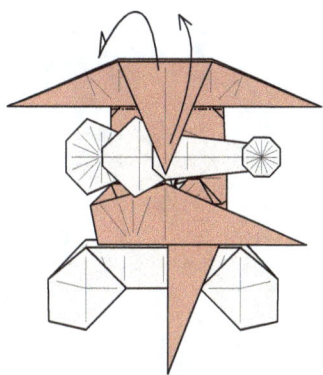

117. Flip the top section.

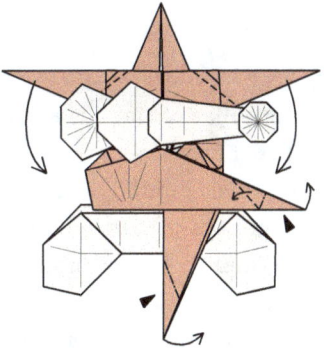

118. Valley fold the top flaps, and squash the bottom flaps as indicated.

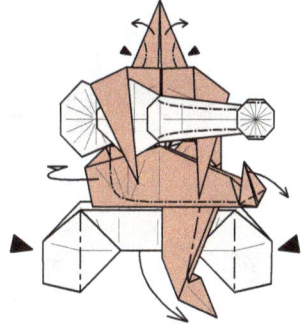

119. Shape and position the player and guitar to taste. Pull out the bench to make it three dimensional, and pull the player over the center of the bench.

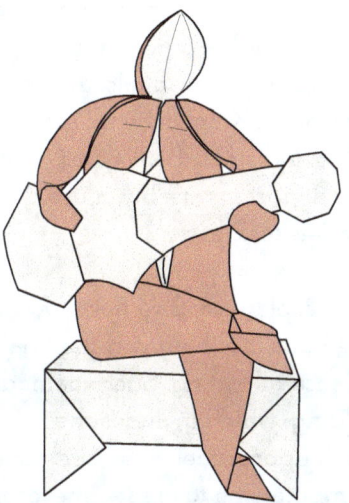

120. Completed *Seated Guitarist*.

Materials and Methods

In theory, the only things required for origami is a piece of paper and a pair of hands. In practice, however, you will want to have the right materials for the project at hand. For initial practice attempts, you will want to use papers that are easy to fold, but not necessarily of presentable quality. The two most popular practice papers are commercial origami paper (sometimes sold as kami) and American foil. Both of these papers are available colored on one side, and white on the other. American foil is preferable as it holds its shape more easily. These papers feature a thin layer of decorative foil that helps your model hold its shape. Most of the origami supply houses sell a 10" version as their largest size, but some thinner wrapping paper can be used if you are looking for something larger. Japanese foil is thinner, and generally easier to fold than the American variety, albeit more expensive. Kami is better for those who have trouble with reverse folds and sinks. Both types of papers will yield adequate results, but almost invariably, more decorative choices will make your models look better.

For display-worthy efforts, you will want to use papers and methods that heighten the final result, possibly at the expense of ease of folding. Such methods include foil-backing and wet folding, which includes the related technique of back coating. Both approaches allow the paper-folding artist to use material combinations to create interesting effects.

Foil Backing

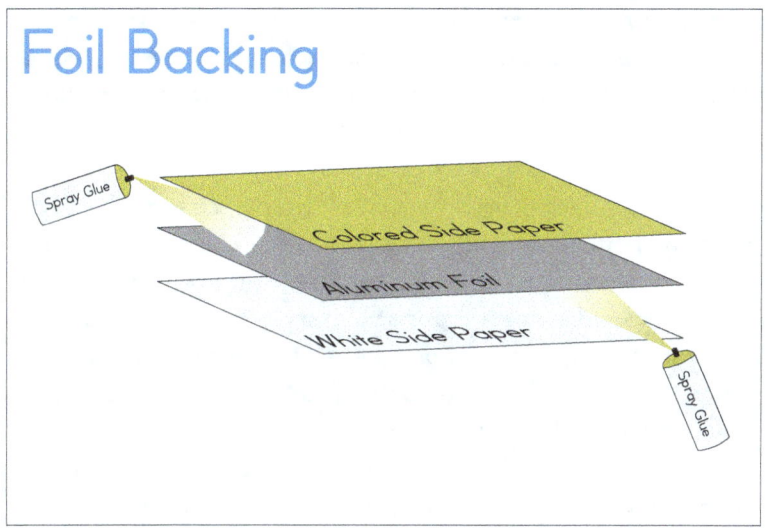

Foil backing is a great way to utilize nonporous materials, and papers with patterns that could get ruined with water (such as newsprint). Foil backing is the process of adding a layer of aluminum foil (yes, the same material you can find at virtually any grocery store) to paper, to give the resulting material unique folding characteristics. A common backing choice is tissue paper, which further enhances the folding properties of the foil (this combination is also known as "tissue foil"). Regardless of the backing material, the metal-like quality allows folds to instantly stay where they are placed. Spray adhesive is used to bond the layers together. This is also known as artist's adhesive or photo mounting spray, and it contains the same glue found on adhesive tape. You can find this at most art supply stores, but you will find it much cheaper at a hardware or office supply store. While I will usually use 3M's Spray Mount, some projects (typically involving very thick papers) will require something like 3M's Super77 Spray Adhesive. All work should be done in a well-ventilated area, as the glue is toxic. You will also want to protect your floor with newspaper. Place a sheet of foil on the floor. Leave the shinier side up first, and use as the surface for the main color. In most cases, the foil will be the limiting factor as far as size is concerned, so use as large a sheet as necessary. Spray the glue onto the surface of the foil according to the manufacturer's directions. If you have a choice of nozzles, use the one with a finer mist. When spraying, be sure to cover the entire surface area of the foil, while paying special attention to the edges. After spraying, you should give the glue about a minute to get tacky.

The next step is to apply your paper to the tacky surface. Start by adhering the bottom edge of your paper to the bottom edge of the foil. Then start working your way upwards until the foil is completely covered. You can also use a baker's rolling pin to apply the paper. Another variation is to start at one corner and work your way to the opposite corner. Try several methods to see which feels most comfortable. For thicker papers, it might be easier to simply drop the paper onto the foil. When you are done, rub out any wrinkles, and then apply another layer of paper on the other side.

To get the largest possible square, cut along the edge of the foil, which should be visible through the layers of paper, provided your papers are translucent enough. If you wish you can also tear through the foil, which is surprisingly accurate (and fun), provided you are using thin enough paper. First, score the paper, unfold, and turn over to leave the resulting crease in mountain fold formation. The paper can easily be torn in this position. Of course you won't get the largest possible square this way, but it is easier to be accurate.

A rotary cutting board is recommended when tearing is not possible, or you cannot see the silhouette of the foil through your backing paper. While a traditional guillotine cutter might suffice, spending an extra $100 or so on a rotary cutter is worth the investment for the serious paperfolding artist. These can be purchased at better art supply stores or photography supply stores. A pair of scissors can be used when a paper cutter is not as convenient.

If you wish to make a square that is wider than your piece of foil, there is a way to accomplish this. First, you have to adhere two (or more) strips of foil together. If you spray along the edge of one piece and attach the other piece along that edge, the results are remarkably seamless. Most likely, the paper you will want to use on the surface will be smaller than the foil piece you have prepared. There is a way around this hurdle as well. First, you should fold your foil in half. The resulting surface area should now be small enough for your paper. Before you use any adhesive, place a sheet of newspaper between the fold to avoid getting any glue on the inner layers. You can now adhere your papers on each side of the foil. When you are done with the gluing part, use a scissor to cut along the folded edge. After you unfold your piece, rub out the crease, and the seam will almost disappear. You can repeat the same process for the other side.

When folding larger models, you might find certain portions to be flimsy. While wire is traditionally used to add rigidity, I have found stuffing layers of foil to be even better. You can fold a piece of foil over upon itself a few times to make it many layers thick. This can be stuffed between the layers of the parts of the model that need more rigidity.

If you are using tissue as the backing paper, where the properties of the foil are at their most extreme, you are in for a radically different folding experience. By themselves, foil and tissue make for flimsy and weak folding materials, but together you have one of the strongest and most resilient materials around. Also, when you make a crease, it will hold very well. It will hold so well that it is difficult to change its direction (i.e., valley to mountain). This makes procedures that require precreasing, such as sinks, difficult to perform. You can unfold the paper after precreasing, rub out the creases that have to be changed, and replace them with new folds that are in the right direction. Unlike commercial foil paper, you can rub out unwanted creases without leaving a trace.

While it is true that foil backing will make folding your model more difficult for most if its stages, its properties are fortuitous at the end of a model's folding sequence. If your model has many layers, it can easily be flattened. In extreme cases, a hammer can work wonders. After your model is as flat as you desire, you can shape and pose it any way you wish. Your model will hold that shape forever, until you decide to reshape it, or someone or something inadvertently reshapes it. The latter scenario is obviously undesirable. If you use a slightly thicker paper (such as the aforementioned Japanese papers), you will lose some of the malleability, but will have a much more solid looking model, due to its increased thickness. It can still be bent out of shape, but is acceptable if being displayed in a controlled environment.

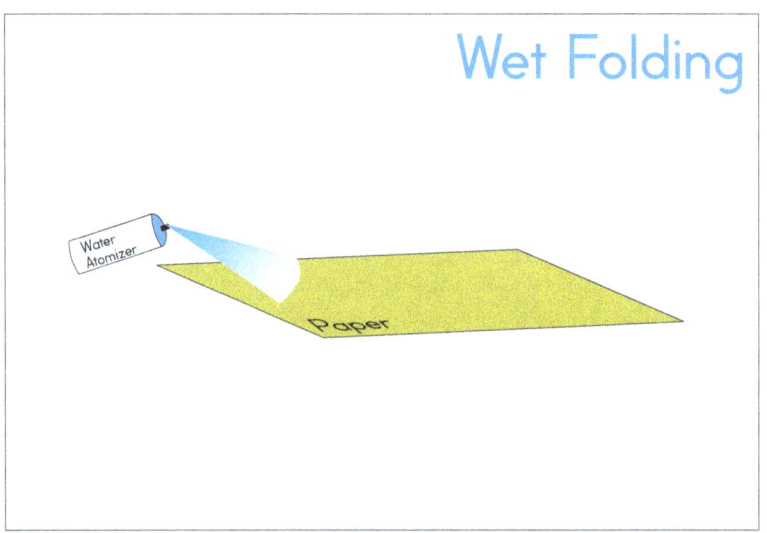

Wet Folding

Foil backed paper looks great in person, but the camera lens often picks up the foil through the backing, even when the backing paper seems to be dense enough. This might be okay for some subjects, but to have a less reflective look, wet folding techniques are more effective. The process might be slower, but the results are more permanent.

Wet folding involves lightly dampening your paper during the folding process, so when it finally dries it will retain its shape. When paper is wet, the sizing (glue-like substance) that holds the paper fibers together is loosened. Once the paper is dry again, the sizing will hold the paper in its new position. Taking advantage of this property of paper enables the folder to hold shapes that seem to defy gravity. Not all papers contain a lot of sizing, so you might have to add a methylcellulose paste to your paper before folding. To do this, you first add the methylcellulose powder (which is sold at many art supply stores) to water, and mix the compound until it is syrupy. You can use about a teaspoon for each cup of warm water. This paste can now be brushed onto your paper with a standard painter's brush. After the paper is dry, it will be even easier to wet fold. To speed up the drying process, you can use a table fan.

When wet folding it is important to realize your paper will expand, often unevenly. This makes accurate folding much more difficult. Also, reference fold crease lines become difficult to see while paper is wet. For these reasons, you may prefer to delay wetting the paper until key folds are in place. When you are ready to wet the paper, it is important not to allow the paper to get soggy. By using an atomizer's mist sparingly, a leathery texture can be obtained from the paper. These spray bottles can be found at many perfume sections; try to find one with as fine a mist as possible.

Holding your model in position while drying can be a creative challenge. Tools that work include twist ties (the plastic coated ones that are often used for electrical wire packing), portable clamps, and painter's masking tape. As an example, you can wind a twist tie around the legs of your insect model, bend them into the desired position, and secure them to a flat surface with masking tape. After further moistening your model with your atomizer, it will retain its stance after it is dry and your bindings have been removed.

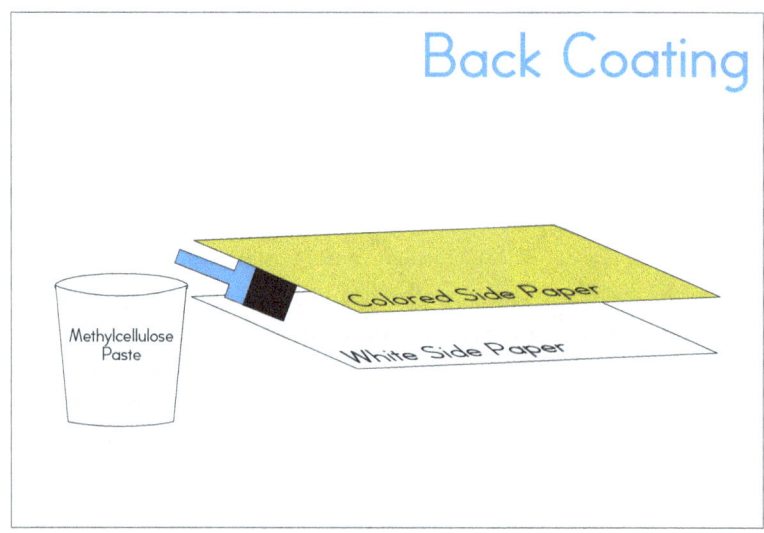

Back Coating

A related technique to wet folding is back coating. Since most specialty papers are monochromatic, the two-toned effect in many origami models is lost. You can use methylcellulose paste to adhere two complementing colors of paper together. Brush the paste on one paper, being sure to work on a smooth surface, as the paper will pick up any texture from your working surface. Apply the second sheet on top, brushing it into place. You can cut your square once it is dry, using a table fan to expedite the process. Again, a rotary cutter is recommended. The materials you chose to mate together should both be porous and fibrous enough to stay together, otherwise you might have to resort to foil backing.

Papers that work well include the Unryu variety (both regular and soft) from both Japan and Thailand. These papers might be labeled as containing mulberry or kozo fiber, but other fibers will work as well. You can also try Yatsuo papers from Japan, which are made from kozo and sulphite pulp, and have a much smoother look than the Unryu papers. These and other fine art papers can be found at better art stores and via mail order. You can expect to pay about three to four dollars for a 25" x 37" sheet.

Other important paper considerations include weight, which is how a material's thickness is described. To give you a gauge of what this means, standard copy paper is often at 20 Gr/M^2 weight. Of course, you will double your thickness if you are bonding two sheets together. Try to keep the total thickness under 80 Gr/M^2. When dealing with lighter colors, you might have to work with thicker papers just to get the right opacity (but you can mate them with lighter weight darker papers if you are trying to avoid additional thickness). As a test, you can hold the paper against a black surface to see how well it eclipses its backing. Sometimes, having the contrasting color show through is a good thing, as your color choices will seem to blend a bit. One thing you would like to avoid is having your paper bleed (having the dye run) when wet. The most temperamental colors tend to be reds and black, but it is a good idea to test out a sheet first if possible. With enough experimentation, you should be able to conceive the perfect material for any model.

Paper Sizes

Most of these models work best as a collective whole. Together, their effect can be enhanced when you choose paper sizes that result in players of a similar size. Since each model has a different reduction ratio, you will have to calculate a starting size for each project. Below are ratios that will give you models that are close proportionately. The thickness of your paper and the way you fold will have an influence on the finished size, but you can make minor height adjustments through the pleats that form the neck and feet.

The models are listed in order of their reduction factor. Multiplying this number by your paper size will tell you large an instrumentalist will be formed. If you know how large an instrumentalist you want, multiply that number by the multiplying factor, which will tell you how large of a piece of paper is needed.

Model	Reduction Factor	Multiplying Factor
Drummer	0.18	5.5555
Pianist	0.24	4.1666
Harpist	0.2647	3.7777
Dancing Couple	0.375	2.6666
Clarinetist	0.4	2.5
Seated Guitarist	0.405	2.468
Saxophonist	0.44	2.2727
Violinist	0.45	2.2222
Guitarist	0.45	2.2222
Conductor	0.525	1.9
Bassist	0.575	1.7391

For example, if an 18" square is the largest size available to you, then the largest "Drummer" possible is 3.24" high (18 x 0.18). For the "Pianist," you could then use a 13.5" square (3.24 x 4.166), to get another 2.88" model. The remaining paper sizes can be obtained by multiplying the multiplying factor by your desired model size (3.24" in this case). As stated before, these are approximations anyway, so you can feel comfortable rounding off your measurements when you are cutting your square. In practice, you will want to use as large a piece of paper as possible.

www.ingramcontent.com/pod-product-compliance
Lightning Source LLC
Chambersburg PA
CBHW081722100526
44591CB00016B/2461